A History of Canada in 15 Moments

HISTORY IN 15

This pioneering new series offers lively perspectives on regional and global histories. Adopting an innovative thematic approach, each title is structured around 15 items, concepts or sources through which the history of a particular region, or the entire world, can be illuminated. From food to films, from cities to songs, this series brings history into focus for students and interested readers.

These approachable books use a consistent set of themes or sources as a lens through which to view the broader history, transforming how the reader understands these items while imparting critical lessons about historical context and analysis. For example, a book on US History in 15 Foods would use 15 foods to examine the history of the nation, covering key topics and themes in US history.

Series Editors: Laura A. Belmonte (Virginia Tech, USA)

Editorial Board:

Maria Montoya, NYU-Shanghai, China

Kyle Longley, Chapman University, USA

Anne Foster, Indiana State University, USA

Julia Irwin, University of South Florida, USA

Fabian Hilfrich, University of Edinburgh, UK

Justin Hart, Texas Tech, USA

Kelly Shannon, Florida Atlantic University, USA

Holly M. Karibo, Oklahoma State University, USA

Ellen Hartigan O'Connor, UC-Davis, USA

Andrew Rotter, Colgate University, USA

Published:

US History in 15 Foods, Anna Zeide

Forthcoming:

US History in 15 Photographs: 1865 to the 21st Century, Rebecca Wingo and Lauren Tilton

Global History in 15 Epidemics, Andrew Robarts

Queer History in 15 Lives, Laura A. Belmonte

Scottish History in 15 Violent Crimes: Gender, Society and the Law, Louise Heren

Global History in 15 Latin American Foods, Elizabeth Newman

Atlantic History in 15 Slave Revolts: Resistance, Rebellion and Abolition from Below, Christian Høgsbjerg

South Asian History in 15 Films, Talat Ahmed

Global History in 15 Disasters: Urban Catastrophes and Reconstruction since 18th Century, Pierre Purseigle

A History of Canada in 15 Moments

Making and Remaking a Nation since 1867

Raymond B. Blake and Jeff Keshen

BLOOMSBURY ACADEMIC
LONDON • NEW YORK • OXFORD • NEW DELHI • SYDNEY

BLOOMSBURY ACADEMIC

Bloomsbury Publishing Plc, 50 Bedford Square, London, WC1B 3DP, UK
Bloomsbury Publishing Inc, 1359 Broadway, New York, NY 10018, USA
Bloomsbury Publishing Ireland, 29 Earlsfort Terrace, Dublin 2, D02 AY28, Ireland

BLOOMSBURY, BLOOMSBURY ACADEMIC and the Diana logo are
trademarks of Bloomsbury Publishing Plc

First published in Great Britain 2026

Copyright © Raymond B. Blake and Jeff Keshen, 2026

Raymond B. Blake and Jeff Keshen have asserted their right under the Copyright,
Designs and Patents Act, 1988, to be identified as Authors of this work.

For legal purposes the Acknowledgements on p. xi constitute
an extension of this copyright page.

Cover image: Kryssia Campos via Getty Images

All rights reserved. No part of this publication may be: i) reproduced or transmitted in
any form, electronic or mechanical, including photocopying, recording or by means of
any information storage or retrieval system without prior permission in writing from the
publishers; or ii) used or reproduced in any way for the training, development or operation
of artificial intelligence (AI) technologies, including generative AI technologies. The rights
holders expressly reserve this publication from the text and data mining exception as per
Article 4(3) of the Digital Single Market Directive (EU) 2019/790.

Bloomsbury Publishing Plc does not have any control over, or responsibility for, any
third-party websites referred to or in this book. All internet addresses given in this
book were correct at the time of going to press. The author and publisher regret
any inconvenience caused if addresses have changed or sites have ceased
to exist, but can accept no responsibility for any such changes.

A catalogue record for this book is available from the British Library.

A catalog record for this book is available from the Library of Congress.

ISBN: HB: 978-1-3504-0823-4
       PB: 978-1-3504-0822-7
       ePDF: 978-1-3504-0825-8
       eBook: 978-1-3504-0824-1

Series: History in 15

Typeset by Integra Software Services Pvt. Ltd.
Printed and bound in Great Britain

For product safety related questions contact productsafety@bloomsbury.com.

To find out more about our authors and books visit www.bloomsbury.com
and sign up for our newsletters.

CONTENTS

List of Illustrations ix
Preface and acknowledgements xi

Introduction 1

1   Joseph Howe and 'Better Terms', 1869:
    Making the nation work 13

2   The hanging of Louis Riel, 1885:
    Managing cultural genocide 27

3   The *Komagata Maru* incident, 1914:
    Racism, immigration and xenophobia 41

4   Anti-conscription riots in Quebec City, 1918:
    War and society 55

5   Agnes Macphail, MP, 1921: The changing place
    of women in Canada 69

6   The Windsor auto strike, 1945: The rise of social
    citizenship in Canada 83

7   Lester Pearson and Suez, 1956: Decolonization and
    the British world 99

8   Saskatchewan doctors' strike, 1962: Universal health
    care for Canada 113

9   Canada, 1967: The centennial and searching
    for a better Canada 129

10 The charter of rights and freedoms, 1982:
    Remaking the nation 143

11 The free trade election, 1988: Towards a new nationalism
    for Canadians 157

12 The Quebec referendum, 1995: To leave or
    to stay in Canada? 173

13 Same-sex marriage, 2005: A changing nation 189

14 Statement of apology, 2008: Activism, dialogue,
    truth – towards reconciliation 203

15 The freedom convoy, 2022: Canada in the
    Covid-19 pandemic 219

Index 232

ILLUSTRATIONS

1   Joseph Howe, former premier of Nova Scotia, 1869. Photo by Topley Studio, Library and Archives Canada/PA-025486 12
2   Portrait of Louis Riel, the Metis leader and political figure. Library and Archives Canada / Jean Riel fonds PA-139070 26
3   Sikhs on board the *Komagata Maru* in English Bay, Vancouver. Library and Archives Canada, Box OS 0075.5, Item 3238584 40
4   Parade against conscription in Victoria Square in Montreal, 1917. Library and Archives Canada / C-006859 54
5   Agnes Macphail, MP for Grey County. New Paramount Studio / Library and Archives Canada / PA-127295 68
6   'Windsor, Ontario, November 5th – Barricade by Pickets Creates Traffic Jam'. Image courtesy of AACA Library & Research Center, Hershey, Pennsylvania, USA 82
7   Lester Pearson, 14th Prime Minister of Canada. https://lop.parl.ca/sites/ParlInfo/default/en_CA/People/Profile?personId=531. Public Domain 98
8   Tommy Douglas being named as the first leader of the federal New Democratic Party, 4 August 1961. Vern Kent, Saskatchewan Film Board 112
9   Thirty-five Yukon Indian teenagers brought to Toronto as a centennial project. Mario Geo/Toronto Star via Getty Images 128
10 Despite the rain, the Queen and Prime Minister Trudeau walked amongst the spectators on Parliament Hill in Ottawa, on 17 April 1982 as they sign into law the new constitution of Canada. The Canadian Press/Tim Clark, CP212661177 142
11 Signing of Mexican president Carlos Salinas, US president George H.W. Bush and Canadian prime minister Brian Mulroney participate in the signing of the North American Free Trade Agreement in October 1992. Unknown Author, George Bush President Library and Museum. Public Domain, https://commons.wikimedia.org/wiki/File:Nafta.jpg 156

12 Rally for a united Canada in Montreal, five days before Quebec voters cast ballots on the sovereignty referendum. https://www.gettyimages.ca/detail/photo/canadians-rallying-for-unity-royalty-free-image/535321470?searchscope=image%2Cfilm&adppopup=true 172

13 Michael Stark and Michael Leshner celebrate their marriage following a successful Ontario court ruling, 10 June 2003. https://globalnews.ca/news/628246/10th-anniversary-of-same-sex-marriage-in-canada/10th anniversary of same-sex marriage in Canada | Globalnews.ca. The Canadian Press/Tim Clark, CP174945751 188

14 In Act of Reconciliation, Canada Apologizes for Aboriginal Abuses. Canadian Prime Minister Stephen Harper and National Chief of the Assembly of First Nations Phil Fontaine pause before walking into the House of Commons on Parliament Hill, 11 June 2008 202

15 Part of the truckers convoy that shut down downtown Ottawa, 22 January 2022. https://www.alamy.com/ottawa-ontario-canada-28th-january-2022-sign-saying-truckers-for-freedom-on-front-of-large-truck-during-the-blockades-of-freedom-convoy-protest-image470267643.html?imageid=CCCFD88C-4F66-4446-803B-65402DA55C5B&pn=1&searchId=9b66dec487da299abca2140cde9d1044&searchtype=0 218

PREFACE AND ACKNOWLEDGEMENTS

This is the seventh book that we have co-authored since we left York University as recent PhD graduates many years ago and headed to Department of History at the University of Alberta in Edmonton. We took different paths in the academic world, but we never lose sight of the importance of collaboration in writing and researching about Canada's history. Our research interests often intersected and while collaborative writing has its challenges, we have also found that it has its rewards. We both learned much from our PhD supervisor, Dr Jack Granatstein, and he remains an inspiration. For him, being a university professor was caring for our students and equally important, putting pen to paper and publishing. Jack is not only an inspiration and mentor but also a friend who has never lost interest in his students nor his commitment to scholarship. It is to him that we dedicate this book.

As with all of our publishing, we have benefitted from the encouragement and support of our families and colleagues. In preparing this volume, we would like to acknowledge two excellent University of Regina history student research assistants, Jack Nestor and Mason Hausermann. Our gratitude also goes out to Dr Stephen King, who works in the President's Office at the University of Regina, and to Kate Baltais for her exceptional editorial work that significantly improved our chapters and for helping to ensure that we write with a single voice. At Bloomsbury, Maddie Smith has been encouraging and generous from the very beginning and her colleagues (Paige Harris, Niamh Coffey, Hemapriya Siva, Prasona Binu) great to work with. We wish to acknowledge and thank two anonymous readers who offered sage advice for improving the book, and also the hundreds of students that we have had the pleasure of teaching at a number of universities in Canada and internationally over the past two decades but especially those bright and engaging students at the University of Regina.

Introduction

History is granular, filled with discrete events and moments that, like the individual grains of sugar in a bowl or the sand on a beach, cannot signal their true significance when looked at individually and without context. Taken together, however, they form a serviceable whole. Singular moments in the life of a nation and its people are similarly useful. Each such moment is important in and of itself, while also helping us understand the whole story. How Canada was made and remade from Confederation to the present day is a narrative that builds through a piecemeal examination of sequential, yet discrete moments through time that reveal incipient trends, continuities, and remarkable changes in the nation's story.

Canada, like any nation, has starkly contrasting histories to draw upon. For an exceptionally long while, the country's normative story – or what we might call the national history – told of how the politicians in British North America came together in the 1860s to create Canada and then how over ensuing decades Canadians successfully overcame various challenges and obstacles to their well-being. In that history, there were great leaders (mostly men) and valiant citizens who worked together to shape the nation by triumphing over the forces that threatened to destroy it. To be a critic of that approach and write a different narrative was too often seen not only as 'bad' scholarship and ahistorical, but unpatriotic as well. The normative history, Canadians would constantly be reminded, was a wonderful story of progress and triumph. That story was not only integral to the nation's history, but also essential to the national project itself. This approach contributed its fair share of myth-building, dominated by heroic figures and momentous events of triumph. Any troubling aspects about Canada's past or the people who were marginalized and did not share in the nation's bounty were largely ignored. Canadian historians, for a long time, largely ignored much that could be construed as negative in the nation's past, especially the perniciousness of colonialism, racism, xenophobia, sexism, homophobia, environmental degradation and the exploitation of marginal communities and regions that did not support their narrative of what they then considered to be and called progress.¹ Even in the 1970s and 1980s, one historian has noted, national sentiments 'fueled the expansion of history departments in the postwar era, and were critical to the "Canadianization" movement that shaped much of English-Canadian cultural life in the 1970s and 80s'.²

That is not today's normative story of Canada, even if the nation-state remains the primary unit of historical analysis. Nor should it be as history must include all aspects of a nation's past, the good, the bad and the ugly. Today there is a new 'national' history. At the risk of oversimplification, we might say the new 'national' history similarly has a largely singular focus, but not on heralding progress.³ Now much of Canada's 'national' history is likely to be a narrative of the nation as a racist, xenophobic, colonizing, hierarchically gendered, violent and unjust nation of white privilege where the capitalist exploitation of labour and the ecosystems victimized many, ushered in a regime of violent dispossession, and destroyed the environment. While pockets of military or political history can be found in universities across the country, there is a clear leaning towards social, cultural and gender history as historians and scholars in complementary disciplines, influenced by postmodernism, critical theory and what has been termed the 'reflexive turn' found that the past is heavily influenced by eurocentrism, racism and post-colonialism.⁴ Some will argue that it is in that approach to history where we will find the roots of many of Canada's current and long-endured problems. The Canadian Historical Association, which represents more than 600 professional historians from across Canada, even issued a statement on 1 July 2021 (Canada Day) that there was a consensus among historians that the profession had 'contributed in lasting and tangible ways to the Canadian refusal to come to grips with this country's history of colonization and dispossession'. It criticized historians for failing to tell the story of Canada 'for what it is, and the ways that it lives on into the present'. That history 'has served to perpetuate the violence, [and] it is time for us to break this historical cycle'. It encouraged Canadians to 'recognize this history for what it is: genocide'.⁵ Not surprisingly, the statement prompted

---

¹See, e.g., Carl Berger, *The Writing of Canadian History: Aspects of English-Canadian Historical Writing since 1900*, 2nd ed. (Toronto: University of Toronto Press, 1986), 218–22; Donald Wright, *Donald Creighton: A Life in History* (Toronto: University of Toronto Press, 2015).
²Adele Perry, 'Nation, Empire, and the Writing of Canadian History in English', in Michael Dawson and Christopher Dummitt, eds., *Contesting Clio's Craft* (London: Institute for the Studies of the Americas, 2008), 123–40.
³Paul Litt, 'The Romance of Canada: Nationalism and Canadian Historiography', *Canadian Historical Review* 102, no. s4 (2021): s907–76.
⁴Shirley Tillotson, 'The Canadian Historical Review at One Hundred Years', *Canadian Historical Review* 100, no. 3 (2019): 315–48.
⁵Canadian Historical Association, 'Canada Day Statement: The History of Violence against Indigenous Peoples Fully Warrants the Use of the Word "Genocide"', CHA Website, 30 June 2021, https://cha-shc.ca/advocacy/the-history-of-violence-against-indigenous-peoples-fully-warrants-the-use-of-the-word-genocide/.

an intense reaction, most notably from those historians who feared that the Canadian Historical Association represents 'an illiberal tendency' when academic organizations take political stances in ways that threaten academic freedom and suggest there is only way to write a nation's history.[6]

The goals of more recent history as represented by the statement by the Canadian Historical Association are lofty and, indeed, important. But history must strive to reveal the past with all its complexities. To focus solely on failings in Canada's past while ignoring its many accomplishments and failing to recognize the important changes in various policies and, indeed, in the direction of the nation over time is to miss much in the study of the past, even if historians – both past and present – believe that through the study of history we can explain the Canada in which they live and write about while expressing hope for a better future.

In this book, we are taking from both the earlier and the newer approach in writing Canadian history. In all fairness, the nation's story cannot be defined as one of simple celebration, as there are too many moments that are truly awful and must be exposed for what they really were. Nor can that history be one of simply condemning and emphasizing the nation's failings. Both approaches are needed for a full understanding of Canada's past and for moving forward in creating a better nation. Both approaches are needed to understand Canada's messy and complex history and how Canada is a work in progress, a different nation today from what it was in 1867 or even in 2000 or at any other time in the past. The past is, indeed, complex and messy, and we often see that only when we view the past from the distance of time. And, we should remember, we never know how decisions made today will turn out in the future.

Canada has emerged as a nation quite different from the one that was forged in 1867 even if a number of features that defined what we might call the nation-building era have remained constant. Canada was then and remains a negotiated nation, a constitutional monarchy with a parliamentary democracy, but Canada's monarch, now King Charles III, is a ceremonial head of state and the British government, unlike in the early years of union, has no constitutional role in Canada: political and constitutional power rests with elected officials in Ottawa, in the provincial and territorial capitals, and increasingly with First Nations and other Indigenous governments. Through territorial expansion, Canada has become the second-largest country in the world by land mass, stretching from the Atlantic Ocean in the east and to the Pacific in the West and the Arctic Ocean in the North. Most of its citizens, however, reside in the southern reaches of the country, not far from the Canada-United States border. Despite moments of instability and resistance to state actions, it is a politically stable nation, seen as a progressive, liberal

---

[6]Christopher Dummitt and P. Whitney Lackenbauer, 'Debating Genocide in Canada: A Response to Steven High', History Reclaimed, 6 October 2021, https://historyreclaimed.co.uk/debating-genocide-in-canada-a-response-to-steven-high/.

state and known for its universal healthcare and strong social programmes, official multiculturalism and a variety of policies and constitutional guarantees that promote inclusion and diversity, strong protections for civil liberties and liberal policies such as marriage equality, legalized cannabis, medically assisted dying and a decades-long commitment to open immigration. It actively promotes reconciliation with Indigenous peoples even if many contend that progress has been slow on this issue. It is also among the world's wealthiest nations, driven particularly by resource development (especially oil, gas and mining), technology, manufacturing and services. Internationally, it is respected for its diplomacy, peacekeeping and commitment to multilateral organizations such as the United Nations, NATO and the G7 and it maintains strong ties with the United States, its largest trading partner, despite quarrels over tariffs during the Trump era. It is a nation that has learned the importance of compromise and negotiation, especially at the national level, and it remains a work in progress. Canada has never had a single, fixed identity. Its national story began as fundamentally bicultural (English and French) and became multicultural with strong Indigenous foundations. Even its constitutional arrangement is under construction as new treaties are negotiated with Indigenous nations. It is an evolving, incremental project, a nation in the making, a story of unfinished identity and ongoing negotiation, which has privileged gradual, cautious and evolutionary change rather than revolutionary breaks or radical transformations. Rather than a fully completed, static nation-state, its identity, governance and societal agreements are future-oriented. The debate over who 'we' are continues to be negotiated, contested and reshaped as it has been since its inception in 1867.

We examine here fifteen key historical moments to show how Canada became that incremental nation and what it is today. We believe that focusing on key moments is a valid and effective approach to studying Canada's past. Through an examination of significant events or individuals, we gain a deeper understanding of historical processes and their lasting impacts while also demonstrating how specific actions or ideas shaped the course of Canada's development. This approach reveals cause-and-effect relationships and illustrates how some moments represent crucial turning points in history, marking significant change in political, social or cultural structures. By studying specific moments, we can demonstrate how historical events influenced and changed the path Canada travelled throughout its history and provide insight into the past and help us better understand past behaviour. Each moment was recognized as important at the time and either reflects a change occurring in Canadian society or helps to propel change. Each was important in helping to create a new and different nation and, we believe, represent pivotal moments in the emergence of modern Canada while helping us to understand our values and gain a clearer sense of what mattered most in the life of the nation. Each of the moments continued to have an impact long after it had passed. There were many other pivotal moments in the nation's past and since significance is a decision that we make, it means that different people can decide that different things are significant, or that they can disagree about the reasons a particular person, event, place or idea is important. Some will reject our selection, but no study of the past can include everything that has ever happened. It is important to remember as well that what we consider to be important will change. Some events which were considered significant a decade ago may not be important to us now. Alternatively, we may consider something historically significant today that no-one will care about in a generation.

We have selected those moments that describe leadership. Among Canada's most momentous and influential leaders were its prime ministers, who have come from every province except Newfoundland and Labrador and Prince Edward Island; its provincial politicians, both English- and French-speaking; and its rebels and activists, both Indigenous and non-Indigenous, urban and rural. As we show in the pages that follow, a focus on leaders does not minimize the role of societies, citizens and culture in the making of a nation. Leaders reflect and are shaped by the economic, cultural, political and social realities of their times and by issues and concerns that the national communities have prioritized. The major economic, political, social, cultural and constitutional issues important to the nation have often pushed individuals into important historical roles. That has been the case with individuals such as Louis Riel and Agnes Macphail, for instance. The fifteen moments considered are presented chronologically, but do not have to be read in order; each chapter can be read on its own. Set in the context of their time and place, with explanatory background information, each moment has had both a local and national impact, has generated an interesting and often problematic historiography, and collectively, these moments shaped Canada's unique identity within North America and the world.

And a unique nation it is, even as Canada continues to deal with new realities, new challenges and new contingencies. Through it all, its national character has been one of finding mutually acceptable accommodations. Conflicts between provinces and the federal government – and the struggle to resolve them – have become normative elements in the story of Canada, even a hallmark of Confederation itself. A flexible federalism became not only an instrument for obtaining political consent for Canada, but also a means of achieving stability and unity in the federation. Canada has been reasonably successful at managing an ethnically and regionally diverse nation even if the process in too many cases has taken too long to achieve. What began in the 1860s as a nation forged by two founding nations – French and English – it has since become a nation of three founding peoples who have been joined by ethnic communities from the world over. Multiculturalism has long been a Canadian ideal, and the recognition of strength in diversity is more than a campaign slogan dreamed up by a political party; most Canadians see diversity and differences as essential national virtues and while the Canadian state has not always been accommodating or even accepting of its minorities, nation builders in 1867 and since have been concerned about the place of minorities whose treatment has remained a major theme in Canada's history. Today, Canada is paying the price for many of its misguided steps in this regard, but it has entered a redemptive moment and is trying to now recall and re-institute the original promise of Confederation based on respect for and recognition of all communities that constitute the nation. This is particularly the case with Indigenous peoples who were victimized by the state for decades, but nearly fifty years ago, the Canadian Constitution recognized three groups of Indigenous peoples (First Nations, Inuit and Métis) and Canada has now apologized for historical wrongs and is working towards the reconciliation with Indigenous people. While Canada remains a work-in-progress as all nations must be, it has become a modern, progressive and liberal state that embraces the values of varying and sharing, equity and fairness for all, together with a strong commitment to inclusion and diversity.

In studying a federated union, meaning a union of parts, region and regional issues warrant attention. Canada is such a union. Not surprisingly, one or another of its regions – its provinces and territories – has at time railed against the centre, that is, the federal government and it has had to respond. Regional interests were a feature from the earliest days of Confederation. Chapter 1 brings them to the forefront while backgrounding the many dimensions of Canada's founding in the 1860s, the strong personalities, the various and sometimes intractable perspectives and agendas brought to the negotiating tables, and the horse-trading involved in nation-building from the country's earliest days. Of course, the politicians themselves were already accustomed to the importance of compromise but the support of Great Britain, the 'mother country' for union of its North American colonies, and an increasing fear of US aggression and talks of annexation sometimes made compromise easier. Our first moment centres on Joseph Howe of Nova Scotia and his quest in 1869 to negotiate 'better terms' for his province.

Indigenous peoples were not included in Canada's nation-building process. Not twenty years after Confederation, the country had to contend with the Northwest Rebellion, led by the Métis activist Louis Riel, who was tried and hanged for treason in 1885. Centring on that moment, Chapter 2 opens the wider discussion on colonialism and the Government of Canada's ill-treatment of Indigenous peoples, which include Inuit and Métis, as well as noting, in view of his partial French background and devout Catholic faith, that hanging Riel created a fissure that long coloured Anglo-French relations in Canada.

Canada's racist laws were not, however, directed only at its Indigenous peoples. White Anglo-Saxon Protestant (WASP) dominance was, for a long time, at the fore in terms of whom the country sought and accepted as immigrants and accounted for the pressures put upon many new arrivals to reject the ways of their original homeland. The federal government's handling of the arrival of the SS *Komagata Maru* in Vancouver in 1914 and its decision to not allow the passengers from India to disembark in

Canada is an illustrative example of this policy. Chapter 3 more generally also explores race, immigration and xenophobia in Canada, as well as the dominion's relationship to the British Empire.

Close constitutional and affective ties to Great Britain and the Empire drew Canada into the Great War. Contributing more than 600,000 military personnel, including 3,500 enlisted Indigenous men, from a population of some 7 million, Canada's involvement in the war was massive and impressive. Canada's involvement also brought great and lasting turmoil to the home front, especially in response to the federal government's implementation of conscription. Chapter 4 focuses on the 1918 Easter weekend anti-conscription riots in Quebec City. This moment allows us to examine more broadly how war shaped the nation, how it badly strained French-English relations to the point of leaving the country fractured, despite the pride and more intense nationalism that participation in the war had generated across much of English-speaking Canada.

Women, too, were not included in Canada's nation-building process of the 1860s. During the First World War, Canada's suffrage campaign achieved some success, and in 1918 the federal vote was extended to all female British subjects living in Canada, if they were twenty-one years of age or older. Ontario's Agnes Macphail, with her electoral win in the general election of 1921, the first after the Great War, became Canada's first woman Member of Parliament. This moment signalled enormous change for the place of women in Canadian society, as did the Person's Case, a few years later, which recognized women as persons in the constitution, and thereby redefined the meaning of Canadian citizenship. Chapter 5 examines these changes and how they came about.

The focus of Chapter 6 is 1945 and the beginning of what even today some refer to as the postwar period, a period that entrenched 'social citizenship' with the public's expectation that the government has a responsibility for maintaining the general welfare. People did not want to see a return to the laissez-faire approach that many believed had exacerbated the harrowing difficulties they experienced during the Great Depression. The singular moment examined here is the 1945 auto strike in Windsor, Ontario. Bitter labour disruptions engulfed large sectors of Canada's economy on many occasions. Often these were met with stiff, even violent, resistance from employers, in many cases assisted by governments, who would portray strikers as socialists or communists and, as such, a threat to constituted authority. Especially in the postwar period, to reduce confrontations and to bring about greater social stability, state accommodations were enacted, such as laws guaranteeing collective bargaining and union rights.

The Second World War, like the First, amplified Canadian nationalism. Loyal to Britain and the Empire, Canadians made tremendous sacrifices, achieved notable successes in combat and mobilized massive economic support for the Allies during the war – and increasingly bristled against British oversight. A pivotal moment in this development was the leadership

Canada took in defusing the 1956 Suez Crisis. Alone among the white Commonwealth countries to do so, Canada voted against the positions taken by Britain and France (with Israel's support), against Egypt's nationalization of the Suez Canal. For several tense weeks, it looked as if the United States and the Soviet Union, the world's two main nuclear superpowers, were going to be engaged in armed conflict against each other in support of one or other of the parties to the dispute. External Affairs Minister Lester B. Pearson, who was awarded a Nobel Peace Prize for this initiative, proposed instead that an armed, impartial peacekeeping force (what became the United Nations Emergency Force, UNEF) be drawn up to enforce a ceasefire and stabilize the situation. And that worked. Chapter 7 shows how Canada's involvement in the Suez Crisis contributed to a new national narrative, to Canada's maturation into an independent middle power, squarely at the forefront of decolonization efforts in the developing world, and with a new national identity, clearly separate from Great Britain's.

Hugely forwarding the nation's maturing identity, and certainly the most significant advancement in Canada's social citizenship agenda, is the country's universal government-run Medicare system. This medical insurance programme was first implemented in Saskatchewan, in 1962, by the Cooperative Commonwealth Federation (CCF) Premier, Tommy Douglas, who many consider to be the greatest Canadian ever. Douglas took this step in the face of an unprecedented and bitter doctors' strike, which is the moment at the centre of Chapter 8. The strike attracted worldwide media coverage, the striking doctors were defeated, and the programme not only went ahead, but was taken up by the rest of the country. Enjoyed by all Canadians today, in 1984 all previous Medicare acts were consolidated in the Canada Health Act (CHA) that also set national standards for health insurance. Medicare was a pivotal moment in the development of Canada's social welfare system and changed forever the role of government in Canada.

The next moment we examine is the Centennial in 1967. At no time before or since has there been such an explosion of nationalism among Canadians as throughout the entire centennial year, the moment that is the focus of Chapter 9. As Canada moved towards its centenary, the 1960s saw this spirit intensify, with government-funded undertakings and preparations for events under way everywhere and in every possible field of endeavour. Pearson, now prime minister, saw the realization of his long-held dream of a new, unique national flag for Canada, with the red Maple Leaf on a white background with red bars on either side replacing the Red Ensign as Canada's national flag in 1965. Yet, this same decade also witnessed the rise of a robust Quebec nationalism, the Quiet Revolution, with widely supported slogans like *maîtres chez nous*/masters in our own house and *je me souviens*/I remember, which is now the official motto of Quebec and to be found on all licence plates in the province. At times, this nationalism turned violent, as its more extreme elements sought liberation from Canada.

Pierre Elliott Trudeau followed Pearson. More than any other prime minister, Trudeau, with his policy of multiculturalism and by patriating the constitution, changed Canada's national narrative. The country's exclusionary, British and French-centric ethnic nationalism was replaced with a rights-based civic nationalism and the country's complete independence. A central moment in this process was the promulgation of the Canadian Charter of Rights and Freedoms, which forms part 1 of Canada's Constitution Act, 1982. Individual rights and freedoms are entrenched in the Charter, and these supersede ethnic, regional or other group nationalisms. The process of achieving the new constitution, which is the subject of Chapter 10, brought bitter divisions. Many felt left out or inadequately represented, perhaps most blatantly Quebec, which is still not a signatory to the constitution. More recently, some have argued that Trudeau's promotion of rights and multiculturalism, in fact, has provided a basis, if tacit, for discrimination and racial violence, allowing Canadians to ignore the harsh lived reality of many minorities, while refuting the claim that racism is alive and well in Canada.

Canadians' fear of domination by, and perhaps even absorption into, a much more powerful United States had also influenced the development of the country's independence and direction. This fear often resulted in a national policy of economic protectionism that was not without controversy. Protectionism was seen to benefit particularly manufacturers in Quebec and Ontario (Central Canada) by protecting and enriching its industrial interests, while disadvantaging the rest of the country. People in rural areas and throughout the prairies saw tariff protectionism as hampering their ability to sell their products widely and to obtain needed inputs, such as agricultural equipment and other manufactured goods, more cheaply. On several occasions, such as in the 1891 and 1911 general elections, the topic of free trade with the United States came to the fore but was ultimately scuttled because of fears raised that it would result in the end of Canada. Prime Minister Brian Mulroney was able to get Canadian voters to change their minds on free trade, as evidenced by the results of the 1988 general election, a seminal moment in the country's history. He insisted that economic nationalism stunted Canada's potential, and his determination, put to a national vote, resulted in the Canada-United States Free Trade Agreement (CUSFTA) in 1988 and later superseded by the North American Free Trade Agreement (NAFTA) in 1994, which included Mexico. Chapter 11 examines the history of protectionism in Canada, how free trade rallied Canadians who were both for and against it in 1988, and the massive impact of continental economic integration since the policy of protectionism, or economic nationalism, was abandoned. For thirty-six years, most Canadians were content with the new trading relationship and their growing economic dependence on the United States but when America's forty-seventh president, Donald J. Trump, introduced punitive tariffs on Canadian imports in early 2025, Canadians rallied around the flag and celebrated as its new prime minister, Mark Carney, who vowed to make the US pay for its treatment of Canada and promised a new trading relationship not only with the United States but with the whole world.

Forever bedevilling Canada and Canadian unity is Quebec's place in the federation. Quebec is still the one province that has not approved the 1982 constitution although it is bound by its contents. The federal government's efforts at accommodation through the redistribution of federal-provincial powers and finding an acceptable means to amend the 1982 constitution have so far failed to produce common ground. Chapter 12 examines Quebec nationalism in response to these constitutional disagreements. A more energized separatist movement sprung up and reached its apogee in the 1995 Quebec referendum, the chapter's central moment, the razor-thin results of which came within a whisker of demonstrating that a majority of Quebec voters favoured leaving Canada.

Gay, lesbian, bisexual, transgender and other non-binary people in Canada were faced with prejudice and discriminatory laws from the earliest days of Confederation. June 2003 signalled a huge moment on this front, when the Ontario Court of Appeal ruled that prohibiting gay couples from marrying is unconstitutional and in violation of the Canadian Charter of Rights and Freedoms. This decision led to the 2005 Civil Marriage Act, by which Canada became the third country in the world to make same-sex marriage legal; nearly half of Canadians polled at that time said they supported gay and lesbian marriage. This sea change from long-standing, punishing legislation and public attitudes was noticed in many places, with even the *Economist* claiming that 'a cautious case can be made that Canada is now rather cool' because of 'a certain boldness in social matters', in particular, such 'excellent liberal ideas as the plan to legalise gay marriage and decriminalise marijuana'.[7] Chapter 13 explores how this change came about, the long struggle against prejudice that homosexuals in Canada waged and the degree to which members of 2SLGTBQ2AI+ communities still face inequality and discrimination.

On 11 June 2008, Canada, for the first time, officially took responsibility for its decades-long policy of attempting to assimilate Indigenous, Inuit and Métis children by placing them, for the most part forcibly, in government-sponsored schools. On that momentous day, on behalf of the Government of Canada, Prime Minister Stephen Harper offered a full apology for the Indian Residential Schools system. Chapter 14 analyses that statement and also considers what has happened since 2008, including Canada's landmark Truth and Reconciliation Commission (TRC) and its 2015 Report which concluded that the residential schools enacted a policy of cultural genocide, with the deliberate destruction of the traditions, language and life skills of Canada's

---

[7]'Canada's New Spirit', *The Economist*, 25 September 2003, https://www.economist.com/leaders/2003/09/25/canadas-new-spirit.

Indigenous peoples and communities. This national shame is examined, as well as the broader history of policies regarding Canada's Indigenous people, of brutally controlling them not only through Residential Schools with their appalling social conditions, but also through the actions of the authoritarian and racist agents of the Department of Indian Affairs, unresolved treaty and other issues, countered by the growth of organized nationwide Indigenous activism and demands for Indigenous self-governments.

Finally, we turn to a very recent, but also stunning moment in Canada's history: the 2021 Truckers Freedom Convoy. In convoys of several hundred rigs, truckers snarled highways and city streets across the country. The convoy settled in downtown Ottawa, shutting down the city for several weeks. Protesters were opposed to the federal government's imposition of mandates and restrictions in its attempts to manage the Covid-19 pandemic, and they accused the government of undermining fundamental freedoms and imperilling civil liberties specified in the 1982 Charter. The protests also laid bare broader frustration and anger directed at Prime Minister Justin Trudeau not only for imposing restrictions, but also for boosting progressive social politics. The convoy and reactions to it seemed to reinvigorate social conservatism in Canada. Feeble and uncoordinated attempts by police to break up the protest and get the truckers to leave the capital, Ottawa, failed. Then, for the first time ever, the federal government invoked the 1988 Emergencies Act, immediately rekindling memories of Pierre's Trudeau's deployment of the War Measures Act in 1970, in response to FLQ activities in Montreal. Within a week the trucks had cleared out of Ottawa; however, a mandatory federal investigation of invoking the Act followed, as well as law suits by various parties in the courts. These issues remain far from resolved.

Each of the fifteen moments chosen for this book marked not only its own unique time and place, but also revealed and helped shape many longer-term developments in Canada's history. They bring to light a complex story of triumphs and failures, hopes and anxieties, and change, survival and renewal. With both discord and achievements having a place in Canada's still-evolving story, these moments help build the national narrative of transformation from a British colony into the modern, economically powerful, socially diverse, culturally rich and sovereign nation that is Canada today.

IMAGE 1 Joseph Howe, former premier of Nova Scotia, 1869. Photo by Topley Studio, Library and Archives Canada/PA-025486.

1

Joseph Howe and 'Better Terms', 1869: Making the nation work

At a public meeting in Halifax in late May 1867, just weeks before the Dominion of Canada came into formal existence on 1 July, Joseph Howe, journalist, publisher, politician and former premier of Nova Scotia, vowed to 'punish the scamps' who had dragged Nova Scotia into Confederation. 'I believe from the bottom of my heart', he said,

> that this union will be disastrous. At present we have no control of our revenues, our trade and of our affairs; and I have no hesitation in saying that if it were not for my respect for the British flag and my allegiance to my Sovereign – if the British forces were withdrawn from the country and this issue were left to be tried out between Canadians and ourselves, I would take every son I have and die on the frontier before I would submit to this outrage [Confederation].[1]

Three months before this, Queen Victoria had given royal assent to the British North America Act, the founding document and constitution of the new country. Section 16 of the BNA Act made Ottawa the national capital. The federation initially comprised the British North American colonies, now provinces, of Nova Scotia, New Brunswick, Quebec and Ontario. No sooner had the new nation come into being than one of the provinces – Nova Scotia, especially in the person of Joseph Howe – attempted to repeal its decision to join it. Howe's anti-Confederation efforts, perhaps surprisingly at the time, did not destroy the union. Working out a mutually acceptable accommodation between a disgruntled member province and the federal government became a cornerstone in the development of Canada's national character.

---

[1] *Morning Chronicle*, 19 May 1867.

A quarter of a century before Confederation and several years before the publication of *A Tale of Two Cities*, Charles Dickens visited parts of British North America. Those were not, of course, the places he was thinking of when he opened that iconic novel with the memorable lines, 'It was the best of times, it was the worst of times … it was the season of Light, it was the season of Darkness, it was the spring of hope, it was the winter of despair'. Nevertheless, these words capture brilliantly the feelings expressed across Canada in 1867. For George Brown, editor of Toronto's *Globe* and one of the champions of Confederation, it was the best of times. 'The history of Old Canada, with its contracted bounds and limited divisions of Upper and Lower, West and East, has been completed', he wrote jubilantly on that first of July in 1867, 'and this day a new volume is opened, New Brunswick and Nova Scotia uniting with Ontario and Quebec, to make the history of a greater Canada, already extending from the [Atlantic] ocean to the headwaters of the Great Lakes, and destined ere long to embrace the larger half of this North American Continent from the Atlantic to the Pacific'. Soon, Brown proclaimed, Canada would be a transcontinental nation, attractive to many people around the world who would join with Canadians to settle the country's virgin farmland and build great towns and cities. 'Together, they would construct a great nation'.[2]

On Canada's east coast, it was for many people, including Howe, the worst of times. Writing in the *Eastern Chronicle and Pictou County Advocate*, editors Robert McConnell and W. B. Alley captured the despair: 'You are now said to be Canadians, by Act of Parliament, against your wishes', they reminded their readers. 'Do you accept the will of the despots who have forced this measure upon you, or do you reject the imputation as an insult upon your intelligence, and a trampling upon your right to be heard in deciding your own destiny?' The perception of Nova Scotians was that they had been sold to the Canadians, and only their respect for the Queen and constituted authorities prevented violence. The first of July 1867 in Nova Scotia was a 'day of humiliation' marked by 'quite a number of flags upside down and half-mast, with several black pennants, and a black flag'. There was no ringing of church bells, no firing of guns to welcome the 'infant monster Confederation'. In Howe's Nova Scotia, it was the season of darkness. The extent of the anger towards Canada would be borne out in the coming elections for the provincial House of Assembly and for members of the federal Parliament.[3] When Nova Scotians voted later that summer, anti-Confederates took thirty-six of thirty-eight seats in the provincial legislature and eighteen of nineteen seats in the House of Commons; only

---

[2]George Brown, 'Confederation Day: The Dominion of Canada – Historical Notes, How Confederation Has Been Brought about, Statistics of the United Provinces', *The Globe* 24, no. 156 (1 July 1867): 1.

[3]'Dominion Day', *Eastern Chronicle and Pictou County Advocate* 25, no. 49 (3 July 1867): 2.

Halifax favoured being part of Canada.[4] The single Confederate survivor was Charles Tupper who had led the fight in Nova Scotia for Confederation and eighteen anti-Confederates, including Howe, who sat in the Dominion Parliament were dubbed the 'Noble Eighteen'.

By 1866, both Prince Edward Island and Newfoundland had decided to stay out of Confederation. With just four provinces to begin with, resentment and anger in Nova Scotia – as well as lukewarm support in Quebec and strong anti-Confederate sentiment in New Brunswick – could have spelled disaster for the new nation. It is not what happened. On 1 December 1869, Canada more than doubled in size when it acquired Rupert's Land from the Hudson's Bay Company, adding to the Dominion the vast tract of land from Labrador in the east, across Quebec and Ontario, to encompass the present-day prairie provinces all of the way to the Rocky Mountains. In fact, within six years of Confederation, three provinces joined the federation (Manitoba in 1870, British Columbia in 1871 and then Prince Edward Island in 1873), extending the country across the continent from sea to sea and northward towards the Arctic Circle. Railways were being built to link central and eastern Canada with the west. The new nation encountered and weathered crises from its earliest days. John A. Macdonald, the dominant figure in the push for Confederation and Canada's first prime minister, resigned in 1873 amid charges of corruption, and the country witnessed the peaceful transfer of power to a new political party and a new prime minister, Liberal Alexander Mackenzie. Little more than a decade later, Canadians quashed a Métis uprising, known as the North-West Resistance of 1885, led by Louis Riel, who was hanged for his efforts – and years later honoured as the founding father of Manitoba – in the huge territory acquired from the Hudson's Bay Company (see Chapter 2).

Quarrels and conflicts between provinces and the federal government – and the struggle to resolve them – became normative elements in the story of Canada, even a hallmark of Confederation itself. In 1867, Nova Scotia's Joseph Howe was only the first to rail against the centre and achieve 'better terms' for his province. A study of Howe's crusade against the Confederation arrangements brings region and fragmentation to the forefront of Canada's story, while demonstrating that the federal principle, embodied in the British North America Act, was designed to be flexible and accommodating if the new nation were to survive. A flexible federalism became not only an instrument for obtaining political consent for Canada, but also a means of achieving stability and unity.

The Dominion of Canada was born during a period often referred to as 'the age of nation building'. In the mid-nineteenth century, smaller geopolitical units in various parts of the world were coalescing into larger political

---

[4]Peter Busby Waite, *The Life and Times of Confederation 1864–1867: Politics, Newspapers, and the Union of British North America* (Toronto: University of Toronto Press, 1962), 202.

entities, seen to be economically and militarily advantageous. In Europe, nationalist movements arose in Italy and Germany, and in the southern hemisphere in Peru and Australia. In the seven British North American colonies, too, there was a growing desire for a larger union. In fact, Joseph Howe himself had talked of the possibility of intercolonial union since the late 1830s. New Brunswick Premier Leonard Tilley urged politicians 'to bind together the Atlantic to the Pacific by a continuous chain of settlements and line of communications for that [was] the destiny of this country, and the race which inhabited it'.[5] Like other nation builders of their day, Howe and Tilley belonged to an emerging middle class that saw larger nation-states as necessary if they were to capitalize on the technological advances of the era. The Industrial Revolution was changing the way economies were structured and, together with increasing urbanization, this placed new demands on the state. The surge in railroad construction, especially, made many people conclude that a national market was desirable. Howe and Tilley and like-minded others saw considerable benefit in nation-states with strong central governments that would have the authority and the fiscal and legal capacity to facilitate the development of larger and more efficient economies that would, in turn, provide a wide range of public goods and services.

The story of what began as the Dominion of Canada in 1867 had little to do with the decolonization movement and the establishment of post-colonial states that have marked more recent global history. Those early Canadian politicians were happy colonials, largely content with the imperial arrangements already in place in British North America. The legislation creating the new nation was itself an imperial statute of the British Parliament and, for more than a century, could be amended only there. Nation-states like Canada and the politicians that drove the nation-building initiatives were not being merely economically pragmatic. They were witness to and certainly concerned about what they deemed to be democratic excess that they surmised had led to the collapse of the US constitutional arrangements and the outbreak of the American Civil War that raged from 1861 to 1865. Canada's 'fathers of Confederation' proceeded on the premise that political ties could be forged between diverse linguistic, religious and ethnic groups, ties that would integrate majorities and minorities into an inclusive power arrangement across a large geographical space called Canada. Shared language and culture were largely irrelevant in the nation-building initiatives of the mid-nineteenth century; virtually all the nation-states that emerged at the time, whether in Europe or elsewhere, were ethnically diverse.

Nation builders in British North America explicitly determined who qualified for full membership in the nation, with a voice in the nation's affairs. At the risk of being crude or anachronistic, they were heavily

---

[5]Chris M. Wallace, 'Tilley, Sir Samuel Leonard', in *Dictionary of Canadian Biography*, vol. 12 (University of Toronto/Université Laval, 2003), accessed 9 August 2024, https://www.biographi.ca/en/bio/tilley_samuel_leonard_12E.html.

influenced by prevailing views of 'civilization' and of who counted as 'civilized'. Indigenous peoples were given no voice unless it was determined they had been assimilated to the economic and social customs of European settler societies. People of African heritage were similarly seen to be lacking in 'civilization', and excluded from political participation. Women were not viewed as autonomous individuals or, indeed as 'persons' (on this, see Chapter 5 and the Persons Case of 1929), and were also excluded from full membership in the nation in their own right. Only white men twenty-one years of age or older, owners of property and British subjects were, with voting rights, considered to be full members of the new nation that became Canada.

British North America was not a homogeneous community. Nation building, of necessity, became a political enterprise rather than a cultural or ethnic one. As in other nation-building efforts at the time, it was believed that Canada's political communities could embrace different cultures and ethnicities and, at the same time, through statecraft administer vast territories and allow people who did not share common cultural and racial bonds to live together despite their differences. The goal was to represent rather than to resolve most of the regional and ethnic differences that existed throughout the British colonies. This approach to nation building is what historian Benedict Anderson, more than a century later, in 1983, famously termed 'imagined communities': in his view, nations could rise above differences created by religion, region and ethnicity and bring together within a single state people who would never meet each other in person but who might together develop a workable state and aspire to a shared national identity.[6]

The first formal steps towards the creation of Canada began at a conference in Charlottetown in September 1864. Various forces and motives drove the Confederation process. Politicians in the Maritime colonies had agreed to meet to discuss union. They shared an enthusiasm for railways, industrial and economic development, and a belief that as part of a larger political entity they would have enhanced access to credit to achieve their common objectives. Politicians in the Canadas (East and West), facing their own political, economic and cultural challenges, asked to be invited to present their idea of a federal union of all of British North America. At Charlottetown, Macdonald, his long-time political partner George-Étienne Cartier, and George Brown explained the benefits of such a larger, federated union. The Maritimers had already been thinking along those lines and agreed with the Canadians.

Thirty-six colonial politicians gathered at a second conference, held in Quebec City the next month. They faced numerous challenges from various perspectives and considerable pressure from London to work out

---

[6]Benedict Anderson, *Imagined Communities: Reflections on the Origin and Spread of Nationalism*, Rev. and extended ed. (London and New York: Verso, 1991).

an agreement on union. Nova Scotians could claim they had achieved a measure of self-government without breaking a single pane of glass. Canada East and Canada West, together comprising the Province of Canada from 1841 to 1867, had both survived rebellion in the 1830s and were struggling to find a workable union between French and English Canada. Mounting public debt was a reality for all the delegates, as they eyed further railway and industrial expansion. They believed their constituencies had reached their potential as separate entities and that it was time to form a larger unit. They all worried, too, about what might happen when the United States emerged victorious from its Civil War: would it then train its sights on British territory to the north and realize its ambitions to drive European powers from North America for good? After all, before the end of the war the United States had announced plans to terminate the Reciprocity Treaty that since 1854 had given the British colonies unfettered access to the US market. London was pushing for a new imperial framework whereby colonies would assume greater responsibility for themselves, for the costs associated with their own well-being – particularly in matters of defence and transportation.

Arrangements accommodating diversity and regional interests were worked out at the Quebec Conference. Delegates agreed on seventy-two resolutions that would form the basis for the British North America Act, which specified shared responsibilities between provincial and national interests, balanced unity and diversity and while enabling the building of a national economy, provided a design for social cohesion. Macdonald and Cartier were long-time political allies and two of the important politicians in the making of Canada. They held differing visions of what Canada should be, however, and the BNA Act accommodated them both. Macdonald imagined an economic union that would have a strong federal government with various general powers and overarching authority to supervise the provinces and develop a national economy. Macdonald's idea of a centralized federation held little traction with the Maritimers, or with Quebec. Cartier insisted that the new arrangements had to provide for Canada's distinct minorities. He understood that through a series of geopolitical, economic and historical realities two settler communities – one French-speaking and the other English-speaking – were firmly entrenched; if the new nation were to succeed, the constitution establishing it had to prevent the national majority from assimilating those minorities that were already very much a part of Canada's cultural identity. Tilley and others from the Maritimes worried about losing all local control to a distant central government; they were for a constitution that mandated strong provincial governments and the equitable distribution of federal monies throughout the new federation. No delegate gave much attention to Indigenous peoples except to embrace the existing plan to assimilate them into Canadian-settler society.

Federalism was the political mechanism by which diversity could be reconciled with unity. In his February 1865 speech during the debates on

Confederation in the Legislative Assembly of the Province of Canada, Cartier explained that in such a constitutional arrangement the federal government would be dealing with national, not local matters; the federal government, he assured sceptics, could pose 'no danger to the rights of French Canadians, Scotchmen, Englishmen or Irishmen'.[7] The Canadian state would not require conformity to one culture, or even to two cultures.[8] Canada was to be a country with a single political – or civic – nationality, but also a country where multiple cultural identities and multiple allegiances could develop and flourish. The embrace of federalism, Cartier insisted, created a Canadian political nationality to which all peoples could belong without surrendering their cultural or regional identity.[9] 'United together, if union were attained', Cartier continued, 'we would form a political nationality with which neither the national origin, nor the religion of any individual, would interfere'. He did note that 'it was lamented by some that we had this diversity of races, and hopes were expressed that this distinctive feature would cease'. Cartier then pointed out that the 'idea of unity of races was Utopian – it was impossible. Distinctions of this kind would always exist ... in the political world'.[10] He expressed hope in what was being created: 'In our own Federation we should have Catholic and Protestant, English, French, Irish and Scotch, and each by his efforts and his success would increase the prosperity and glory of the new Confederacy ... we were of different races, not for the purpose of warring against each other, but in order to compete and emulate for the general welfare'.[11] For Cartier, especially, diversity was a fact that could not be erased from the Canadian polity, and Canadians had to learn to reconcile diversity with the need for unity. In British North America, he said, 'we are five different peoples living in five separate provinces' and with Confederation, we would form 'a political nationality independent of national origin, or the religion of any one individual'.[12]

---

[7]Allan Smith, *Canada, an American Nation? Essays on Continentalism, Identity, and the Canadian Frame of Mind* (Montreal and Kingston: McGill-Queen's University Press, 1994), 135.

[8]'The Rights of Each and Every Citizen Will Be Protected', speech by George-Étienne Cartier, 17 May 1867. Available at Macdonald Laurier Institute Confederation Project, https://www.macdonaldlaurier.ca/the-rights-of-each-and-every-citizen-will-be-protected-may-17-1867-speech-by-george-etienne-cartier/.

[9]Samuel V. LaSelva, *The Moral Foundations of Canadian Federalism: Paradoxes, Achievements, and Tragedies of Nationhood* (Montreal and Kingston: McGill-Queen's University Press, 1996), 34–8.

[10]See George-Étienne Cartier, Speech in the Confederation Debates – 7 February 1865, Macdonald Laurier Institute, Confederation Series, 7 March 2017, https://macdonaldlaurier.ca/18740/.

[11]Cited in Canada, *Parliamentary Debates on the Subject of the Confederation* (Quebec: Hunter Rose, 1865), 60, Reference re Secession of Quebec, [1998] 2 S.C.R. 217, https://scc-csc.lexum.com/scc-csc/scc-csc/en/item/1643/index.do?site_preference=normal.

[12]Canada, *Parliamentary Debates on the subject of the Confederation*, 55–9.

In a classic federal system, the power to legislate is limited to that allocated in the constitution. The two orders of government in Canada – federal and provincial – are each assigned exclusive powers, and it is understood that neither level of government can encroach upon the powers or jurisdiction of the other. The federal government was given clear responsibilities in national matters, in areas such as defence, developing a national transportation system, and creating a nationally integrated economy through its control of, for example, currency and weights and measures. It was also given jurisdiction over international trade and commerce. Section 121 of the BNA Act provided for a common market, claiming that 'all articles of the growth, produce or manufacture of any one of the Provinces ... shall be admitted free into each of the other Provinces'. At Quebec City, the delegates from Canada East and the Maritimes insisted that the provinces retain autonomy over education, religious and civil institutions, property rights, and such social institutions as public workhouses, reformatories, prisons, hospitals, asylums and charities.

Those who made Canada understood it was to not be a classic federal system. The preamble to section 91 of the BNA Act outlines Ottawa's responsibilities. It includes a clause that empowers the federal government to make laws for the 'Peace, Order and Good Government of Canada'. Frequently referred to as the 'POGG' clause, it clearly establishes for the federal government the sense of a national jurisdiction to meet national needs and govern for the good of the nation; and second, it provides the federal government with general and wide-ranging powers, while leaving provincial jurisdiction to deal with local matters and interests. Moreover, the federal government was given the authority to encroach on provincial jurisdiction, including the power of disallowance and reservation of any bill from the provincial legislatures. Both powers have been seen as providing a supervisory role for the federal governments over the provinces, which unmistakably indicated Ottawa was the dominant power. Unlike in the United States, where the Constitution gives all residual powers to the states, in Canada's Constitution all residual powers rest with the federal government.

From the beginning, Canada's founders were concerned about the country's minorities, and the treatment of minorities would continue to be a major theme throughout Canada's history, as we will see in the chapters that follow. The federal government was given the responsibility to protect the educational rights of religious minorities as they existed by legislation at the time of Confederation. If a provincial majority decided to impose any tyrannical measures against a provincial minority, section 93 of the BNA Act gave to the federal government the authority to protect minority education rights existing at the time of union. Although Canada has too often treated its minority groups shabbily, the politicians who created Canada in the 1860s recognized the importance, especially of religious minority rights that at the time trumped virtually all other rights. The rights of Indigenous peoples, however, attracted but little attention at Confederation, because, for one thing, in Eastern Canada they were thought to be quickly disappearing or adopting a European lifestyle.

The BNA Act did not contain an amending formula explaining how it might be changed, and this was because everyone assumed that changes would be done in concert with the British government in London. Canada's founders believed they had reconciled the necessities of creating a nationally integrated economic union and succeeded in uniting the scattered colonies of British North America through crafting a constitution based on the federal principle that shared responsibility between competing provincial and national interests. Richard Simeon, one of Canada's pre-eminent federalist scholars, once noted that 'federalism is not an end in itself'. Rather, it must be evaluated on its functional effectiveness, that is, its ability to 'enhance or frustrate the capacity of government institutions to generate effective policy and respond to citizen needs'.[13] It should be noted, however, that the making of Canada was hardly an exercise in democratic splendour and inclusion. Women, Indigenous peoples and various minorities were excluded. We know all too well that the Canada created in 1867 assumed the role of colonizer and embarked on several misguided and evil policies, especially towards Indigenous peoples, the legacies of which are still very much evident today.

At the heart of Canadian federalism remains the question of jurisdiction and which order of government has which power. To their, and Canada's credit, Canadian politicians have successfully managed moments of conflict between provinces and the federal government for more than 150 years. This point is amply demonstrated by examining how, in the weeks and months after Canada came into existence, the nation dealt with attempts to change the Confederation agreement – or take Nova Scotia out of Confederation.

The roles of Maritime politicians such as premiers Leonard Tilley of New Brunswick and Charles Tupper of Nova Scotia have often been overshadowed by those of Macdonald, Cartier and Brown, but that does not mean they were less important to the making of Canada. They shared in the national spirit and were firm supporters of a broader union of the British North American colonies. They also supported a federal union as was agreed to at Quebec City in 1864 for many of the same reasons that Cartier insisted on such a constitutional arrangement. Once they returned home, however, and the seventy-two resolutions were published, they were faced with considerable opposition. Throughout the region, many people believed that the Quebec Resolutions did not adequately meet their needs and concerns. In fact, both Newfoundland and Prince Edward Island were so disappointed that they opted not to join the union. Tilley put the issue to a vote in New Brunswick and lost the election badly to the anti-Confederate Albert Smith. By 1866, however, Smith's government was in turmoil and through the

---

[13]Jean Leclair, 'The Supreme Court of Canada's Understanding of Federalism: Efficiency at the Expense of Diversity', *Queen's Law Journal* 28 (2003): 411–14.

machinations of Arthur Gordon, the British-appointed lieutenant governor of New Brunswick, new elections were held. This time everything aligned for Tilley and the Confederates. The campaign had generous funding from the Canadians. Moreover, it began just as the Irish-American Fenians turned their attention to invading Britain's possessions in North America to force the British out of Ireland. As the Fenians amassed on the colony's border with the United States, Tilley was able to convince his constituents that a larger union would provide a better defence system than New Brunswick could muster alone. Even the Catholic Church came out in support of union. Once Tilley was back as premier, the New Brunswick legislature quickly passed a resolution in support of Confederation.

The situation unfolded differently in Nova Scotia, even though the opposition to Confederation there was better organized and more determined. Premier Tupper believed elected members in the legislature had the authority to decide the issue, and he refused to hold an election to let Nova Scotians decide on their colony joining the British North American union. He delayed calling a vote on Confederation in the Nova Scotia Legislature until he was sure of winning it. The moment came in March 1866, with the Fenians seemed poised to attack in New Brunswick. Promising changes to the Quebec Resolutions, Tupper convinced enough legislators wary of union to endorse a motion in favour, by a vote of thirty-one to nineteen. It was a shabby manoeuver for a colony that was the first in British North America to win Responsible Government, or self-government. Opposition outside the provincial assembly soon mounted. It thrust Joseph Howe, journalist, public servant, former premier and firm believer in some sort of imperial union to the centre of Nova Scotian politics once again and made him leader of the anti-Confederation forces.

On 11 January 1865, shortly after the terms of union were released, Howe published the first of twelve anonymous Botheration Letters in Halifax's *Morning Chronicle*. At the time, he was fisheries inspector for the British government and, as a civil servant, he was not permitted to publicly voice his opinion on Confederation. In those letters, and later as president of the League of the Maritime Provinces (known more generally as the Anti-Confederate League), he refined his opposition to union, but he was preaching to the converted: opinion had already swung against Confederation by then, but Howe soon became the leading spokesperson against union. He feared that the plan devised at Quebec City would create a highly centralized union and that in Ottawa Nova Scotia would have only limited influence on important matters. Of particular concern to Howe was the matter of tariffs that the Province of the United Canadas had adopted. If those tariffs were extended to Nova Scotia, it would be devastating for the province.[14] Nova Scotia needed low tariffs to encourage trade with Great

---

[14]*Halifax Morning Chronicle*, Botheration Letters no. 3, 14 January 1865.

Britain and other locations around the Atlantic. Moreover, higher tariffs would raise the cost of imported goods. Howe was deeply concerned, too, that the people of Nova Scotia had not been given the opportunity to vote on Confederation, and he often noted the discord that had emerged in Ireland and Scotland when their legislatures were destroyed through what he called coercion and deception. The manner in which Tupper and his party had made union possible, Howe insisted, was undemocratic and flew in the face of responsible government which he had helped bring to Nova Scotia a decade earlier.

Howe turned his attention to London, hoping the British Parliament would not pass the legislation that would create Canada; however, he found that the British government, particularly the Colonial Office, favoured union and had little time for its detractors. Howe continued agitating against union. In the general election of 18 September 1867, he won a seat in the House of Commons along with seventeen other anti-Confederates. He went to Ottawa to repeal Confederation, or at least to get Nova Scotia out of the union. Among the first acts of the new Canadian Parliament was harmonizing the tariff throughout the Dominion, setting the rate at 15 per cent rather than the normal rate of 20 per cent which had been the case in the Canadas (Quebec and Ontario) before Confederation. It was moderately protectionist policy and considerably higher than the more or less free-trade policy of what Nova Scotia had previously. Howe seized upon the change, arguing that the initiative would lead to undue hardship on the poor of his province, but more importantly, it demonstrated that Nova Scotia's interests could not be protected in the federal government. The secessionist threat gained momentum.

Howe continued to lobby London for his cause, but his pleadings there still fell on deaf ears. All legal means of extricating Nova Scotia from Confederation had apparently failed. Howe reasoned that he was left with two options: (1) continue the agitation, rachet up the anger and rhetoric, which he feared might lead to open insurrection or an armed uprising against Canada, or (2) accept Nova Scotia's place in Confederation and work within the federal system for better terms. Violence was a non-starter for Howe. He took the pragmatic option of working within the federal system to try and protect the interests of his province (as members of the sovereigntist parties in Quebec and reformers in Western Canada would do in future decades). He realized that Nova Scotia would have to be an active participant in the Dominion Parliament regardless of any desire to remove the province from Confederation. In some ways, Howe's fellow Members of Parliament were not unlike the modern Bloc Québécois, a political party that promotes Quebec's interests and Quebec sovereignty in the House of Commons today.

In Ottawa and at the same time, Macdonald realized, too, that he had to address the anti-Confederate sentiment in Nova Scotia. Nova Scotia remaining in Canada was critical to the success of the new nation. It had a well-developed economy and was site of a major Royal Navy base. If it left the new union, New Brunswick might follow and Britain might cool on the whole idea of Canada as the new British Prime Minister, Liberal William Gladstone, dismissed the importance of the colonies like Canada. Macdonald travelled to Halifax and met with Howe. It was not only about pacifying Howe and the Nova Scotians. He continued to hope that Prince Edward Island and Newfoundland would soon join the federation as would British Columbia which was then a Crown colony on the West Coast. If those colonies could be added, Canada would become a nation that was trans-continental just like the United States. It was an ambitious project, and it could not be jeopardized by continued anger and resentment towards the union in Nova Scotia. Macdonald offered to negotiate better financial terms for Nova Scotia within Confederation as well as a seat in his Cabinet for Howe and one other Nova Scotian. All legal options being closed, Howe was open to Macdonald's overtures. In January 1869, Howe and fellow Nova Scotian MPs reached an agreement with Sir John Rose, Macdonald's minister of finance, offering 'better terms' to Nova Scotia. Ottawa agreed to absorb all of Nova Scotia's provincial debt of approximately $2 million and extend a federal subsidy by $166,734 for ten years and $85,000 thereafter. Joseph Howe joined Macdonald's Cabinet as president of the Privy Council and was given control of federal patronage in Nova Scotia.[15] As was required at the time, he had to resign his seat in Parliament and contest a byelection. It was a bitter campaign with the anti-Confederate, Monson Henry Goudge, who was nick-named 'Roaring Billows', falling just 300 votes short of unseating Howe. While some have dismissed Howe's acceptance of a Cabinet post as self-serving opportunism, Macdonald warned that 'better terms' could not be carried without some assurance that the secessionist agitation cease and the best way to achieve that was for Howe to enter the Macdonald's Cabinet. Howe's Nova Scotia allies, including Premier William Annand, never forgave him but Howe himself believed it was necessary to sit at the Cabinet table to protect the interests of Nova Scotia in Ottawa.[16] Evidently, John A. Macdonald knew he would have to deal with other discontent in the federation, and in doing so, he created a template for dealing with dissent and dissatisfaction that prime ministers have by and large followed ever since. Perhaps ironically, Howe's protests helped centralize the power of the federal government.

How national governments seek to accommodate the goals and aspirations of various subnational entities or provinces has been one of the pressing concerns of all federalist states. Canada has wrestled with this

---

[15]Joseph Howe, 'Letter from Hon. Joseph Howe: To the Electors of the County of Hants', *British Colonist*, 27 July 1872, 2, https://babel.hathitrust.org/cgi/pt?id=aeu.ark:/13960/t3320fh5r&seq=5.
[16]Ibid.

dilemma from its very beginnings. Intense conflict between the provinces and the federal government has been a regular feature of Canada from its inception. Among additional noteworthy examples of such quarrels – that some see as evidence of federal-provincial dysfunctionality – occurred in the period right after Confederation when some provincial premiers, notably, Ontario's Oliver Mowat, in the 1870s, resisted Macdonald's determination to increase the power of the federal government at the expense of the provinces; in the 1930s, when premiers sought a greater share of national revenue; in the various constitutional battles in the 1980s and early 1990s, particularly between Ottawa and Quebec; and in the disputes over energy in the 1980s, when Western premiers resisted Prime Minister Pierre Trudeau's plan to create a national energy policy; and most recently, when Prime Minister Mark Carney introduced a regulation that ceased the application of the Greenhouse Gas Pollution Pricing Act (carbon tax) after considerable opposition from the provinces. Sometimes the courts have resolved jurisdictional conflict between the two orders of government, but the survival of federalism – and Canada itself – rarely depended only on the judiciary. Often the solution was found in a political agreement between the constituent parts that make up the country.

Joseph Howe and John A. Macdonald not only reshaped the Nova Scotia–Ottawa relationship in the late 1860s, but they also helped shape Canada and Canadian federalism. When Howe agreed to accept union and Macdonald negotiated 'better terms' for Nova Scotia, they both demonstrated that Canada and Canadian federalism would be a work in progress, a living organism that could change and accommodate contingencies and adapt to new and emerging dynamisms. They recognized, too, that as a political community, Canada consists of provinces and communities, each with particular and distinctive ways of life and different needs and aspirations that must be met for the nation-state to survive and thrive. Those politicians demonstrated that Canadian federalism – and, indeed, Canada itself – works effectively across geographical space, languages and cultures when political actors practise accommodation and compromise and are willing to move beyond the original texts of federalism and constitutionalism to find workable solutions to the nation's problems.

IMAGE 2 Portrait of Louis Riel, the Métis leader and political figure. Library and Archives Canada / Jean Riel fonds PA-139070.

2

The hanging of Louis Riel, 1885: Managing cultural genocide

The *New York Times* was one of several newspapers that despatched a correspondent to report on the hanging of Louis David Riel in the jail yard of the Northwest Mounted Police barracks in Regina on Monday, 16 November 1885. Riel was executed for high treason against the Crown. The previous morning, a Sunday, Riel had awakened early and asked to see Edgar Dewdney, lieutenant governor of the North-West Territories and Indian commissioner appointed by Prime Minister Macdonald. The correspondent reported he accompanied Dewdney to Riel's cell, where Riel told Dewdney a guardian angel had visited him during the night, 'revealing to him that he would rise three days after his execution and share the Premiership of Canada with Sir John Macdonald'. The angel had also informed Riel that he would remain three years more in the Northwest and 'obtain the liberty of the half breeds'. Dewdney must have wondered about Riel's mental state as during the trial Riel's lawyers attempted to portray him as insane, but he simply replied that he had brought with him the warrant for Riel's execution. 'Riel was rather dazed by the news, but said, with a sickly smile: You bring a grand announcement; I shall soon be out of my trouble'. 'Ah, mon cher', he said to the Governor who had asked if Riel had any final requests, 'I shall not be weak ... When the moment arrives, I shall have wings to carry me up to God, who sent me to liberate the half breeds, and who will send me back very soon' to fulfil his divine mission as a prophet to lead the rebellion. Riel asked for his body to be sent to St Boniface for burial. The *Times* coverage noted there was considerable debate about Riel's state of mind, even his insanity, and noted that in Ontario the Protestant Conservatives were feeling 'inward satisfaction' that the court order for the execution had been carried out but in Quebec, there was anger and outrage. Effigies of prominent Conservatives politicians, including Hector Langevin, Sir Joseph-Adolphe Chapleau and Macdonald, were burned as crowds marched to Champ de Mars in Montreal and then roamed through the English quarter singing

French songs.[1] It was nowhere mentioned that the Canadian government had actually hanged an American citizen. Riel had become a US citizen two years earlier.

In 1884–5, Riel led the Northwest Resistance, an uprising of the Métis against the encroachment of Canadian settlers on their lands in what are now Saskatchewan and Alberta and has become one of the most controversial figures in Canadian history. To the Métis he is a hero, an eloquent spokesperson who rallied against their being ignored when their homeland was transferred to Canada without any consultation and later, it was again Riel who sought to redress their mistreatment in the decades after Confederation. Many in the Northwest in 1885 saw him as a villain but today he is seen as among the first in Western Canada to protest the lack of political and economic power of the region within the federation. As a French-speaking, Roman Catholic Métis, French Canadians saw Riel as a victim of Ontario religious and racial bigotry and as a warning of the dangers they faced in Canada, despite the promise of Confederation that the new nation would protect its minority communities.

Indeed, the leading politicians involved in designing what became Canada's constitution, the British North America Act, 1867, recognized the importance of diversity and differences. One of their principal goals was to assure a stable political order for their new nation. No attempt was made to unite the parts around a single new national loyalty; instead, the founders made it their task to join together several British North American colonies into what could become a united people within a federal arrangement. Coexistence rather than the vanquishing of minorities was the underlying premise, amid concern about possible American encroachment and aspirations to expand across the continent.[2] Soon after Confederation, the country was put to the test. The provocation centred on Canada's acquisition of Rupert's Land and the North-Western Territory, to be combined under the new name, North-West Territories, and at the centre of it all was Louis Riel, a 25-year-old St Boniface native who spent much of the previous ten years at the Petit Séminaire de Montréal, as a clerk in the Montreal law firm of Toussaint-Antoine-Rodolphe Laflamme, and working precariously in Chicago and St Paul before returning to St Boniface in July 1868.

A few months later, in October 1868, George-Étienne Cartier, minister of militia and defence, and his colleague at public works, William McDougall, travelled to London to negotiate with the British government and the Hudson's Bay Company (HBC) terms for the sale and transfer to Canada of a vast area that had been granted to HBC in 1670: Rupert's Land and the North-Western Territory. It would be one of the largest land sales in history.

---

[1]'The Rebel Chief Hanged', *The New York Times*, 17 November 1885.
[2]This history is explored in David Robertson Cameron, 'An Evolutionary Story', in Janice Gross Stein et al., *Uneasy Partners: Multiculturalism and Rights in Canada* (Waterloo: Wilfrid Laurier University Press, 2007), 71–94.

Under section 146 of the BNA Act, the British government admitted these territories to Canada, effective 15 July 1870. Simultaneously, the province of Manitoba was created, under the Manitoba Act.

In the part of Rupert's Land called the District of Assiniboia, there was a significant, mostly Métis settlement at Red River. From 1821 to 1870, a governor and the Council of Assiniboia administered the colony. With a population of about 12,000 mostly francophone and anglophone Métis – a French word meaning 'mixed blood' and applied to those born to European fathers and Indigenous mothers or descendants of these marriages – the Red River Settlement was one of the centres of Métis society. Young Louis Riel was emerging as one of its leaders. Born in 1844 to parents who were both born in the West, he is said to have had one-eighth Indigenous blood from his paternal grandmother, a Franco-Chipewyan Métisse. While attending the Catholic school in St Boniface, Riel attracted the attention of Bishop Alexandre-Antonin Taché and was sent to a private secondary school in Montreal run by Sulpicians, where he studied from 1858 to 1864. Returning to Red River, Riel discovered that numerous Protestant Canadians from Ontario and a handful of Americans had settled in his community. These newcomers were generally hostile to Catholicism and to the social and economic values that the Métis community had developed over decades. The Canadians were hoping to annex the colony to Canada, while Riel and others were worried about what exactly annexation would mean. Riel believed his people represented a nation in its own right and were a distinct community; he even talked about the colony's nation-building aspirations. No Indigenous people living in the territory, including the Métis, were included in the negotiations over the sale of Rupert's Land to Canada and then over the transfer from London to Ottawa of the whole North West. Riel was convinced that the people of Red River were fully justified in stopping the transfer of their land and their community to the Dominion of Canada.

More than half of the Red River Métis were French-speaking and Roman Catholic. Over time, they had divided the land along the Red River into long narrow lots running back from the river, a necessity for travel and food, and as was customary in Quebec. They had created their own economic and cultural traditions, as well as their own legal system. A strong sense of identity had emerged among the Métis, and they were prepared to defend themselves against intrusions from Canada and the Canadians intent on extending their influence on the western lands. Discontent and anxiety prevailed in Red River. A severe grasshopper plague devastated much of the harvest in 1867 and 1868, causing widespread hunger and hardship. The situation was further aggravated by a dramatic decline in the buffalo population on the eastern plains in the wake of US military operations against its Indigenous population, advancing settlers and the indiscriminate slaughter of the herds. The huge bison herds on the North American plains were rapidly approaching extinction, declining from as many as 30 million in the mid-seventeenth century to a few hundred by the end of the nineteenth, making it one of the worst ecological and environmental disasters of all time. Aside from the roughly 12,000 Métis, there were some 60,000 Indigenous people throughout the region divided into five cultural groups belonging to three linguistic families. The Algonkian family included the Ojibwa, Cree, Blackfoot. The Assiniboine, known as Nakota (or Nakona), were part of the Sioux family and lived on the northern Great Plains. An Athapaskan tribe, the Chipewyan, occupied the basins of the Churchill, Athabasca and Mackenzie rivers. There were also about 3,500 Europeans who worked mostly at HBC trading posts or had settled at Red River.

Canada's federal government planned to take control of Red River in December 1869. What little information the people living there did obtain about the transfer or about how the new owners of the land would govern the territory came largely from the local newspaper, *The Nor'Wester*, which was controlled by the Canadians in the colony. For them, annexation to Canada was the only path forward. This idea had long been promoted by many of the men who had participated in the Confederation process from 1864 to 1867, including George Brown of *The Globe*, William McDougall and others. The Canadians in Red River saw the land as essentially empty and theirs for the taking. Like Canada's first Prime Minister, John A. Macdonald, they linked the destiny and prosperity of Canada to the occupation and development of the North West. Ontario, especially, was fuelling the expansionist sentiment, driven by the lack of arable land in that province. A West filled with farmers would be an important market for manufactured goods coming from Quebec and Ontario, as well as a source of raw materials for their factories. Thomas D'Arcy McGee, among Canada's most fervent nationalists, captured the expansionist sentiment when he said in 1868 that 'the future of the Dominion depends on our early occupation of the rich prairie land'.[3]

Macdonald and his government were increasingly worried about the Americans, who were developing their own western lands and looked with interest to the British-held prairies.[4] Minnesota had become a state in 1858, and farmers were pouring into the Red River Valley there and in the Dakotas. Americans already exerted considerable influence in the British side of the border through the St Paul and Pacific Railroad that ran along the international border and cornered virtually all the trade with the Red River Settlement and nearby Fort Garry. Eager to annex the territory, the Government of Canada – like the Hudson's Bay Company and like the British government – gave no thought to consulting or negotiating

---

[3]Quoted in Doug Owram, *Promise of Eden: The Canadian Expansionist Movement and the Idea of the West, 1856–1900* (Toronto: University of Toronto Press, 1992), 77.
[4]A balanced interpretation of Macdonald can be found in Patrice Dutil, *Sir John A. Macdonald & the Apocalyptic Year 1885* (Toronto: Sutherland House, 2024).

with the people living in the region about the impending transfer of their land to Canada.

The Canadians in Red River were mostly young and well-educated from middle-class Ontario families. They were associated with a group known as 'Canada First', a nationalistic political movement that offered little space in Confederation for Indigenous people and French Canadians, who they saw as a 'bar to progress'. Founded in 1868, its members included Ontarians George Denison, Henry Morgan, Charles Mair, William Foster and Nova-Scotia born Robert Grant Haliburton. Dr John Schultz, a medical doctor, merchant and land speculator who had arrived in Red River from Canada West in 1859, was also a member. In January 1867, they started a petition asking that the area be united with Canada. Such petitions played a significant role in shaping Canada's perception of the Red River colony as a place anxious to join the new Canadian nation. The Canadian party in Red River did little to cultivate support among the Indigenous population and saw any manoeuvrings led by Riel and the Métis as acts of lawlessness, not the actions of a self-determining people.

What followed has been called the Red River Resistance of 1869–70. The Métis were horrified when in the fall of 1869 John Stoughton Dennis arrived at the Red River Settlement. Despatched by William McDougall, who was the lieutenant governor designate of the North-West Territories, Dennis was a temporary employee of the Canadian government sent to survey lots for prospective settlers. He had been given specific instructions to respect the Métis river lots, although the Métis saw no reason for any survey in the first place. They certainly had no desire to see their lands divided on the American section system which would have threatened their existing river lot holdings. Dennis stayed with Dr Schultz, adding to suspicions. The Métis challenged the survey to be conducted without their consent, and despite assurances that their land holdings were secure, on 11 October 1869 they were able to stop the survey team from doing any further work. A few days later, they formed the National Committee of the Métis and called for an independent Métis republic. Dennis wanted the HBC Governor of Assiniboia and of Rupert's Land, William MacTavish, to punish the perpetrators. MacTavish refused. He criticized the Canadian government for its refusal to consult the inhabitants of Rupert's Land about the pending transfer and its apparent attempt to assert its authority in Red River before the transfer of title had even taken place.

News arrived back in Ottawa of Métis dissatisfaction with the process, and the Canadian government at last realized it would not be acquiring empty land and came to understand that the right of self-determination was important to the Métis. When word reached Macdonald that there was some uncertainty in Red River about the transfer, and that quite possibly John Dennis had exacerbated the problem, he wrote to Cartier, saying, 'All that those poor people know ... is that Canada has bought the country ... & that they are handed over like a flock of sheep to us; and they are told that they lose their lands ... Under these circumstances it is not to be wondered at that they should be dissatisfied and should show their discontent'.[5] And dissatisfied, they were. Riel told the Council of Assiniboia and the National Council of the Métis that they 'would prevent the entry of McDougall or any other governor unless the union with Canada was based on negotiations with the Métis and with the population in general'.[6]

Macdonald had appointed McDougall to lead the colonial administration as its first lieutenant governor until the colony was ready to become a province. McDougall arrived in Pembina, Dakota Territory, on 30 October 1869. Several days earlier, on 21 October, the National Committee of the Métis had ordered McDougall to not enter the settlement. Macdonald similarly advised McDougall not to assert any authority in the region, as Canada did not yet own Rupert's Land, and he did not want trouble with the colony. McDougall, however, attempted to do precisely the opposite. On 30 November, McDougall was met at Pembina by Janvier Ritchot and André Nault, who gave him a letter from the National Committee of the Métis ordering him to not enter the Northwest without permission of the Committee. The Métis had seized Upper Fort Garry, where the Council of Assiniboia met and where the Hudson's Bay Company had its main administrative offices in the region. On 8 December, Riel, along with and French and English-speaking Métis and a number of English-speaking settlers, formed a provisional government to negotiate the terms of the colony's entry into Confederation ensuring that the rights of the local populations were respected. Riel became its president, and he participated in the Convention of Forty (with twenty English Métis and twenty French Métis delegates) held from 25 January to 10 February 1870 to determine the region's political future. They drafted a 'List of Rights' (entitling it the Bill of Rights) that proposed the entry of the region into Canada with representation in the House of Commons, guarantees of bilingualism in the legislature, a bilingual chief justice, and arrangements for free homesteads and treaties with Indigenous peoples. Many in the English-speaking population did not think the demands were unreasonable, and indeed, they became the basis of the Manitoba Act, 1870.

This was an auspicious moment in Canadian statecraft. British North American politicians, among them men now sitting in the House of Commons in Ottawa, had just recently created a new nation-state: a political union within which there would be a common citizenship with specific obligations and entitlements, but also one that included the recognition of distinct political identities that gave rise to special arrangements and protections for minority communities. Would the Government of Canada

---

[5]Quoted in *Dictionary of Canadian Biography*, 'The Challenge of Red River and the Manitoba Act', https://www.biographi.ca/en/theme_macdonald.html?project_id=98&p=13.
[6]Ibid.

under Macdonald's leadership extend those protections and arrangements to the Métis and Indigenous peoples of the new territory about to be acquired and which would put them under the administration of the Canadian government? Louis Riel was ready and anxious to participate in the new Canadian nation on terms that respected diversity and inclusion. His version of Confederation aligned perfectly with the vision that was articulated at the 1864 conferences in Charlottetown and Quebec City. As M. Max Hamon demonstrates in *The Audacity of His Enterprise: Louis Riel and the Métis Nation That Canada Never Was, 1840–1875*, Riel's mission was more about nation building within Canada than resistance to it.[7] Riel understood that the Métis as a people had come to define themselves as a distinct nation in the borderlands between the United States and British North America. In his view, '*Je suis métis moi*' was an indication that the Métis were a people built on the concepts of *wahkohtowin* (kinship) and *otipemisiwak* (those who own themselves), and they deserved recognition of that identity and distinctiveness. Riel hoped that the Métis would be fully accepted into the Canadian federation where the idea of difference, it seemed, had already been institutionalized and no community would be subordinated and colonized by another.

At first, it seemed that Riel's objective and the demands of the Métis provisional government would be accommodated. Macdonald noted, however, that McDougall and Dennis had 'done their utmost to destroy our chance of an amicable settlement' with the Métis, and he attempted to solve the growing crisis. He despatched Donald Alexander Smith, the Hudson's Bay Company (HBC) commissioner of the Montreal department that managed HBC's eastern operations, to Red River as a special envoy to help defuse the growing tensions with Riel and the provisional government. After negotiations that included recognizing the inhabitants' land titles and the promise of a territorial council, along with an offer of amnesty, money and employment to Métis leaders, Riel and the provisional government agreed that a delegation would go to Ottawa to formally negotiate terms for entry of the prairie territory into Confederation. Smith promised that such a delegation would be given 'a very cordial reception'.[8]

With such an approach, Macdonald continued the process of negotiation and accommodation that had marked the Confederation process from its beginnings. Archbishop Taché of St Boniface visited Ottawa at Macdonald's request in early February 1870. He met the prime minister and some of his Cabinet and described the mood as conciliatory. He obtained the promise

---

[7]Max Hamon *The Audacity of His Enterprise: Louis Riel and the Métis Nation That Canada Never Was, 1840–1875* (Montreal and Kingston: McGill-Queen's University Press, 2019).
[8]Quoted in Lewis H. Thomas, 'RIEL, LOUIS (1844–85)', in *Dictionary of Canadian Biography*, vol. 11 (University of Toronto/Université Laval, 2003), accessed 4 November 2024, https://www.biographi.ca/en/bio/riel_louis_1844_85_11E.html.

of a complete and general amnesty to the inhabitants of Red River who laid down their arms. Donald Smith's negotiations with Riel had prepared the way for a delegation from Red River to negotiate the colony's entry into Confederation. This was achieved in May 1870 with the Manitoba Act which satisfied most of the demands of Riel and the Métis. It promised Red River settlers secure tenure of the river lots already occupied by them and a reserve of 566,580 hectares to be allotted to the next generation of Métis. The remaining land in Manitoba and Rupert's Land was deemed Dominion Land to be used for national purposes and, therefore, beyond the authority of the Manitoba legislature. The Manitoba Act also provided for denominational schools and the use of French as a language of record as well as for debates in the provincial assembly, although in the 1890s the French-speaking Métis would have their linguistic and school rights taken from them. French-Canadian leaders, especially in Quebec, were extremely pleased with the Manitoba Act, as it fulfilled the promise of the French–English duality of Canada. In Ontario, however, the Act caused some resentment and disappointment: Ontarians had seen the North West as their hinterland and as a fertile land for the children of Ontario farmers. That was Macdonald's hope, too, for the newly acquired territory; indeed, he confided to Sir John Rose, his former finance minister, that the Métis 'must be kept firmly in hand until they are submerged by the influx of settlers'.[9]

Louis Riel and Red River became a serious issue for the Canadian government when events spiralled out of control and inflamed emotions across the country. A group of Canadians in Red River, led by Dr John Schultz, John Dennis and others, opposed to Riel and the provisional government had established their headquarters at Schultz's general store which the Métis raided, taking the Canadians prisoners. They soon released those who promised to leave the territory or abide by Métis laws. Schultz refused and remained imprisoned, only later to escape and lead his supporters in an attack on the provisional government at Fort Garry. The Métis suppressed the uprising, but this time, events would unfold differently. Within a month, the uprising turned bloody, and the tide turned against the Red River Resistance. Several of the insurgents, including Thomas Scott, a 28-year-old recent arrival from Ontario, member of the anti-Catholic Orange Order and a vehement anti-Catholic, were captured at Fort Garry. He was part of the Canada First group, along with Schultz and Charles Mair, a poet and columnist in Red River for *The Globe*, who attempted to overthrow the provisional government. Their leader, Major Charles Arkoll Boulton, was sentenced to death for treason by the provisional government, but Riel intervened to save his life. Scott, on the other hand, was not so fortunate. He tormented his guards with insults and contempt and threatened to shoot Riel

---

[9] Jean Hamelin, 'Taché, Alexandre-Antonin', in *Dictionary of Canadian Biography*, vol. 12 (University of Toronto/Université Laval, 2003), accessed 4 November 2024, https://www.biographi.ca/en/bio/tache_alexandre_antonin_12E.html.

if he was ever freed. When a beating failed to silence him, he was charged with insubordination and treason. On 4 March 1870, Thomas Scott was convicted, sentenced and executed by a firing squad. Riel reluctantly agreed to Scott's execution to placate his men – upset over the death of one of their own in a previous altercation – and as he said later, 'We must make Canada respect us'.[10]

Events in Red River would soon have repercussions throughout Canada, as they threatened to accentuate racial and religious divisions within the new nation. Macdonald had to choose a course of action that would minimize the tension between Ontario and Quebec while, at the same time, resolving the conflict with Riel and the Red River colonists. He negotiated with Riel and his supporters to demonstrate to Quebec that he was fulfilling the promise of the French–English duality of Canada. Scott's execution had added fuel to the nationalist fire raging in Ontario where the news of his death precipitated a public outcry for retribution, particularly from the Orange Order, one of the most powerful organizations in English-speaking Canada. In Ontario, Riel was denounced; in Quebec, he was a hero.

Macdonald lamented to Adams G. Archibald, the new lieutenant governor for Manitoba, of his dilemma in offering amnesty for Riel. If Scott had not been murdered, the situation could have been resolved to the satisfaction of both Quebec and Ontario. To appease Ontario, though, Macdonald despatched troops to Manitoba in July 1870 on the pretext of preventing further trouble. The Red River Expeditionary Force of more than 1,000 Canadian troops, commanded by Colonel Garnet Wolseley, arrived in Manitoba that August. It became an occupation force. Amid reports of assaults, rapes, murder, arson and assorted acts of mayhem against the Métis near Fort Garry, newspapers in Red River and in eastern Canada described the behaviour of the expeditionary force a 'reign of terror'. Escaping such an intolerable climate of violence and fear, a number of the Métis moved from Manitoba to present-day Saskatchewan.[11]

With Manitoba's entry into Confederation, the situation changed markedly. The Métis soon became outnumbered by incoming Ontarians and French Canadians. These newcomers were often hostile to the Métis' desire to assert their hard-won rights. The Métis were persecuted for their role in the Red River Resistance and the execution of Thomas Scott. Macdonald encouraged Riel to flee to the United States, and rumours persisted that Macdonald even offered him money to remain there. Twice elected to the

---

[10]Thomas Flanagan, *Louis 'David' Riel: Prophet of the New World* (Toronto: University of Toronto Press, 1979), 29–30; and Matthew McRae, 'What's in a Name? Thomas Scott and the Curious Case of the Forgotten Memorial', *Active History*, 4 March 2020, https://activehistory.ca/blog/2020/03/04/whats-in-a-name-thomas-scott-and-the-curious-case-of-the-forgotten-memorial/.

[11]Charles A. Boulton, *Reminiscences of the North-West Rebellions* (Toronto: Grip Printing and Publishing, 1886), 102; *Toronto Telegraph*, 4 October 1870.

House of Commons, Riel was prevented from attending. Mackenzie Bowell, the Ontario Orange leader, and later prime minister of Canada (1894–6), introduced a motion in 1873 to expel Riel from Parliament. In 1875, Riel took the offer of an amnesty in exchange for agreeing to five years' banishment from Canada. At the time, it seemed that the Métis had achieved their objective. Canada had been dissuaded from annexing their land without consultation with them, and they had won entry into Canada as a province with legislative guarantees that their land, religion and language would be secure within the new Canadian regime.

The British North America Act gave the federal government jurisdiction over 'Indigenous people and Land reserved for Indigenous people', and Canada continued the process initiated by the British in the eighteenth century of dealing with Indigenous titles and rights. Between 1871 and 1921, the Canadian government negotiated eleven 'numbered treaties' that covered much of present-day Ontario, Manitoba, Saskatchewan, Alberta and some of the Canadian North. It was implicit in the treaty process that there would be colonial settlement on First Nations territory and when this settlement took place, the laws of Canada were to apply to First Nations communities. Let there be no mistake, however; those treaties provided for the cession of land by the First Nations to allow expansion of white settlement into Western Canada. In these negotiations, Indigenous leaders were not without purpose, however. In addition to the promise of reserve land and annual gratuities, they demanded the continuation of their economic practices, including hunting and fishing rights, the provision of agricultural implements and livestock, schools and a variety of other benefits to protect them from hunger and disease. They also demanded an exemption from the most onerous obligations of citizenship (taxation and conscription), for receipt of social benefits, and for preservation of religious and cultural integrity. Some First Nations made it clear to government officials that they wanted treaties, as treaty making was a way to assert their sovereignty over the land. Others believed they needed some sort of accommodation with the Canadian government, especially given the rapid depletion of the resources they had relied on for centuries. There was clearly an element of intercultural accommodation between settlers and First Nations; however, in most instances, the situation never turned out as Indigenous peoples had hoped: the reserve system led to widespread hunger, starvation and disease that the government had promised to prevent, and in time, schools, especially residential schools, almost destroyed Indigenous peoples and their cultures.

One can make the case, too, that it was the intention of the Canadian state and settler colonialism to abridge the treaty relationship as soon as they had the political capacity to do so. Unlike with the early fur trade, agricultural settlers did not require a productive relationship with Indigenous peoples, and there was a sense among newcomers that the original peoples would disappear. From the time of the Royal Proclamation of 1763, the British government had determined that Indigenous land could only be alienated by treaty through the Crown. It was also believed that Indigenous peoples would be inculcated in European ways and assimilated into the settler culture. A series of government initiatives was adopted in the pre-Confederation era to facilitate that policy. Chief among them was the Province of the United Canadas 1857 Act for the Gradual Civilization of Indian Tribes. The goal was to promote the assimilation of Indigenous people into newcomer society through various means, including residential schools to educate First Nations children and have them gain full citizenship rights and become successful farmers. Of course, Indigenous peoples resisted, even appealing to the Prince of Wales when in 1860 he visited Canada.

The Government of Canada continued with its assimilationist policies after 1867, particularly when it passed the Indian Act in 1876, which was an attempt to bring all the laws and regulations governing Canada's Indigenous peoples under a single statute. This Act virtually turned Indigenous peoples into wards of the state, as government policy became steadily more interventionist in their lives and more controlling. The Act set out conditions for the sale of reserve lands, and mandated elections for band councils despite traditional practices of Indigenous governance. It effectively decided who could and could not be considered 'Indian' under the law. Any woman who married an Indigenous male would be considered an 'Indian', but any Indigenous woman who married a non-Indigenous male ceased being one and lost all privileges under the Act. Indigenous peoples of mixed ancestry, such as the Métis, had to choose to either take an 'Indian' identity and become part of a treaty or take scrip (land certificates) and remain outside the treaty arrangements and away from reserve lands. Métis scrip could be used only to acquire lands from the Dominion Lands Office, but many of those land vouchers or certificates were purchased by land agents and financial institutions at considerable discount and then flipped at huge profits to immigrant homesteaders. The scrip process left many Métis landless and without a community base. The Indian Act provided for the establishment of residential schools for Indigenous children between the ages of five and sixteen; attendance became compulsory in 1895, with terrible consequences for Indigenous society. The Indian Act was intended to speed the process of assimilation; it was regularly amended as the federal government searched for the most effective policies with which to accomplish its objectives.

In just over a decade after the Red River Resistance and enactment of the Indian Act, the Métis would again call upon Louis Riel to defend their interests. In the mid-1880s – as in 1869 – the Métis had legitimate grievances. Those who had settled in the Qu'Appelle Valley of Saskatchewan after leaving Red River were struggling, as were many of the First Nations on reserve lands. Indian agents appointed by Ottawa were generally unsympathetic to the plight of Indigenous peoples, and their leaders soon complained that Ottawa was not fulfilling its treaty obligations. European settlers in the Northwest were equally disappointed with Ottawa for ignoring their concerns; an important issue for them was the lack of representation in the

House of Commons, which did not happen until 1887. They also demanded provincial status and self-government, which, they maintained, would be the only way to deal with the lack of schools, roads and other infrastructure in the territories. European settlers also complained that land speculators and officials connected with the federal Conservative Party wielded too much power in the region and benefitted immensely from their connections, usually at the expense of the settlers and Indigenous peoples. The result was another uprising against the federal government. Known as the North-West Rebellion or the North-West Resistance, this armed uprising in what is present-day Saskatchewan was led by Louis Riel, with about 250 armed Métis, 250 Indigenous fighters and at least one white man (Honoré Jackson). On the government's side were 900 Canadian Militia (the nascent Canadian army), armed North-West Mounted Police officers and armed local residents, some 5,500 men in total. Battles and other outbreaks of violence in the spring of 1885 left ninety-one people dead. Within months, the rebellion was put down, and on 16 November 1885, Riel was hanged for treason.

Louis Riel became an important symbol for Métis and Indigenous peoples, not only as a martyred leader but also as a visionary who fought for their rights.[12] Just over a hundred years after his death, on 10 March 1992, the House of Commons unanimously passed a resolution recognizing Louis Riel as the founder of Manitoba and one of the fathers of Confederation. Nowadays, it is John A. Macdonald who is being named the villain. Rigorous efforts by Macdonald and others who followed him to the prime minister's office to remove the culture, language and life skills of Indigenous communities have been called cultural genocide. Some might contend that without defining Canada by the stories of oppression and cultural homicide that took place there can be no subsequent story of repentance and reform and, hence, no serious national project of thoroughgoing decolonization and reconciliation.

After Manitoba joined Confederation in 1870, Canada failed to uphold its original promise to Métis and Indigenous peoples, and it failed in the decades after to accept diversity and differences and allow all communities within the nation to flourish. Métis and Indigenous peoples have demonstrated that culture – and identity – cannot be easily destroyed by the state, and all attempts to pursue a policy of cultural degradation and elimination result in social dysfunction and bitterness that cannot easily be reversed through compensation and inter-community engagement. Decades of national shame in the treatment of First Nations and all Indigenous peoples in Canada reside not only with John A. Macdonald but with all of Canada's prime ministers, who, like too many Canadians, failed to grasp the enormity and extent of the past treatment of Indigenous peoples through residential schools, Indian agents and brutal social conditions. For too much

---

[12]Raymond Blake, Jeff Keshen, Norman Knowles and Barbara Messamore, *Narrating a Nation: Canadian History Post-Confederation* (Whitby: McGraw-Hill Ryerson, 2011), 63–70.

of its history, the Government of Canada never regarded the numbered treaties as being signed between sovereign autonomous communities, but as real-estate transactions to assimilate if not extinguish Indigenous peoples and their cultures and rights and acquire land for settlement.[13] Much has changed between Indigenous and Métis peoples and the Government of Canada since the first of the Numbered Treaties were signed in 1871. Most recently, on 30 November 2024, Gary Anandasangaree, minister of Crown-Indigenous Relations in the Government of Canada, and David Chartrand, President of the Manitoba Métis Federation, signed the Red River Métis Self-Government Recognition and Implementation Treaty, the first-of-its kind Self-Government Treaty that reaffirms Indigenous Peoples' right to self-government and self-determination. It recognizes the Red River Métis have an inherent right to self-government and law-making powers over its own citizenship, elections and other operations.

Today, the treaties have been finally recognized as constitutionally binding agreements between Indigenous peoples and the Crown, but the episodes involving Louis Riel and the treatment of Indigenous peoples more generally demonstrate that when Canada put aside its founding principles of respect for diversity and difference and its concern for the well-being of any of its minority communities, it invited instability and disorder that one day it would have to redress. For Canadians, that day of reckoning has come, and the nation struggles to deal with social dysfunction in many Indigenous communities, with protracted struggles over land claims, bitter negotiations between governments, resource developers and Indigenous peoples over the exploitation of resources, with a healing response to atrocious cultural degradation and with Indigenous self-government. Important steps were taken with the Constitution Act, 1982, that recognizes three distinct groups of Indigenous peoples in Canada, namely, First Nations, Métis and Inuit, as well as their constitutional right to protect their culture, customs, traditions and languages. Moreover, the Charter of Rights and Freedoms does not abrogate or derogate from any Indigenous treaty, or other rights or freedoms that pertain to the Indigenous peoples of Canada, including the rights and freedoms recognized in the Royal Proclamation of 1763 and any rights or freedoms that now exist by way of land claim agreements or may be so acquired. The Government of Canada has officially apologized to Indigenous peoples for their treatment in residential schools and established the Truth and Reconciliation Commission in 2008 to facilitate reconciliation among former students, their families, their communities and all Canadians. Canada has clearly entered a redemptive moment and is trying to now recall and re-institute the original promise of Confederation based on respect for and recognition of all communities that constitute the nation.

---

[13]On those points, see John D. Whyte, 'Federalism Dreams', *Queen's Law Journal* 34, no. 1 (2008): 1–28.

IMAGE 3 Sikhs on board the *Komagata Maru* in English Bay, Vancouver. Library and Archives Canada, Box OS 0075.5, Item 3238584.

3

The *Komagata Maru* incident, 1914: Racism, immigration and xenophobia

To escape grinding poverty in their homeland, by the beginning of the twentieth century, about a million Punjabis were living and working abroad, typically as cheap labour. In many parts of the British Empire, however, in countries dominated by whites, they were unwelcome. Exacting requirements for language competency excluded large numbers of them from Britain itself, and this strategy was pursued also in Australia, New Zealand and South Africa. Numerous historical examples speak to this. One of the most blatant incidents barring new, non-white immigrants involves the SS *Komagata Maru*, a steamship that arrived in Vancouver in 1914 carrying mostly Sikhs from Punjab province, India, a colony in the British Empire. All of these passengers were British subjects, and as such could have been supposed to be eligible to enter Canada.

Xenophobia was widespread in Canada. For years before the *Komagata Maru* incident, race relations in Vancouver and elsewhere on the Pacific Coast were strained, with the Anti-Oriental riots of September 1907 representing a culmination point. Labour unions and small businessmen led demands for action to be taken against Asian immigration. After the riots, the federal Liberal government made William Lyon Mackenzie King, deputy minister of Canada's new Department of Labour, head of the Royal Commission Appointed to Investigate Methods by Which Oriental Labourers Have Been Induced to Come to Canada. In its first attempt to restrict immigration, on 8 January 1908, the Canadian government issued an order-in-council prohibiting the immigration of persons who 'in the opinion of the Minister of the Interior' did not 'come from the country of their birth or citizenship', separate from British subjecthood, 'by a continuous journey and or through tickets purchased before leaving the country of their birth or nationality'.[1] This meant that for new arrivals to be admitted into Canada, the vessel transporting them could not stop, dock and presumably pick up other passengers anywhere between its point of origin and Canada – and because of the great distances involved, this essentially applied to people from India and Japan, though not those from Europe.

Moreover, particular concern had arisen over the presence and possible arrival of additional radicals from the Punjab. In June 1913, the Ghadar Party was formed, mostly by Sikhs in the United States and Canada. An Urdu word derived from Arabic, Ghadar means 'revolt' or 'rebellion'. With Sikh Punjab independence from Britain as its stated goal, the Ghadar Party had members among British Columbia's still small South Asian community.

Determined to test Canadian immigration laws, Gurdit Singh, a Sikh leader, businessman and supporter of the Ghadar Movement, established the Guru Nanak Steamship Company. He chartered a Japanese ship, the *Komagata Maru*, to transport people, mostly Sikhs, to Canada. Both the British and Canadian governments monitored the vessel throughout its preparation and departure. Convinced that the ship was carrying Sikh revolutionaries, British colonial officials initially stopped it at Budge Budge in West Bengal. There, authorities attempted, but failed, to arrest Gurdit Singh and twenty of his supporters. In the chaos that erupted, nineteen passengers were killed, but Singh and many of his allies escaped. The ship sailed on. It was an arduous trip. Built in 1890, the *Komagata Maru* was not a large or spacious vessel; just over 300 feet long and 41 feet across, it moved at a top speed of 30 knots. Fifteen of the passengers were quartered in its small number of private cabins; all others were crammed into steerage, where they slept on bunks. Departing from Hong Kong, the steamship stopped in Shanghai to drop off and pick up passengers, and it stopped again in Moji, Japan, to obtain coal. It had 376 passengers on board, 80 from India, and the rest Indians living in the Far East; the total comprised 340 Sikhs, 24 Muslims and 12 Hindus, all of them of Punjabi background.

When the *Komagata Maru* arrived in Vancouver on 23 May 1914, its passengers expected to simply be processed and granted immediate entry into Canada. Eager and excited about starting a new and more promising life, many of them dressed in the very best clothes they had brought with them. But things quickly turned sour. The vessel was ordered to anchor about a kilometre offshore, in Burrard Inlet. After two weeks, reports circulated of supplies growing critically short, and of the health of several passengers deteriorating, to which Canadian authorities appeared indifferent. A court case in the name of a passenger, Munshi Singh, was started to test the exclusion laws and the passengers' rights as British subjects. For the

---

[1]'Continuous Journey Regulation, 1908', The Canadian Museum of Immigration at Pier 21, https://pier21.ca/research/immigration-history/continuous-journey-regulation-1908.

South Asian community in Canada — and for those who wanted to join it — the court case was a test of the rhetoric of Empire: was it possible for any British subject, regardless of colour or creed, to settle anywhere in the British Empire? For the Canadian government, it was a test of whether the country would be able to exercise the power to decide who would get in and who would be kept out. The decision rendered on 6 July supported the federal government's right to refuse their entry into Canada. Although Singh claimed that he had no interest in violent revolution, many of the men on the *Komagata Maru* were ex-soldiers and targets of Ghadar propaganda. Moreover, Singh's supporters in Vancouver had ties to the Ghadar Party and Canadian officials worried that some of those on the *Komagata Maru* in 1914 were bringing their battles with Britain to Canada. For another seventeen days, as the case was unsuccessfully appealed, those aboard the *Komagata Maru* waited, in what were terribly overcrowded, hot and increasingly squalid conditions. Tensions with Canadian authorities rose, and some passengers armed themselves with clubs. About thirty-five men, many of them members of the local militia, were sworn in as special immigration officers and armed with Ross rifles (the standard issue for Canada's army). Joined by nearly 100 police officers, they tried to seize the vessel in a 19 July nighttime raid. Several passengers violently resisted, throwing hunks of coal, fire bricks and scrap metal.

The Government of Canada then ordered its only naval vessel on the Pacific Coast, the HMCS *Rainbow*, to force the *Komagata Maru* out of Canadian waters. Of its 376 passengers, 20 were admitted into Canada; only these 20 had not violated the exclusion laws. The ship was forced to leave for Asia on 23 July, exactly two months after its arrival in Vancouver. Once back in India, several passengers were removed for interrogation. Some defied authorities. The police and military fired on the crowd, killing twenty of the passengers and wounding twenty-two. Those who returned to India were never allowed to re-enter Canada. Punjabi men were granted permission, in 1920, to bring their wives and children to Canada, and in 1947 — the year that separate Canadian citizenship was created — immigrants from Asia, including from India, were extended the right to vote in all Canadian elections. In 1951, the yearly maximum admissible number of immigrants from India was set at 150, from Pakistan at 100, and from Sri Lanka at 50.

The *Komagata Maru* incident remained little known in Canada, not covered in school curricula until the 1970s. This change reflected a multicultural Canada that was now celebrating diversity as a national strength. Canada, in recent decades, has welcomed large numbers of Hindus and Sikhs, and next to the United States and Great Britain, it has the world's largest expatriate Indian community, exceeding half a million by the early 2000s.

Ironically, the Canada into which those aboard the *Komagata Maru* sought entry was, in fact, experiencing an immigration boom. Posters, pamphlets and government advertisements presented the Prairie West as a land of boundless opportunity. Canada's Immigration Branch offered a bonus to agents of steamship companies and colonization organizations for each successful agricultural immigrant they attracted. Many groups in Europe faced persecution, especially Ukrainians and Jews, the latter often confronting deadly, violent, state-sanctioned pogroms. Religious groups, including Mennonites and Doukhobors in Russia, were not permitted to hold land communally nor always, as pacifists, excused from compulsory military service.

Immigrants were promised 160 acres of free land if within three years they made specified improvements to the property. Initially, Canada focused on attracting people who wanted to farm, and particularly those from the British Isles. Land was expensive in Britain, and the rigid class structure there prompted those of more modest means to consider Canada. Fewer than 1,200 individuals from the British Isles moved to Canada in 1900. By 1905 that annual figure had reached 65,000 and in 1912–13 it peaked at 150,000. Significant numbers also came from the United States, as America's west was filling up. Some 19,000 people moved to Canada from the United Sates in 1900; this figure reached 58,000 in 1905 and 139,000 in 1912–13.

Although the Canadian government was seeking farmers, many newcomers, even those who headed West, did not go directly into land ownership; rather they became wage labourers in the agriculture, industrial and resource sectors. Although many immigrants came from preferred areas like Northwest Europe, Britain and the United States, the federal government considered the overall number from these areas unsatisfactory. Canada turned elsewhere: to Central Europe and to the Ukrainian farmer. Minister of the Interior Clifford Sifton, Canada's lead on immigration, expressed hope, but also cultural condescension, when in a speech to the Toronto Board of Trade in March in 1922 he declared, 'I think a stalwart peasant in a sheep-skin coat, born on the soil, whose forefathers have been farmers for ten generations, with a stout wife and half-a-dozen children, is good quality'.[2]

Getting established in Canada was a hard slog for new immigrants. Many lived in sod huts with poor ventilation in the summer and inadequate insulation in the winter. Breaking the ground was arduous work, still done with primitive equipment; tractors did not disseminate widely in the Prairies until after the First World War. Though many immigrants were successful, their economic progress did not translate into social acceptance. Ukrainians were cast as disposed to crime, violence and excessive drinking. Some who were poor did take petty articles, such as seeds or a spare part for a machine, mostly from better-off members of their own ethnic group; nevertheless, the entire

---

[2]https://dchp.arts.ubc.ca/entries/men%20in%20sheepskin%20coats. Also see John Douglas Belshaw, *Canadian History: Post-Confederation – 2nd Edition*. 5.4. The Clifford Sifton Years, 1896–1905, https://opentextbc.ca/postconfederation2e/chapter/5-4-the-clifford-sifton-years-1896-1905/.

community was frequently labelled as thieves by more established settlers. Ukrainians in rural areas tended to settle near one another, and this made it easier to propagate negative stereotypes, as the Ukrainians remained strangers; block settlement patterns built resentment from the host society over the supposed unwillingness of Ukrainians to assimilate.

The more groups remained separate, the more they were denounced, even though Anglo-Canadians themselves were not disposed to mix with newcomers. Doukhobors were among the late-nineteenth-century wave of immigrants. They and others who lived in separate, communal settings faced considerable suspicion and were pressured to assimilate. But arriving at a time when Canada was in desperate need of settlers, the federal government accepted their differences, and the Doukhobors' demands, including guarantees of never having to serve in the military and control of the schooling of their own children. Still, their pacifist and religious ways, determination to remain separate and the fact that they did not speak English generated resentment. Doukhobors had mostly settled in the Prairies, and by the beginning of the twentieth century they were finding the Canadian government increasingly intolerant towards them. The tendency grew to deny them land title transfers, as it was felt that their communal ways undermined the concept of private property ownership. Government inspectors visited their holdings, and, in many cases, confiscated land where it was deemed that improvements had not been made in accordance with the original homesteading agreement. In 1908, many Doukhobors left the Prairies, heading to land their leader, Peter Verigin, had purchased in the Nelson/Grand Forks area of British Columbia; by 1912, some 5,000 of them lived on self-sufficient communal farms there. Increasingly, the surrounding Anglo population demanded that Doukhobors pay taxes, register for vital statistics and educate their children in public schools, to which many children were forcibly relocated. This produced a Doukhobor group called the Sons of Freedom, who set fire to numerous public schools, right up until the 1960s, when state interference finally subsided.

Between 1904 and 1914, nearly 400,000 immigrants to Canada indicated they wanted to farm, but this accounted for only 28 per cent of those who arrived. Many new immigrants ended up in resource sectors, as labourers in mining, forestry and fishing, and in railway construction. Often, they faced horrendous working conditions; between 1904 and 1911, of the 9,340 on-the-job fatalities in Canada, 23 per cent were in the railway sector. No matter where they settled, the belief prevailed that for immigrants to succeed they had to assimilate into the mores of the host society. This was strongly encouraged at institutions such as public schools. Immigrants, who did not quickly learn English, who did not know British history or who were seen as failing in other ways to integrate, were portrayed in reports of the Ontario Provincial Education Ministry, for example, as being of inferior intelligence. School textbooks often rated the quality of different races, presenting the Anglo-Saxon as the civilized, moral, intellectual and physical pinnacle.

Annual immigration to Canada increased from the mid-1890s until the First World War. In 1898, the intake was 31,900, and a decade later it stood at 143,326. Immigration peaked in 1913 at 400,870, and from 1910 to 1913 totalled 1,096,953 at a time when Canada's population was some 7.2 million. Newcomers helped facilitate massive economic expansion. But for many long-established and many native-born Canadians, the scope and pace of change brought fear and expressions of hostility. This period was influenced by the creed of 'Anglo conformity'[3] which shaped ideas on whom the Dominion should attempt to attract and what was expected of newcomers. Topping the preference list were arrivals from Great Britain and the United States followed by those from Northwest Europe, while at the bottom were Jews and non-whites.

As the pool of immigrants became more diverse, commentary increased about Canada becoming a dumping ground. In burgeoning cities, newcomers were blamed for slums, crime, immorality, prostitution and increased labour unrest. Few voices criticized the prejudices and poverty that came to oppress the lives of many immigrants. In the late nineteenth century, Montreal's working-class immigrant slum, which the businessman, philanthropist and author, Herbert Brown Ames, called 'The City Below the Hill',[4] held the dubious distinction of having the highest infant mortality rate in North America. Not all immigrants did poorly; some, serving mainly people in their own enclave, for example, by operating businesses, did well. Exacerbating the frustrations of many newcomers, however, were their situation at work. Sixty-hour work weeks were not uncommon, especially for immigrants, who were recruited to fill unskilled positions and viewed as cheap to employ. Routinely, new immigrants were blamed for unionization and labour unrest, cast as having been radicalized, typically with socialist or communist beliefs, in their homelands. Canada amended its immigration rules in 1910 to permit the deportation of individuals promoting 'subversive or anarchistic' views.[5]

Labour unions demanded restrictions on immigration, especially of people thought to work cheap, such as people from China. More generally, the Chinese were portrayed as cruel, barbarous and deceitful, and of bringing opium dens, prostitution rings and Tong gangs to Canada. On Canada's West Coast, where most of the country's Chinese population lived, fears abounded over what was called the Yellow Peril, meaning hordes of Chinese were presumedly trying to enter Canada. Chinese men were first brought to Canada in the 1880s as cheap labour to help construct the

---

[3] Howard Palmer, 'Reluctant Hosts: Anglo-Canadian Views of Multiculturalism in the Twentieth Century', in John Mallea and Jonathan Young, eds., *Cultural Diversity and Canadian Education* (Ottawa: Carleton University Press, 1984), 21–40.
[4] Herbert Brown Ames, *The City below the Hill: A Sociological Study of a Portion of the City of Montreal* (Toronto: University of Toronto Press, 1972). Originally published in 1897.
[5] https://pier21.ca/research/immigration-history/immigration-act-1910.

transcontinental railway. Women were barred so that the Chinese would not settle and grow in numbers. When the Canadian Pacific Railway was completed, in 1885, politicians in British Columbia demanded Oriental exclusion. Ottawa responded with a $50 head tax on each Chinese immigrant. Under tremendous pressure, in 1900 Prime Minister Wilfrid Laurier's government increased the head tax to $100. But that was not enough. In 1903, it was raised to $500, equivalent to an average labourer's annual salary, with the result that only eight Chinese men were admitted into Canada that year.

Japanese and East Asians were also unwelcome. A 1908 Gentleman's Agreement between Canada and Japan – named as such to enable Japan, as an ally of Britain, to save face (it was also known as the Hayashi-Lemieux Agreement) – limited Japanese immigration to 400 annually, less than half the number that had come in each of the preceding three years. Like China, Japan, teeming with people, was perceived to be eager to flood Canada with immigrants. The Japanese in Canada created separate institutions, such as Buddhist temples; this was regarded with suspicion and considered to be evidence that they would not try to assimilate.

Blacks, though few in Canada, also faced campaigns to keep them out. Black men were portrayed as having insatiable sexual appetites and as a threat to the purity of white women. Canada's federal government advertised in the United States to discourage prospective Black migrants; relying upon racist tropes, it warned them, as a so-called southern race, of their inability to cope with the cold Canadian climate. When Edmonton's population stood at 24,900, 3,400 signatures were obtained on a petition against Black immigration, then coming from places like Oklahoma where Jim Crow laws and lynchings subjected African Americans to deadly violence.

In times of crisis, the tendency to focus distrust on those from elsewhere intensified. During the First World War, Canadians grew jittery over potential spies and saboteurs, especially with, until April 1917, a neutral United States on Canada's doorstep containing millions of German Americans. In February 1916, a fire demolished Canada's House of Commons. Although caused by a combination of careless smoking, piles of paper lying about, and highly oiled pine desks, chairs and panelling, in screaming newspaper headlines the fire was initially blamed on German American saboteurs. That spring, the majority Anglo-population in Berlin, Ontario, led a successful campaign to change its name to Kitchener to commemorate the former British Minister of War. During that campaign, soldiers with the 118th Battalion stole a bust of Kaiser Wilhelm I from the German Concordia Club, dumped it into a nearby lake, and sacked the premises, even though the club had ceased operations for more than a year and almost half of its members had volunteered to fight for Canada.

One thing most German Canadians had going for them, however, was that their long-settled status in Canada made them British Subjects. This was not the case with several thousand Ukrainians, many of whom came from the Austrian-controlled province of Galicia, and as such were classified as enemy aliens. Authorities noted that in August 1914 the Western Canadian Ukrainian spiritual leader, Bishop Nicholas Budka, advised his followers 'to support the peace-loving Emperor Franz-Joseph'. Within a week Budka recanted, insisting that all Ukrainians were 'faithful citizens of ... the British Empire'.[6] Understandably, many considered the second comment disingenuous, but unfairly assumed that most Galicians would follow Budka's initial, and subversive, advice.

At this time, Canada interned 8,579 individuals, of whom 3,100 were German reservists, and nearly all the rest were Ukrainians. Internees were sent to remote places in the interior of British Columbia, northern Alberta and northern Ontario. Many were assigned to work in Canada's emerging national parks, such as Banff, where they built roads using pick and shovel, setting the groundwork for what politicians predicted would be a postwar tourist boom with the proliferation of the automobile. Approximately 100 prisoners died from illnesses, and 6 were killed, including those trying to escape. In 1916, as Canada's labour surplus transformed into a labour shortage, most Galicians were paroled, though only if accepting certain work, such as farm labour.

Immediately following the Great War, the federal government moved to clamp down on political radicalism. For those who believed in world revolution, never did it seem so possible. Communist forces had consolidated in Russia and the radical Spartacus movement threatened to seize power in Germany. Labour radicalism peaked in 1919. Strikes mounted across North America, in Canada producing, up to that time, a record 2.1 million workdays lost that year. In most cases, strikers were trying to catch up to postwar galloping inflation; moreover, with union membership having doubled to some 376,000 between 1914 and 1919, labour organizations were trying to prove their worth to workers who, now that the war was over, did not feel the same need to stay on the job.

In Winnipeg, Canada's third-largest city at this time, metal trade workers went on strike on 1 May 1919 to achieve union recognition, something for which they had battled for more than a decade. They were joined by building and construction trade workers seeking better wages. Both groups appealed to the Winnipeg Trades and Labour Council for support; council members endorsed a general strike by an overwhelming margin of 11,000 to 500. Foreign radicals were blamed for the strike. The Winnipeg *Tribune* told its readers, 'Remember, behind ... this strike is a group of revolutionaries – its most active followers are undesirable aliens'.[7] After

---

[6] Joseph Boudreau, 'The Enemy Alien Problem in Canada, 1914–1921', PhD thesis, University of California Berkeley, 1965, 45–6.
[7] Winnipeg, *Tribune*, 21 June 1919, 1.

five weeks, a dawn raid by authorities nabbed the principal strike leaders (none of them new immigrants), and then, on 21 June, there came Bloody Saturday, when Mounties on horseback with revolvers drawn charged into a crowd, leaving two strikers dead. Seven of the eight arrested strike leaders were convicted of seditious conspiracy and received jail terms ranging from six months to six years, though most were released early. Still, the federal government was convinced that existing legislation did not provide an adequate deterrent to those intent on overthrowing constituted authority. In June 1919, section 41 was added to the Immigration Act to provide for the easier deportation of suspected radicals. Despite most of the Winnipeg General Strike leadership being of British background, section 41 was applied only against Slavs and Finns.

Until 1923, Mennonites, Doukhobors and Hutterites – all being pacifist, communal in economic practice and often German-speaking – were banned from immigrating to Canada, as were those from enemy countries during the First World War, as well as Ukrainians and Russians. So intense was the postwar pressure on Mennonites to integrate, especially when it came to the schooling of their children, that in the early 1920s some 2,000 left Canada to establish new settlements in Mexico and Paraguay. Until 1947, the 1923 Chinese Immigration Act kept out immigrants from China and strict quotas remained against the Japanese, kept to 150 annually. Looking for newcomers, the government again turned to Britain and Northwest Europe. In 1922, Canada worked with England to implement the Empire Settlement Act, which funded agricultural colonization schemes for emigrating Britons. Under this programme, almost 24,000 British women came to Canada as household workers between 1923 and 1931.

By the mid-1920s, labour shortages produced increased pressure from several companies for more immigration. The resulting influx also generated harsh reactions, especially because many newcomers from Central Europe were Roman Catholics. In the Prairies, and particularly in Saskatchewan, thousands of Anglo residents joined the racist Ku Klux Klan, whose popularity soared in the American Midwest, also in response to increased immigration and the growth of cities that were cast as centres of debauchery. The Klan offered a social venue, as well as a place where they could express their commitment to maintaining the dominance of white Protestants. In the June 1929 provincial election, the Saskatchewan Klan, some 25,000 strong, threw its support behind the Tories, led by J. T. M. Anderson, who toppled a Liberal administration that had governed the province since its founding in 1905. While Anderson's connection to the Klan remains unclear, his rhetoric took from many of their ideas; for example, he would claim that Saskatchewan was losing its Britishness even though the proportion of its population of non-British origin declined from 54.7 to 47.5 per cent between 1911 and 1931.

The Wall Street crash in October 1929 and the Great Depression that ensued brought additional negative consequences for many new Canadians and those seeking entry into Canada. With the economy in free fall, Canada essentially closed its borders, with immigrants being portrayed as exacerbating unemployment. A 1930 order-in-council specified that only people with adequate capital to set themselves up on a farm would be admitted into Canada, and the next year, all non-agricultural immigrants of non-British background were denied entry. Throughout the 1930s, immigrants were accused of exploiting suffering to spread socialism and communism. There began a concerted effort to locate and, when possible, to deport such people, who did not enjoy due process in the courts. Whereas 1,964 people were deported from Canada in 1929, that number rose to 7,647 in 1932.

Towards the end of the decade, Canada also proved itself to be among the most unwelcoming countries worldwide for Jews trying to flee Nazi Germany. Charles Frederick Blair, the highest-ranking federal civil servant in the Immigration Branch, was determined to maintain Canada's Anglo-British and Christian character, and when it came to Jewish immigration he said, 'None was too many'.[8] In 1939, a petition with 128,000 names on it appeared in Quebec, organized by the traditionalist St Jean Baptiste Society, opposing Jewish immigration. Across the country, Jews were excluded from social clubs and from buying homes in many neighbourhoods. Toronto in 1933 saw several days of rioting by the Christie Pits baseball grounds, located near a Jewish neighbourhood, as youth sympathetic to Nazi propaganda unfurled swastikas.

As had happened during the Great War, the Second World War brought more intense suspicions upon certain ethnic groups. Many people of German origin were fired from their jobs. Those classified as enemy aliens had to regularly report on their whereabouts. Two weeks before the conflict broke out, in September 1939, RCMP Commissioner, S. T. Wood, told Minister of Justice Ernest Lapointe that the police had prepared lists and could immediately arrest all enemy aliens. Arguably the most abysmally treated were Japanese Canadians, 90 per cent of whom lived in the Vancouver area. RCMP surveillance of this population stretching back to the early 1930s had not detected any subversion. British Columbians, however, had long resented Japanese Canadians for their economic success, especially as fishers, and accused them of being loyal to Japan. Demands for their internment hit a fever pitch in December 1941 with Japan's attack on Canadian troops at Hong Kong and on the US naval base at Pearl Harbor, Hawaii. This wave became unstoppable when, on 20 February 1942, the United States introduced an evacuation order from all coastal areas against its Japanese population. Four days later, Canada followed suit, barring 23,000 Japanese – most of whom were naturalized British subjects – from living within 160 kilometres

---

[8]Irving Abella and Harold Troper, *None Is Too Many: Canada and the Jews of Europe, 1933–1948* (Toronto: University of Toronto Press, 1982).

of the coast. Japanese-owned houses and fishing vessels were seized and sold off, often for only a fraction of their value. Numerous communities across Canada refused the entry of the Japanese forced to leave the west coast. Most evacuees went into rapidly constructed, overcrowded and generally nasty government housing complexes in the British Columbia interior. In August 1944, with the tide moving towards Allied victory, Canada's federal government told Japanese Canadians to choose between settling east of the Rocky Mountains or to move to Japan. Initially, just over 10,000 opted to leave Canada. Soon after, nearly half sought to change that decision, as they realized Japan was devastated. Ultimately, just under 4,000 went to Japan and these people were not allowed to return to Canada.

Prejudice remained strong in postwar Canada. Even after learning of the horrors of the Holocaust, one survey taken shortly after the war still placed Jews as among the least-favoured immigrants. While 250,000 Jewish survivors of the Holocaust languished in Europe, Canada accepted only 8,000 by the end of 1948, the year that the creation of Israel provided an outlet for European Jewry.

Still, immigration was changing postwar Canadian society. Between 1946 and 1952, Canada took in 164,000 displaced persons (DPs) from war-torn Europe. Immigration agents targeted people with occupational skills for which Canada had shortages. Newcomers were also selected, however, so as not to significantly alter Canada's white and Christian character. In 1947, in an official *Statement on Immigration*, Prime Minister Mackenzie King spoke of Canada's 'absorptive capacity', meaning not only its need to keep the number of newcomers to a level that would not add notably to unemployment or strain social services, but also to prevent them from altering Canada's racial character. Of the Chinese, Mackenzie King remarked, 'Any considerable Oriental immigration would ... give rise to social and economic problems ... that might lead to serious difficulties'.[9] During the first postwar decade, Canada took in 1.2 million newcomers, nearly 10 per cent of its 1945 population. Canada required labourers, especially in its resource and construction sectors, and for that, it turned to places like Greece, Portugal and Italy, where poverty, political instability and repression made many people anxious to leave. Also, between 1956 and 1958, Canada accepted 37,456 Hungarian refugees fleeing from the brutal Soviet suppression of a failed anti-Communist uprising during the Suez Crisis.

Reflecting an increasingly diverse population, in 1962, Canada's Immigration Act was revised to remove climate adaptability from criteria considered to provide entry. Canada introduced a point system in the late 1960s to attract the most qualified people for needed labour. This opened the door for immigration from a wider array of countries, including to more

---

[9]https://www.lipad.ca/full/permalink/1466185/.

non-whites and their immediate family members. Once having qualified as landed immigrants, such people were permitted to sponsor family members and relatives, as long as the sponsor assumed responsibility for ensuring those joining them would not become a charge on the public purse.

On 8 October 1971, Prime Minister Pierre Trudeau declared in the House of Commons that Canada was a multicultural country, meaning that Canada supported and celebrated all its ethnic and racial groups. Just over a decade later, in 1982, the principle of multiculturalism was enshrined in the Canadian Charter of Rights and Freedoms. The federal government passed the Canadian Multiculturalism Act of 1988 which, in defining multiculturalism as a core characteristic of modern Canada, spoke of eliminating barriers to enable full participation in all aspects of society and ensuring equal protections under the law. Canada also demonstrated a much more empathetic approach to refugees. In the late 1970s and early 1980s, it accepted tens of thousands of Vietnamese 'boat people' who took to the South China Sea in tiny vessels fleeing their homeland under mortal threat. In recent decades, some 10 per cent of refugees worldwide have come to Canada where they have resettled.

Over the past generation, Canada has had among the highest per capita immigration rates in the world. Annual immigration topped 400,000 in the 2020s. Canada's 2021 national census listed more than 450 ethnic groups, and 26.5 per cent of its population as non-white. The Canada of today is far removed from the country where the SS *Komagata Maru* sought to land. Indeed, on 27 May 2016, Prime Minister Justin Trudeau apologized in the House of Commons for the *Komagata Maru* incident, stating: '[N]o words can fully erase the pain and suffering ... experienced. Regrettably, the passage of time means that none are alive to hear our apology today. Still, we offer it, fully and sincerely. For our indifference to your plight. For our failure to recognize all that you had to offer. For the laws that discriminated against you, so senselessly'.[10] His government provided $2.5 million for education and commemoration.

From its earliest days, Canada has been a nation built on immigration, such as when the Loyalists came in the late eighteenth century from the newly independent United States to continue their fidelity to Britain. Yet, for most of its existence, Canada was also a country in which clear preferences existed on who it was best to accept and what was expected of those who arrived. Perhaps there is no starker picture of those sentiments being expressed than that of the throngs of Vancouverites cheering from the dock, as the HMCS *Rainbow* expelled from Canadian waters the SS *Komagata Maru* because its passengers were perceived to be a grave threat to the predominant vision of Canada as a White Anglo-Saxon Protestant country.

---

[10]https://vancouver.citynews.ca/2016/05/18/a-text-of-the-prime-ministers-apology-for-the-komagata-maru-incident/.

The Canada of today has come a long way from that dark episode. And yet, trepidation over large-scale immigration remains. One national poll, taken in October 2024, showed that 58 per cent of Canadians believed the country has accepted too many immigrants.[11] Although far less rooted in overt racism, still evident, however, is the belief that newcomers add to unemployment, increase costs to social services and contribute disproportionately to crime.

---

[11]Keith Neuman, 'Canadian Public Opinion about Immigration and Refugees', 17 October 2024, https://www.environicsinstitute.org/projects/project-details/canadian-public-opinion-about-immigration-and-refugees.

IMAGE 4 Parade against conscription in Victoria Square in Montreal, 1917. Library and Archives Canada / C-006859.

4

Anti-conscription riots in Quebec City, 1918: War and society

As the Great War dragged on, Canadian casualties kept mounting and voluntary enlistment sagged distressingly. Prime Minister Robert Borden felt compelled to introduce conscription, and soon after, in December 1917, a general election. Borden's new Unionist Party won by a landslide. In Quebec, however, the Unionists suffered overwhelming defeat, and in the months that followed, tensions there reached a boiling point.

Traditionally, Holy Week was a period of quiet in Quebec, a predominantly Roman Catholic province. It was a time when people would reflect on the Passion and Crucifixion of Jesus, culminating on Easter Sunday morning with celebrations of the Resurrection. The peacefulness, such as there was in the spring of 1918, started unravelling on the eve of Good Friday. Two members of the Dominion Police Force entered a pool hall in the working-class district of St Roch in Quebec City demanding that every man of military age dressed in civilian clothes produce a conscription exemption certificate. One man was arrested for failing to do so. Papers were soon produced, and the man was released, but the torch had been lit. Almost immediately, a large crowd gathered, enraged over the imposition of conscription and the heavy-handed way in which it was being enforced. The police station was stormed, several officers were beaten and there was significant damage to property. Fearing the rioters would extend their attacks to the city's federal buildings, local military commanders were ordered to be at the ready should they be needed.[1]

The rioting escalated and confrontations continued throughout that entire weekend. On Good Friday morning, 3,000 protestors were in the city's streets, ransacking stands of local newspapers that supported conscription. Their numbers doubled as the day wore on, overwhelming thirty local constables on the scene. People threw rocks and ice, breaking the windows

---

[1] Martin F. Auger, 'On the Brink of Civil War: The Canadian Government and the Suppression of the 1918 Quebec Easter Riots', *The Canadian Historical Review* 89, no. 4 (2008): 503–40.

of federal government buildings and other places where conscripts were to go to register. Mayor Henri-Edgar Lavigueur asked for military support, and the Chief of the General Staff in Ottawa, Sir Willoughby Gwatkin, immediately despatched 300 nearby armed military personnel to help secure order in the province's capital city.

Borden and his Unionist government, deeply unpopular as it was in Quebec, worried things would spiral out of control, perhaps across the entire province. On Saturday, 30 March, Borden invoked the War Measures Act, passed by the federal Parliament in August 1914, suspending basic civil liberties and immediately transferring law enforcement to the federal government through military personnel it put in place. Curfews were instituted and *habeas corpus* was suspended. Anyone could be arbitrarily stopped, searched and arrested.[2]

Troop levels in Quebec City quickly reached 4,000. Nearly all of them came from Ontario and western Canada, amid doubts French Canadians recruits would – should it become necessary – crack down on the rioters. By Easter Sunday, there were reports of stolen rifles, shotguns, revolvers, knives and daggers. Public notices were issued warning against gatherings. Tramway service was discontinued, as was ferry service across the St Lawrence River, and all bridge crossings were closed. Military trucks, mounted with machine guns, patrolled the city's streets. Still, defiant crowds continued to assemble. Cavalry and infantry moved in to disperse them. The mob hurled stones, ice, rocks and snowballs; a few individuals fired bullets from rooftops, alleys, behind snowbanks and other spots from which they could conceal themselves. Foggy weather hampered pinpointing the source of the shots, and troops were ordered to open fire on the rioters. Panic ensued. The crowd dispersed, leaving four people dead and some seventy injured. On the government side, thirty-two were wounded. Over the several days of rioting, the total number of wounded, on both sides, reached more than 150, and $300,000 ($6 million in 2025) in property damages was incurred. Martial law remained in effect for weeks. Some 3,000 troops were kept in Quebec City, while others were assigned to Montreal, and seconded troops did not completely leave the province's capital until early 1919.

The Quebec City riots through Easter weekend in 1918 were the most striking flashpoint of intensified wartime discord between French- and English-speaking Canadians. The roots of this discord lay in the sustained, if simmering French-Canadian discontent that went back to the time of Britain's military victory over the French on the Plains of Abraham in 1760, coupled with French Canada's continued struggle to defend its culture and language and insistence that its people were not to be subjected to Anglo-Canadian loyalties to Great Britain and its Empire.

---

[2]See Robert Borden, *Robert Laird Borden: His Memoirs*, vol. 2. 1938 (Toronto: McClelland and Stewart, 1969).

The United Kingdom entered the Great War on 4 August 1914. At that time, Canada still had no final say over its own foreign policy. As part of the British Empire, Canada was obligated to stand with 'the motherland', although decisions about the men and materiel it supplied remained under Canadian control. Initially, Canadians' support for the war effort was unequivocal, enthusiastic and, though more tepid in Quebec, nationwide. Enemy Germany was viewed as militaristic, autocratic and aggressive – and to be stopped. Equally widespread was the sentiment that the conflict would be brief, with Britain and its allies destined for a quick and decisive victory. At first, men clamoured to enlist, naively seeing the war as a great adventure. In 1914, at Acadia University, in Wolfville, Nova Scotia, for example, twenty-seven of twenty-nine men in their final year volunteered. They could not possibly have foreseen the terrifying bloodbath that would ensue over four horrific years along a largely unmovable maze of trenches that would mark the Western Front. Moreover, this occurring soon after a steep prewar economic recession, many young men saw military service as a steady job, starting at $1.10 per day for a private, with all meals and lodging covered.

Recruitment was chaotic, with little centralized coordination at first. Canada's charismatic, bombastic and endlessly energetic Minister of Militia and Defence, Sam Hughes, depended for volunteers on local militia units and formations rapidly created in locales across Canada. In the first months, and arguably for the first year of the war, in many parts of the country there were more volunteers than spots available. That, however, changed. The conflict dragged on and casualties mounted. April 1915 alone saw 6,000 Canadians killed and wounded at Ypres, Belgium. A fact not noticed by many this early in the war was that two-thirds of the men in Canada's first overseas contingent were born in Britain; thus, these were men with particularly strong ties to the Mother Country. Certain demographic groups felt greater motivation to enlist than did others. One hotbed was Toronto, at the time 80 per cent Anglo-Protestant. As of February 1916, 47 per cent of Canadian volunteers identified as Anglican when, across the country, just one in seven declared that as their faith. By October 1917, 86 per cent of Toronto's males eligible for military service had at least tried to enlist.[3]

Volunteer levels sagged sharply as the war progressed. Over the course of 1915, to increase numbers, the military reduced height, weight and chest measurement requirements, as well as dental health requirements. Starting that August, a husband no longer required his wife's formal, written permission to sign up. To reach growing enlistment targets, recruiters began haranguing and shaming men in public places. 'Give Us His Name' campaigns sprang up in many communities; people were urged

---

[3]Desmond Morton, *When Your Number's Up: The Canadian Soldier in the First World War* (Toronto: Random House, 1993).

to send in the names of individuals to whom recruiters should make a personal visit. Women assisted by handing out white feathers – indicating cowardice – to men viewed as being of military age yet wearing civilian clothes. High school teachers and university professors, clergy and others in positions of authority, including, of course, political leaders, joined this chorus of pressure.

Enlistment lagged in rural areas. Farms needed workers to help meet the increased demands on output, but now there were well-paying war jobs in urban centres, and many men saw these as a better option than military service. Despite strict censorship and inspiring stories of daring and bravery among Allied troops, ever-expanding casualty lists and the return home of wounded soldiers seriously dampened enthusiasm for enlisting. The most glaring weakness about enlistment numbers was in French Canada; at a time when Canada's military personnel neared 300,000, just over 14,000 of these volunteers came from French-speaking Quebec.

Sam Hughes squandered early enthusiasm for the war in some quarters by failing to create a French-speaking battalion, instead dispersing French-Canadian men among Anglo-dominated formations. Hughes eventually realized that this was a poor approach and that a French-Canadian formation would provide pride and encourage esprit de corps; in mid-1915, the Royal 22nd Regiment, known in English as the 'Vandoos', was established, but in trying to fill its ranks it had to recruit from across Canada. Hughes exuded endless confidence in the patriotism of the Canadian people, and the ability of local units to drive recruitment.

The prime minister ignored warnings both from Canada's Chief of the General Staff that conscription would result, and from others, like the president of the Canadian Pacific Railway, Thomas George Shaunessy, of severe labour disruptions: on 1 January 1916, the Borden government committed Canada to a volunteer army of 500,000 men. The expanding scope of the war overseas led to ever louder calls for conscription, which the United Kingdom implemented from January 1916, starting with unmarried men aged eighteen to forty-five. New Zealand followed suit that April. But six months later, in a very divisive public referendum, Australia rejected conscription – with its still-robust voluntarism, belief that conscripts would besmirch its proud military reputation, not to mention pronounced opposition from its large Irish-Catholic population with its long-standing antipathy to Britain.[4]

In the first three months of 1916, Borden's bold challenge for Canada to stand tall among its allies with a half-million-man volunteer army saw a bump in enlistment. After that, however, recruitment entered a persistent downward trend. Pressure was mounting on Canada to conscript men for overseas service. That April, in Ontario, the Hamilton branch of the

---

[4]Carl Berger, ed., *Conscription 1917* (Toronto: University of Toronto Press, 1969).

Citizens' Recruiting League articulated a demand for *equality of sacrifice* from all parts of the country. This prompted groups like the Canadian National Service League to highlight Quebec's laggard performance. With a quarter of Canada's population, by 1917 Quebec provided only about 14 per cent of recruits, the majority coming from the province's 18 per cent anglophone contingent.

Some people tried to encourage positive dialogue about unity and shared civic duty. Standing out among these was the Bonne Entente movement. It was led by prominent Toronto lawyer and Liberal John Milton Godfrey and in Quebec by Premier Jean Lomer Gouin and Jean-Georges Garneau, the first president of the National Battlefields Commission (which manages the Plains of Abraham site in Quebec City), serving in that role from 1908 to 1939. The Bonne Entente movement raised millions of dollars for a series of high-profile and well-attended conferences in both Ontario and Quebec. But the gatherings produced little more than platitudes. Indeed, there was some speculation that their real purpose was economic, to rope in many business leaders with the goal of mitigating growing calls in Quebec to boycott Ontario goods as a protest over that province's Regulation 17 undermining bilingual schools.

Much of the anger in Quebec was stoked by the prominent and influential Henri Bourassa. A former Liberal Member of Parliament, Bourassa had parted ways with Wilfrid Laurier over the latter's decision, when prime minister, to send a battalion of volunteers to assist the British in the 1899–1902 Boer War. Soon after Bourassa left the House of Commons, he was elected to the Legislative Assembly of Quebec. In 1903 he started the Ligue nationaliste canadienne, and in 1910 he founded the influential newspaper, *Le Devoir*, which railed against the federal government for supporting British Imperial interests either through cash contributions to its Royal Navy or by creating a Canadian navy that would, in times of emergency, be put at Britain's disposal.[5]

Bourassa also led opposition to Ontario's Regulation 17. Passed in 1912, it eliminated French-language or bilingual instruction in schools beyond the first grade. Through *Le Devoir*, and at large rallies, Bourassa would ask why French Canadians should fight to retain democratic rights overseas when they were denied basic civil liberties at home. Anger also exploded on the ground, most directly, in October 1915, at Ottawa's Guigues elementary school, named for Monsignor Joseph-Eugène-Bruno Guigues, that city's first Roman Catholic bishop. Seeking to protect teachers who were defying Regulation 17, parents occupied the school, and several women stood guard, armed with hatpins, to hold off authorities. Borden received a petition with 60,000 names organized by the Association catholique de

---

[5]Damien-Claude Bélanger, 'Review of Geoff Keelan, *Duty to Dissent. Henri Bourassa and the First World War*', *Revue d'histoire de l'Amérique française* 74, no. 4 (2021): 89–93.

la Jeunesse canadienne-francaise condemning Regulation 17. In Montreal, at one rally, 10,000 people gathered in protest. Quebec Liberal MP Ernest Lapointe introduced a motion in the House of Commons urging the Ontario legislature to rescind Regulation 17. The motion was defeated by the Borden Conservatives, asserting that the matter fell under provincial jurisdiction and not under section 93 of the British North America Act, 1867, then Canada's constitution, which does refer to minority schooling rights, nor under its section 133, which denotes several domains in which both French and English are official languages. Even Pope Benedict XV expressed his sympathy for French speakers and urged compromise, as did Canada's highest court at the time, the London-based Judicial Committee of the Privy Council. Nevertheless, Regulation 17 remained in force until 1927, even though French-language schools in Ontario were not officially recognized under the provincial Education Act until 1969, with the first French-language high schools in the province officially opening in late 1969 and 1970. On 22 February 2016, Ontario Premier Kathleen Wynne apologized in the Legislative Assembly on behalf of the Government of Ontario for Regulation 17 that effectively outlawed public French-language education in primary schools for more than a decade. French-Canadian disenchantment was augmented when Manitoba in 1916 further restricted bilingual education, and Saskatchewan, soon after, made English the sole language of instruction past first grade, except for one hour per day.

The defects of Canada's locally administered recruitment for the war effort had become glaringly apparent by mid-1916. Parts of the country remained little impacted, while others suffered from labour shortages that crippled local production. That spring the Legislative Assembly of New Brunswick passed a resolution urging the federal government to organize recruitment along scientific means, meaning to balance military enlistment with homefront needs. Sam Hughes resisted this call, casting the suggestion as unnecessary, impractical and involving too much bureaucracy. Hughes was determined to retain for himself unchallenged control over Canada's military effort. Borden by this time was increasingly seeing Hughes as a political liability. A recent Royal Commission investigation had revealed that the militia minister's friend and appointee to the Shell Committee (created in 1914 to manufacture shells and bullets for both the Canadians and the British), J. Wesley Allison, had taken kickbacks for distributing munition contracts; moreover, in London, Canadian arms production was considered deficient, thus leading to the 1915 creation, in Canada, of the British-controlled Imperial Munitions Board.

Hughes travelled to London in April 1916 to reassert control over extraterritorial Canadian training and to receive a peerage that had been arranged at Borden's request. Yet, rather than displaying gratitude for the honour, throughout the visit Hughes denounced Ottawa for deciding to establish the Ministry of Overseas Military Forces of Canada to manage military matters outside Canada. In a final effort to retain his power,

Hughes attempted, without Borden's permission, to organize a 'Sub-Militia Council' directly answerable to him – an action that resulted in his dismissal from Cabinet.

While Hughes stirred up trouble abroad, Borden authorized changes to Canadian enlistment practices. In August 1916, Thomas Tait, head of the Montreal branch of the Citizens' Recruiting League, was installed at militia headquarters in Ottawa as Director General of Recruiting. To relieve pressure on areas exhausted of labour and to provide for a more effective sweep of the land, Tait appointed senior army officers to coordinate activities in nine military districts that were subdivided into precincts and then parcelled out among recruiters from various regiments. The following month, to further improve the system and to hopefully avoid conscription, Tait's position evolved into director of the newly created National Service Board (NSB) which, among other things, set priority classifications on jobs so that recruiters could focus on occupational groups whose absence would not cripple the domestic economy.

Many military authorities concluded that such reorganization had come too late and was incapable of reversing the downward trend of voluntary reinforcements. The direction was clearly moving towards compulsory service. Throughout the latter part of 1916, Ottawa received entreaties from London to put a fifth Canadian division in the field to compensate for massive Allied losses sustained at the Somme, starting with the ill-named and disastrous Big Push on 1 July and continuing throughout that summer and fall. The NSB, which advised on labour supply, launched a nationwide campaign to convince men of working age to mail back by 7 January cards – amounting to registration cards – that it had distributed seeking answers to questions dealing with matters such as age, health, marital status and occupation. The NSB emphasized that this was to secure the most efficient use of labour and made no mention of conscription. Although suspicion persisted among those opposed to compulsion, the campaign proved reasonably successful; more than 80 per cent of the cards were returned, though of that number 15 per cent were blank or incomplete. The returns led to the conclusion that some 475,000 Canadian men were fit for military service.

It was not only in Quebec that distrust grew over the federal government's true intent. An increasing number of union leaders demanded that before men were conscripted, the same occur with wealth in the form of higher progressive taxes. Accusations abounded that many business, industrial and financial leaders were profiting excessively from Canada's war effort. Critics portrayed new corporate and income taxes introduced in 1916 and 1917 as minimalist. Leadership of the Trades and Labour Congress of Canada, the country's sole national union body, criticized the federal government – and, indeed, all provincial governments – for still not having legislation guaranteeing unions recognition from employers when most employees supported a particular union. In Winnipeg, a hotbed of union support, with much of it leaning towards socialism, the city's Labour Council urged workers not to fill in the registration cards. Several unions threatened strikes should conscription come to pass.

Anger grew in rural Canada. Farmers were being urged to produce more with decreasing numbers of labourers resulting from recruitment and migration to better-paying urban war jobs. If conscription did come to pass, farmers demanded that those who worked to support agriculture be exempted. By 1918, nearly 20,000 schoolchildren had been prepared to assist under the Canada Food Board's programme called Soldiers of the Soil, together with about 2,500 young urban women volunteers called 'farmerettes' who worked on vegetable, fruit and truck farms; however, the numbers were inadequate, and the participants were regarded as too inexperienced. Shortages of labour were also costing farmers more: over the first three years of the war, the annual salary in Ontario of a farm labourer rose from $323 to $610, though, fortunately for farmers – but not consumers – this was offset by rising commodity prices.

Throughout English-speaking Canada, the desire for conscription was fed by the belief – and prejudice – that French Canadians, especially those in Quebec, were not pulling their weight. In all, fourteen French-Canadian battalions were established: eleven from Quebec, one from New Brunswick, one from Alberta and one from Eastern Ontario. However, only three achieved their full strength of 1,100 recruits. Calls for Quebec to help save their brethren in France had little impact, as in this deeply religious province, there was the widespread view that the war was divine punishment on France for having become a republic in which the Church had little or no influence on government.

Canadian casualties mounted with costly battles at places that included St Eloi in the spring of 1916 and Courcelette that September. The next spring, Canada's successful, pride-producing, but bloody attack to capture Vimy Ridge resulted in 24,000 killed, wounded and missing. Over the course of 1917, casualties approaching 123,000 nearly doubled enlistments which were at just under 64,000. The United States entered the Great War on 4 April 1917. This was welcomed in hopes of turning the tide, but it also came with US imposition of compulsory selective service which increased pressure on Canada to do the same. Among key members of the British Empire, Canada's response, while impressive, still lagged; Great Britain now had 17 per cent of its male population in uniform, New Zealand had 12 per cent and Australia had 11 per cent, compared with the Canadian proportion of barely 10 per cent.

In London for meetings of the Imperial War Cabinet in early 1917, Prime Minister Borden was extremely aware that the overall situation remained gloomy. In Russia, the czar's collapse to Communist supporters was imminent, thus permitting Germany to transfer more soldiers to the Western Front. Italy was faltering against Austria, and morale among French troops was collapsing to the point where, after costly battles that May in the Champagne

District, a mutiny resulted. America's declaration of war offered new hope, but its mobilization would take months. Most military experts predicted high Allied casualties continuing well into 1919. While overseas, Borden also visited wounded Canadian soldiers, promising them the country's full effort. He arrived at the conclusion that it was essential and, in fact, a solemn duty, to introduce conscription in Canada. As the bill establishing conscription was brought before parliament, Borden pleaded with its members: 'If we do not pass this measure ... if we do not keep our plighted faith, with what countenance shall we meet them [soldiers] on their return'.[6]

The act classified men of military age, with the highest category for conscription being single, widowed and childless men between the ages of twenty and thirty-four. The aim was to conscript 100,000 men. To mitigate potential discord, Borden approached Opposition Leader Wilfrid Laurier with the idea of forming a coalition government. Expressing respect for those – including within his own party – who supported conscription, Laurier nevertheless rejected the offer, citing philosophical antipathy towards compulsion, displeasure over Borden's introduction of the Military Service Act before offering the partnership, and most important of all, his fear that such collaboration would hand Quebec over to the more extreme francophone nationalist forces led by Henri Bourassa, tear the nation apart and perhaps even precipitate civil war.[7]

On 11 June 1917, Borden introduced the legislation in the House of Commons. Debate was contentious; ninety-nine MPs spoke on the proposed act. On the second, and most critical reading of the measure, only two MPs from Ontario and two from Western Canada opposed it, while just seven in Quebec offered their endorsement. On 28 August, the bill passed third and final reading, 119 to 55; all francophone MPs from Quebec present in the House voted against it. That evening, authorities in Montreal had to disperse an angry mob. Implementation of the act would, however, wait until after a general election, scheduled for 17 December.

Many Liberals stuck by their long-time leader, former prime minister and, for numerous MPs, revered elder statesman, Wilfrid Laurier. But cracks soon appeared. Several Liberals from English-speaking Canada agreed that conscription was necessary; others, aware of public opinion, worried about defeat. On 12 October, a coalition of former members of the Conservative Party and some pro-conscription Liberal MPs was officially announced with a Cabinet intended to project national unity to include fourteen former Conservatives and ten Liberals, though only three of the latter came from Laurier's caucus and the rest from provincial Liberal ranks in Ontario and western Canada. Behind the new Union Party's high-sounding public

---

[6]Tim Cook, *War Lords: Borden, Mackenzie King and Canada's World Wars* (Toronto: Allen Lane, 2012), 103.
[7]See Canada, House of Commons Debates, particularly 2–5 April 1918, 236–9, 284–6, 336, 378–463.

pronouncements about country over party, however, was bitter infighting between former Conservatives and Liberals on who would run for office and serve in Cabinet. Indeed, beyond supporting conscription and condemning its opponents as disloyal, the Unionists did not present a cohesive platform. This election, however, was not about policies; it devolved into raw emotion over conscription.

The Unionists, backed by major business donors, amassed an election cache of $1.5 million, five times higher than when Borden first ran for the prime ministership. To ensure victory, they bent election rules to their advantage. That September, through closure that limited parliamentary debate, they passed two controversial statutes. The first, the Wartime Elections Act, denied the ballot to conscientious objectors and those of enemy background naturalized as British subjects after 31 March 1902; this group, particularly western Canada's large Ukrainian population, consistently voted Liberal. It also extended the franchise – at a time when women in Canada did not yet have the right to vote in federal elections – to the wives, widows, daughters and sisters of those in uniform, an agglomeration assumed to be sympathetic to conscription, especially with leading suffragists strongly endorsing the war effort. The second, the Military Voters Act, permitted the governing party to determine the provincial distribution of overseas soldier ballots, also reasonably presumed to be overwhelmingly pro-conscription. In making certain the desired result, Liberal election scrutineers complained about being kept physically away from overseas military polling stations where they quite rightly alleged election boxes were stuffed, and officers watched enlisted men as they marked their ballot. It was therefore no wonder that approximately 90 per cent of soldiers supported the Unionists. In justifying these two pieces of legislation, which shifted an estimated fourteen parliamentary seats away from the Liberals, Arthur Meighen, speaking for the government, argued that the women extended the ballot were being given the opportunity to take the place of men whose responsibilities in uniform prevented them from voting; that Canadians relatively recently arrived from enemy countries might be divided in their loyalties; that conscientious objectors had the "trade off" of not being compelled to fight; and that it was unrealistic for those in uniform, facing incredible challenges, to recall their exact home riding. Moreover, the Unionists offered strategic bribes to ensure their victory. Families that already had a member in the military were promised lower priority over other men eligible for conscription. To solidify rural support, Borden's government passed an Order-in-Council – meaning that it did not have to go through parliamentary debate – stating that famers' sons engaged in agricultural production would be exempt from conscription or if recently enlisted, could obtain an honourable discharge.[8]

---

[8] Patrice A. Dutil and David MacKenzie, *Embattled Nation: Canada's Wartime Election of 1917* (Toronto: Dundurn, 2017).

The 1917 election campaign saw the creation of the Union Government Publicity Bureau which flooded the country with inflammatory posters, pamphlets and press advertisements, for example, charging Laurier, and by implication Quebec, with 'deserting our men ... and trailing Canada's honour in the mud'.[9] Chief Justice Charles Fitzpatrick of the Supreme Court of Canada and Quebec Archbishop Paul Bruchési both warned Borden of potential violence. There were plenty of signs for worry. In early 1917, an anti-conscription mob in Quebec City had smashed the windows of the pro-government newspapers *L'Événement-Journal* and the *Québec Chronicle-Telegraph*. Increasingly, there were reports of troops being attacked throughout the province. That August, a bomb made from stolen dynamite was left at the door of the mayor of Outremont, a Montreal suburb, a known supporter of the federal government, though a subsequent investigation concluded the explosives were inactive. Also at this time, the chauffeur of Hugh Graham, publisher of the pro-conscription *Montreal Star*, was murdered. Throughout the election campaign, it became necessary for Union Party candidates to use bodyguards when in Quebec. Indeed, the new coalition had trouble fielding candidates in Quebec as many of those approached to run feared for their physical safety. Throughout much of English-speaking Canada, the campaign became a crusade against Quebec, namely, to compel the province to shoulder its duty. 'The Flag will not come down', declared the London Free Press. 'The Canadian soldiers at the front will not be deserted. Quebec shall not rule Canada'.[10]

The Unionists won a huge majority that December, taking 153 of the 235 seats up for grabs. In their ranks were 37 who formerly had been Liberals. But this was far from a government of national unity. The Liberals took 62 of 65 seats in Quebec, but only 20 of 167 in English-speaking Canada. In Ontario, 62 per cent voted Union, while in Quebec, only a quarter of the vote went that way. Meanwhile, in the Legislative Assembly of Quebec, MLA Joseph-Napoléon Francoeur proposed a motion that Quebec separate from Canada; although defeated, this motion was debated all through the first month of 1918 and garnered considerable sympathy. Enforcement of the Military Service Act, starting on 1 January 1918, required despatch of Dominion Police Force officers into Quebec to try to track down resisters, who in some cases armed themselves as they went into hiding.[11]

Only 24,132 conscripts made it to France from Canada. If forcing the same wartime sacrifice from Quebec constituted a major aim, the

---

[9] Desmond Morton and Jack Lawrence Granatstein, *Marching to Armageddon: Canadians and the Great War, 1914–1919* (Toronto: Lester & Orpen Dennys, 1989), 183.
[10] Cook, *War Lords*, 113.
[11] Jack Lawrence Granatstein and J. Mackay Hitsman, *Broken Promises: A History of Conscription in Canada* (Toronto: Oxford University Press, 1977).

government came up short. Of the 115,602 men in Quebec called up under the Military Service Act, 113,291 (i.e., 98 per cent) sought an exemption. Only 23 per cent of those drafted were French speaking from Quebec; those from agricultural families, in particular, were successfully able to convince conscription tribunals that they were needed at home.

In defence of the prime minister, it was impossible in 1917, or even through most of 1918, to predict that Germany would collapse so quickly after its initially successful spring offensive fizzled. Still, Borden's steadfast support for conscription led him to back initiatives that, in the words of his most respected biographer, 'did him no credit'.[12] It was sadly ironic that, in the cause of trying to arouse Canadians to what was presented to them as a higher standard of service, Borden capitalized on bigotry, displayed gross disrespect for democracy and implemented propaganda that tore deeply into the nation's delicate English-French duality. When Robert Borden left office, Canada was more fractured than ever before.

Division continued to fester after the Great War. In large parts of rural Canada, resentment persisted, especially as, in April 1918, in the wake of Germany's spring offensive, the Unionist government cancelled all exemptions to conscription. The war intensified rural depopulation, with the explosion of war jobs in urban localities. Soon after the cessation of hostilities, commodity prices collapsed, in response to which the federal government offered but little assistance. Feeding off long-standing grievances over an economic and political system perceived to be geared to the benefit of central Canada's urban manufacturers and other elites, much of rural Canada turned to new farmer political movements that, over the decade following the war, captured power in several provinces and, in the 1921 general election, won the second-largest contingent of seats in the House of Commons.

Organized labour came out of the First World War angrier because of intensified inflation, charges of wartime profiteering and continuing lack of legislative protections, even in factories that were run by the Imperial Munitions Board which, furthermore, was accused of paying meagre wages. During and following the war, with socialism spreading throughout Europe, and the Russian czar's overthrow by Communist forces, more Canadian workers and unionists expressed radical language and aims to dismantle capitalism. Much of organized labour in Canada had cast conscription as unfairly falling most heavily on working people. Fearing the threat of violence, as had transpired in the Easter weekend anti-conscription riots in Quebec City in 1918, the federal government passed legislation outlawing socialist and communist groups, infiltrated unions, arrested many of their leaders and, in some circumstances, violently

---

[12]Robert Craig Brown, *Robert Laird Borden: A Biography*, vol. 2 (Toronto: Macmillan, 1975), 101.

crushed strikes – most famously in response to the April 1919 General Strike in Winnipeg that left three dead.[13]

The impact of conscription lasted longest in Quebec. Being forced into combat in the First World War brought anger to unprecedented levels and, in sparking the Quebec City Easter weekend riots, precipitated panic in the federal government with tragic results. The riots and their aftermath were long remembered, destroying Conservative fortunes in the province for a long time to come. In the 1921 general election, the first following the war, Liberal leader William Lyon Mackenzie King painted the Conservatives, and particularly their new leader, Arthur Meighen, as the party of conscription. Indeed, throughout his long and successful political career, Mackenzie King, who remained prime minister for all but five years from 1921 to 1948, always kept in mind the catastrophic impact of conscription on national unity. Throughout the late 1930s this worry saw him delay rearming Canada in the face of expansionist European fascism for fear of indicating that Canada had accepted the inevitability of war. For most of the war, he confined conscription to the defence of Canada, initially for one month starting in Spring 1940, and the next year, extending the length of service for as long as the war continued. It was only in November 1944 that he finally relented, authorizing 16,000 men – the bare minimum demanded by military leaders – to be compelled to move from home defence to overseas service, as King feared an imminent cabinet revolt and the loss of power. Recalling the fate of his political mentor in 1917, King remarked in his dairy, 'It is perfectly plain to me that in pretty much all particulars my position is becoming identical to that of Sir Wilfrid Laurier's where his supposedly strongest colleagues left him, one by one ... '.[14] Conscription in the First World War divided the country as never before, and the Quebec City riots were the most striking manifestation of this divide. Conscription sustained a powerful narrative in Quebec decrying French-Canadian subjugation under British, and then, Anglo-Canadian dominance. The fight to undo that dominance would continue over the ensuing decades and indeed echo throughout the twenty-first century.

---

[13] James Naylor, Rhonda L. Hinther and Jim Morochuk, eds., *For a Better World: The Winnipeg General Strike and the Workers' Revolt* (Winnipeg: University of Manitoba Press, 2022).
[14] Jack Lawrence Granatstein, *Canada's War: The Politics of the Mackenzie King Government, 1939–1945* (Oakville: Rock Mill's Press, 2016), 350.

IMAGE 5 Agnes Macphail, MP for Grey County. New Paramount Studio / Library and Archives Canada / PA-127295.

5

Agnes Macphail, MP, 1921: The changing place of women in Canada

On 6 December 1921, in the first general election since the end of the Great War, Canadian women aged twenty-one years and older could vote, so long as they were not Asian or Indigenous – it would be another four decades before *all* women in Canada got the franchise. In 1921, five women ran for a seat in the House of Commons; one of them was elected: Agnes Macphail for the Ontario riding of Grey Southeast, thus becoming Canada's first woman Member of Parliament.

This pivotal moment was a long time coming. Section 41 of the British North America Act (BNA Act), 1867, as Canada's constitution was then called, expressly gave the franchise to men: 'Every Male British Subject, aged Twenty-one Years or upwards, being a Householder, shall have a Vote'.[1] No mention is made of women in this context. Soon after Confederation, a women's suffrage movement emerged in all of the Canadian provinces. Many feared extending the franchise to women would mean giving them undue influence, while degrading their supposedly higher sense of morality by miring them in the dirty and often corrupt world of politics. Supporters vigorously argued the opposite, insisting that women's participation in elections would have a morally uplifting influence on society.[2]

The first major leader in Canada's campaign for women's suffrage was Dr Emily Howard Stowe, who in 1880 became the second woman licensed physician in Canada; the first was Jennie Kidd Trout, in 1875. Stowe, together with Jessie Turnbull, founded the Canadian Women's Suffrage Association

---

[1] https://www.justice.gc.ca/eng/rp-pr/csj-sjc/constitution/lawreg-loireg/p1t11.html.
[2] Joan Sangster, *One Hundred Years of Struggle: The History of Women and the Vote in Canada* (Vancouver: University of British Columbia Press, 1997).

(formerly the Toronto Women's Literary Guild, established in 1877) to fight for women's rights as well as for better working conditions. They achieved a breakthrough in 1883, when Ontario granted the municipal franchise to widows and unmarried women who owned property. After that things ground to a halt for a time. Leaders in the movement insisted women would use the ballot to achieve a 'purifying, civilizing, and stabilizing influence'[3] and that they had no aspirations whatsoever to challenge male authority. Defined by many historians as 'maternal feminists', these women activists tended to come from upper- and middle-class backgrounds and, in English-speaking Canada, were typically of British heritage. In Quebec, where a conservative Roman Catholic Church held tremendous influence until well into the twentieth century, public expressions of feminism remained comparatively muted.[4]

Many of the women who sought for themselves a greater role in society did so to promote what they considered social uplift. They pursued social reforms, such as to alleviate urban squalor and horrid working conditions. They also attacked what they considered moral and social decay with, for example, campaigns to stamp out prostitution and to restrict immigration from outside Britain and Western Europe, in the belief that certain peoples or races fomented degradation of Canada as a country built on presumedly superior Anglo stock.[5]

Canada's involvement in both world wars necessitated expanded roles for women. By the end of 1914, with the First World War in full swing, the Canadian Red Cross established 100 spots for women to go overseas as nurses. These nurses were typically portrayed in terms of traditional notions of womanhood: as selfless, self-sacrificing 'angels of mercy', attributes reflected even in their quasi-religious uniform of a white, nun-like dress. Women took on a wide variety of jobs to release men for overseas service and to mitigate wartime conditions. Some 35,000 women were hired in munitions plants, almost all in Ontario, though there were far more applicants than available jobs; in Toronto, in 1918, of 6,000 women who applied, only 2,000 were placed. These were overwhelmingly young, single women, as it was considered undesirable that married women and mothers work outside the home. Although doing comparable jobs, women were paid less than men, confined to lower-status positions and, in factories, often kept under watch by female inspectors hired to ensure they not become overly familiar or friendly with their male colleagues.

---

[3]James Pitsula, *For All We Have and Are: Regina and the Experience of the Great War* (Winnipeg: University of Manitoba Press, 2008), 94.
[4]Catherine L. Cleverdon, *The Woman Suffrage Movement in Canada: Second Edition with New Introduction by Ramsay Cook* (Toronto: University of Toronto Press, 1974).
[5]Carol Lee Bacchi, *Liberation Deferred: The Ideas of the English-Canadian Suffragists, 1877–1918* (Toronto: University of Toronto Press, 1983).

Given women's many wartime contributions, more Canadians came to believe women would use the vote to produce a better post-war world. A perceived link between the war and social uplift strengthened demands for female suffrage. Prominent women's groups spearheaded myriad volunteer efforts to support the war effort and helped to successfully lobby for wartime prohibition to save resources and focus labour and production to bolster the fight overseas. Adding momentum was the argument that it was unacceptable in wartime to deny the vote to women of British background, while male immigrants, including those with roots in enemy countries, enjoyed this privilege.

Before she moved to Alberta, Nellie McClung was Manitoba's most prominent suffragist, working tirelessly for both the war and the franchise.[6] A convincing, sardonic and fearless champion for the ballot, she mockingly declared of opponents: 'Is it any comfort to the women who feels the sting of social injustice to reflect that she, at least, had no part in making such a law?'[7] Before the war was over, women could vote in provincial elections in five of Canada's nine provinces. In January 1916, Premier Tobias Norris fulfilled an election campaign promise and made Manitoba the first province in Canada to extend the vote to women. Emily Murphy was a prominent suffragist in Alberta, where she played a leading role in registering women for war-related volunteer campaigns; her province followed Manitoba's lead later in 1916, as did Saskatchewan that same year. In Saskatchewan, a petition garnered 11,000 signatures in support of female enfranchisement on the grounds that women had 'raised patriotic funds, knitted socks, rolled bandages, cared for the wounded ... and surrendered husbands, fathers, and sons to the battlefields'.[8] British Columbia and Ontario followed in 1917, where in both cases the government acted to offset endorsements of female suffrage by their opponents. It would take another decade to see the Maritime Provinces come on board, and in Quebec women did not get the vote until 1940.

Nevertheless, women gained little political presence at the provincial level, and then only in western Canada. Louise McKinney was elected to the Alberta legislature in 1917 as part of the short-lived Non-Partisan League, for which Irene Parlby also won a seat – and held it for fourteen years – in the 1919 provincial election. In British Columbia, Mary Ellen Smith, a Liberal, won a 1918 Vancouver by-election, succeeding her late husband in representing the riding. Nellie McClung sat as a Liberal in the Alberta legislature from 1921 to 1926.

---

[6]Veronica Strong-Boag and The Estate of Michelle Lynn Rosa, eds., *Nellie McClung: The Complete Autobiography* (Toronto: University of Toronto Press, 2003).
[7]Ramsay Cook and Wendy Mitchinson, eds., *The Proper Sphere: Woman's Place in Canadian Society* (Toronto: Oxford University Press, 1976), 315.
[8]Maclean's Magazine, *Women at War* (Toronto: Maclean-Hunter, 1943), 10.

Prime Minister Robert Borden was generally sympathetic to the idea of women's suffrage; moreover, he needed votes in support of his government's Military Service Act of August 1917 that mandated conscription. Accordingly, in September 1917, three months before the general election was held, the Borden government rammed the Military Voters Act and the Wartime Elections Act through Parliament as noted above. The former provided about 2,000 military nurses with the vote, and the latter did the same for servicemen's wives, widows, mothers, sisters and daughters who were twenty-one years of age or older. This is how the federal government enfranchised women who, it believed, would support the contentious policy of conscription. Soon after being re-elected, Borden's government, on 24 May 1918, passed an Act to Confer the Electoral Franchise upon Women. Also known as the Women's Franchise Act, this legislation stipulated that 'women who are British subjects, 21 years of age, and otherwise meet the qualifications entitling a man to vote, are entitled to vote in a Dominion election'.[9] 'It was a proud day yesterday for me and an hour which you and others have by unceasing devotion to the cause, made possible', one woman was moved to write to the pioneering Canadian suffragist, Flora Dennison. 'I may now be recognized by humanity at large, as having a complete number of organs and faculties with more or less average mental ability to use them!'[10] Also, that July, with a change to Canada's Elections Act, enfranchised women gained the right to stand for the House of Commons, although appointment to the Senate remained out of their reach until after the Persons Case of 1929.

Encouraging signs of change for women appeared in the years right after the First World War. The number of female university undergraduates nearly doubled in the 1920s to 7,500, or almost a quarter of Canada's total university population; while women accounted for more than 80 per cent of students in the Arts, they accounted for less than 2 per cent of the students in Medicine and less than 0.25 per cent of those studying Law. The 'Roaring 20s' saw liberalizing fashion trends for women: Corsets and bloomers went out of style. Skirts still rose only to the ankle, though the look was slimmer and more form fitting, suggestive of an independent and active woman. Helped by the changing styles in clothing that facilitated more freedom of movement, more women took part in sports. Lawn tennis and softball became more popular with women, and there were more university women's sports teams. Fanny 'Bobbie' Rosenfeld, whose nickname referred to her short, bobbed hair, became a widely celebrated top-ranked athlete, capturing Canada's first Olympic track and field medals, a gold and a silver, in Amsterdam in 1928. Yet, popular views

---

[9]https://lop.parl.ca/sites/ParlInfo/default/en_CA/ElectionsRidings/womenVote.
[10]Beth Light and Joy Parr, eds., *Canadian Women on the Move, 1867–1920* (Toronto: New Hogtown Press, 1983), 227.

portrayed athletic women as masculine, as risking their reproductive organs, and as likely to have puny babies.[11]

Indeed, consternation mounted over women having fewer children. Between 1921 and 1931, the fertility rate of women aged fifteen to forty-nine dropped by a quarter to just under 100 per 1,000. Critics focused on careerism as the primary threat to women's commitment to the family. In that same decade, the total number of working women in Canada grew by nearly half to reach 665,859, though this translated into only 17 per cent of Canada's labour force. Employment options for women overwhelmingly remained within gender-based stereotypes: secretaries, teachers, nurses, waitresses, textile workers and as ever, domestic servants. Marriage and motherhood continued to be presented as the most important roles for women.

The 1921 general election was a turning point in Canadian political history, for several reasons.[12] The government, under variously changing party names, that had led Canada since 1911 and through the First World War was defeated and replaced by a Liberal government under William Lyon Mackenzie King. This was the first federal election in which (white) women across the country could vote, and for the first time women could campaign for seats in the House of Commons – five did, and one was elected. Until 1921, only men sat in Canada's Parliament. That changed forever with Agnes Macphail's victory in her home riding of Grey Southeast, making her Canada's first woman MP.[13] 'I do not want to be the angel of any home', she later declared about her drive into political life and champion of the less powerful and privileged. 'I want for myself what I want for other women, absolute equality. After that is secured, then men and women can take turns being angels'.[14]

Macphail was nominated as a member of the National Progressive Party. To that point the Progressives were a movement advocating for farmers, as well as for democratic reform. They entered the political arena in 1920 and, led by Thomas Crerar, fielded 129 candidates in the 1921 race. An effective stump speaker, and known for her quick-witted repartee, Macphail ran as a farmer representative. She was nominated against twenty-four contenders, but it took five ballots, as there was considerable uneasiness over a woman candidate. Her Conservative opponent symbolized the status quo; he was Robert James Ball, a 64-year-old accountant, life insurance agent and teacher who had been first elected to the House of Commons a

---

[11]Sharon A. Cook, Lorna R McLean and Kate O'Rourke, *Framing Our Past: Canadian Women's History in the Twentieth Century* (Montreal and Kingston: McGill-Queen's University Press, 2001).

[12]Barbara Messamore, *Times of Transformation: The 1921 Canadian General Election* (Vancouver: University of British Columbia Press, 2025).

[13]Terence Allan Crowley, *Agnes Macphail and the Politics of Equality* (Toronto: J. Lorimer, 1990).

[14]www.brainyquote.com/quotes/agnes_macphail_404178.

decade earlier. Macphail's campaign ran on a shoestring budget of $200, one-third of which came from her own modest savings, but it was fuelled by enthusiastic volunteers. Exuding perpetual energy, she made more than fifty campaign speeches, often several in a single day. Her passion and message resonated, and she won with the largest margin of victory (2,598 votes) in the history of that Ontario riding. Macphail quickly became known as a champion of farmers, the working poor, women's rights and world peace.

Agnes MacPhail's modest, inauspicious, upbringing did not portend a storied future. Born in 1890, she was raised in a log home, and her family worked a humble piece of land. From a young age she was assigned a variety of chores. On farms, women did many, if not most, of the same physical activities borne by men. Macphail, however, displayed a love of books and learning, and at age sixteen qualified as a teacher. In choosing this path, Macphail demonstrated an independence that marked her life, as her parents wanted her to stay and help on the farm. While a young teacher in a one-room rural schoolhouse, she started to become politically active. She spoke out in support of farmers seeking to organize against what were presented as powerful, urban forces, especially manufacturers and other businesses accused of price gouging and profiteering, and against politicians from mainstream parties who supported inequities by maintaining high tariffs to shut out lower-priced items, including agricultural implements, particularly from the United States. She gravitated to movements that supported rural interests, initially the United Farmers of Ontario (UFO), founded in 1914 by the union of various farmers' organizations that had emerged over the previous decade and a half and, in 1919, after a narrow victory at the polls formed the provincial government. Macphail had gained notoriety through speaking at rallies on behalf of the UFO's women's organization, the United Farm Women of Ontario. Adding to discontent throughout that 1921 federal campaign was a sharp post-war recession. Moreover, strains in rural areas during the First World War, especially from the Borden government's broken promise not to conscript farmers' sons, given the wartime rural labour shortages, made things ripe for farmers to organize politically.

Agnes MacPhail's triumph at the polls generated intense media coverage, even in the United States, and she worked hard to champion her constituents' issues and democratic reforms. The press, however, focused on her personal life, on the fact that she was single, childless and dressed plainly, criticizing her for not wearing a hat and gloves in public (a rule she managed to change for women who came into the House of Commons). Newspaper articles presented her as a stern, ambitious, unfriendly shrew. On her first day as a parliamentarian, she found flowers on her desk, later to discover they had not been placed there as a tribute, but as the result of a lost bet that she would not get elected.

Macphail established herself as a serious, focused, and formidable politician and reformer. Early on, she championed striking coal miners in

Cape Breton. On a visit to Glace Bay, she railed against company housing that lacked indoor plumbing and running water and drew attention to the conditions of workers' children who were without proper clothing or decent schools and were plagued by rickets, a consequence of malnutrition. Turning to issues outside Canada, she recommended that Canada break from the British Empire and pursue world peace through the newly created League of Nations. In 1929, she was appointed as Canada's first woman delegate to the League, headquartered in Geneva, Switzerland, where she established herself as a widely respected and powerful voice for peace.

At home in Canada, Macphail spoke at rallies for disarmament. In 1932, she helped gather for the Women's International League for Peace and Freedom, founded in 1915, 500,000 signatures on a petition for global disarmament. She battled to see women attain equality not only in getting the vote, but also as participants in the workplace. She pushed for equality for women within marriages, such as for joint ownership of property, and advocated for divorce courts that would simplify and speed the process of divorce, as many women were trapped in abusive and exploitative relationships. Macphail earned voters' respect, ultimately winning eight elections. In general elections in 1925, and again in 1926, that saw the Progressives reduced to a small rump in the House of Commons, she defied the odds, winning re-election by wide margins.[15]

Building upon Macphail's presence in the House of Commons, pressure grew for women to be declared as eligible to sit in Canada's appointed Senate. This had been denied on the ground that section 24 of the British North America (BNA) Act identified a qualified 'person' for the Senate with the pronoun 'he'. Five prominent women activists, who became known as the Famous Five – Emily Murphy, Nellie McClung, Louisa McKinney, Irene Parlby and Henrietta Muir Edwards – launched the Persons Case, as it became known. On five occasions between 1920 and 1927, the federal government refused demands to change eligibility for the Senate to include women. Murphy – who, in 1916, became the first female magistrate in the British Empire – noted that, under the Supreme Court of Canada Act, five people, acting as a unit, could petition the Court on interpretations of the constitution. Justice Minister Ernest Lapointe, who sympathized with these women, backed their challenge to section 24. Nevertheless, in April 1928, Canada's Supreme Court ruled against the Famous Five. Adopting a strict interpretation of the BNA Act, the Court concluded that if the term 'person' was meant to include women, the framers would not have specifically linked it to the pronoun 'he'. The case was appealed to the Judicial Committee of the Privy Council in London. In October 1929, speaking for the Privy Council, Lord Sankey compared the BNA Act to 'a living tree capable of growth and

---

[15]Rachel Wyatt, *Agnes Macphail Champion of the Underdog* (Montréal: XYZ Publishing, 2000).

expansion within its natural limits',[16] meaning that the Council considered the Supreme Court's interpretation of a 'person' as too narrow and thus overruled it. Soon after the Privy Council's decision, many advocated for Macphail's appointment to Canada's Senate. She refused, however, stating that being relegated to Canada's appointed and usually quiet upper chamber would transform her status and influence into that of a fossil. The first woman to hold a seat in Canada's Senate was Cairine Wilson, of Ottawa, who was married to a Liberal MP and herself one of the founders, in 1928, of the National Federation of Liberal Women of Canada.

Throughout the Great Depression that ravaged the 1930s, and the widespread suffering it wrought, Macphail devoted her energies to advocating for social programmes, including unemployment insurance, public works initiatives and emergency support for farmers. She made it known that the Depression brought new hardships for women, like being dismissed from jobs to make room for more men. She supported forming a political alignment between farmers and labour as a means of advancing broader and greater fairness for ordinary people. This prompted her move from being a representative of farmers to finding a home in the new social democratic Co-operative Commonwealth Federation (CCF), formally launched in 1933 in Regina, of which she was a founding member. Her effectiveness as a speaker, clear convictions and courage as still the lone female Member of Parliament had some people touting her for leadership of this new party, though that position went to the Reverend James Shaver Woodsworth, a man Macphail deeply respected and admired.

Agnes Macphail, though highly regarded by many, could never escape the intense scrutiny that came with her being a woman. She was regularly accused of dressing frumpy, and her sometimes aggressive tone and sharp tongue – whose motto 'never apologize, never explain, just get the thing done, and let them howl'[17] – often considered evidence of strength for male politicians, became a basis for many to say that she was not ladylike. But, never dissuaded by critics, she continued to relentlessly pursue social change. In the 1930s, this included prison reform, both to alleviate horrid conditions and to emphasize rehabilitation rather than simply punishment. Canadian prisons remained largely unchanged from the nineteenth century, being governed in many respects by vengeance, exemplified by the meting out of physical punishment, including the cat-o-nine-tails. The Great Depression witnessed a sharp rise in Canada's prison population, deteriorating prison conditions and outbreaks of violence at several institutions, including at Stony Mountain outside Winnipeg and at Kingston, Ontario. Investigations revealed practices like the deliberate sharing of dishes and laundry, known

---

[16]John T. Saywell, *The Lawmakers: Judicial Power and the Shaping of Canadian Federalism* (Toronto: University of Toronto Press, 2002), 192.
[17]https://www.brainyquote.com/authors/agnes-macphail-quotes.

to be responsible for the spread of disease. Macphail played a notable role, both in raising this issue in Parliament and in ensuring that information was sent to the press. Shortly after the 1935 federal election, in which Macphail managed to increase the margin of her victory, a Royal Commission on Prison Reform was launched. Delayed in its start to October 1936 because of the death of one commissioner, two years later its report articulated a host of recommendations – which did not, however, begin to be implemented until some seven years later, with the end of the Second World War.

As war clouds were gathering over Europe once again, Agnes Macphail continued her work as a peace activist. She went as far as to say in 1937 that Canada should not enter any war without a national plebiscite authorizing such involvement, and she grew ever more critical of Great Britain as it began to rearm. Then came Hitler's annexation of Austria, the Sudetenland portion of Czechoslovakia, and in early 1939, all of Czechoslovakia: at this point, Macphail rejected appeasement and declared that Hitler had to be stopped. But the damage had been done. She lost her seat in the House in the March 1940 federal election. Canadians considered her, and the CCF, to be too soft on the need to fight in the war, especially with Woodworth voting against involvement.

Ever the fighter, Macphail was not yet finished. She moved to provincial politics, joining the Ontario CCF in 1942. She won office representing the Toronto constituency of York East, as one of two women elected in a contest in which the Conservatives narrowly bested the CCF. As a member of the Official Opposition, Macphail championed rural electrification and the installation of running water as many farms still depended on oil lamps and stand-alone wells with no water connections to the buildings. She advocated for cooperative ownership of the food-processing industry and stronger marketing boards to ensure fair pricing for both farmers and consumers. She continued to advocate for prison reform, as well as better support for elderly people, more subsidized housing, affordable childcare, and enhanced opportunities and equal treatment for women, particularly in the workplace. In the twilight of her political career, she insisted on equal pay for equal work for women based on the 1948 United Nations Universal Declaration of Human Rights, of which Canada was a signatory. With MacPhail playing a leading role, in 1949 the CCF introduced a measure for this into the Ontario legislature, but it failed to pass, prompting her to portray its Conservative opponents who formed the government, as privileged, archaic and insensitive.

Throughout her life, which ended in 1954, Agnes Macphail lived and worked in a legal and social milieu that presented formidable challenges to women. During her early years, most Canadians lived in rural settings where everyone had to pitch in: women worked the fields, in addition to their domestic chores of washing laundry, hauling water, cooking and cleaning, making clothes the family needed, caring for children and tending vegetable gardens. In urban centres, women were responsible not only for the domestic sphere but, in many cases, they also joined the paid workforce and worked for wages that were far below that of men. In 1901, women made up about 15 per cent of Canada's labour force. Popular attitudes did not favour women working outside the home, because that was seen as threatening the breadwinner status of men and as taking women away from household and family responsibilities. Some 90 per cent of women who did work outside the home at this time were single or widowed. Most of them held low-paying jobs, often perceived as an extension of housekeeping or nurturing. Some women entered professions like teaching (almost exclusively at the lower grades) and nursing. Up until the First World War, by far the most common paid employment for women was domestic service. This meant not only long hours of hard labour, but also the risk of sexual exploitation: many of the young girls employed as domestic labour became pregnant by their employers.[18] Both under Quebec's Civil Code and English Common Law, wives shared rights similar to those of children and the insane. They could not obtain credit on their own or exert any legal control over joint property. While adultery by a wife was grounds for the husband to demand a divorce, if the wife demanded such the husband's adultery had to be accompanied by desertion, incest, bigamy or the rape of another woman.

During the Depression, pressure quickly built to dismiss women from the paid workforce so that more men could perform the breadwinner role. Quebec's Legislative Assembly nearly passed a measure that would have required a woman to show financial need to take a job other than as a farm cook or domestic servant. Seeking to eke out some money, more women turned to home-based employment, but here, too, things became harder. One analysis concluded that whereas compensation received for sewing a dozen dresses in 1929 was $5.00, by 1934 it had dropped to just $1.35.

Once again, it was war that accelerated change for women. Within Canada, the increasing scale of the mechanized Second World War intensified economic needs, and with that the potential for social change, but accompanying this was also widespread anxiety over the process. Between June 1939 and the beginning of 1944, some 370,000 women in Canada obtained employment in areas directly connected to the war effort, often in roles that had been the exclusive domain of men. The proportion of women with jobs outside the home grew from 23 per cent to 33 per cent of the eligible female workforce, aged fourteen years and older. Record numbers of working women were married with children. To meet the rising demand for labour, in mid-1942 the federal government introduced income tax breaks for working couples and passed legislation to provide joint federally – provincially funded childcare facilities.

---

[18]Susan Crompton and Michael Vickers, 'One Hundred Years of Labour Force', *Canadian Social Trends*, Statistics Canada, https://www150.statcan.gc.ca/n1/en/pub/11-008-x/2000001/article/5086-eng.pdf?st=FyGyPWQB.

Government propaganda and press commentary conveyed the message that women had taken wartime jobs out of patriotism to release men for military action, and with victory overseas they would return to domestic life. Yet, several accounts, especially those written by female columnists, heralded the workplace contributions of women and spoke favourably of this being the basis for more permanent change. Lotta Dempsey, a future editor-in-chief of *Chatelaine*, then the most widely circulated magazine marketed to Canadian women, wrote in 1943: 'This was the time and the place it really started, the honest-to-goodness equality of Canadian women. It began to happen that hour when Canadian girls left desks and kitchens ... stepped into overalls and took their places in the lines of workers at lathes and drills'.[19] Yet, in the wartime workplace, men still dominated higher-prestige and higher-paid jobs. As during the First World War, some factories employed female inspectors to monitor women's behaviour, to prevent what was deemed excessive fraternization with male co-workers. Still, many women spoke of being changed by their work experience, often in ways that portended ambitions extending beyond traditional female roles. They were proud of having coped with long hours and physically demanding tasks, from successfully performing 'men's' jobs, to earning their own paycheque.

The Second World War also brought unprecedented, but also controversial, new roles for Canadian women as part of the military. By mid-1942, some 50,000 in total joined the Canadian Women's Army Corps (CWAC), the Royal Canadian Air Force Women's Division (RCAF(WD)) and the Women's Royal Canadian Naval Service (WRCNS). The federal government assured Canadians that precautions were in place to prevent femininity from being compromised in the rough military world, for example, by providing uniforms designed by fashion experts to flatter the female form. Initially, women who enlisted earned two-thirds the male pay rate and were mostly confined to lower-graded jobs that reflected gender stereotypes. As of March 1945, 62 per cent of CWAC personnel were administrative clerks and 8 per cent were cooks. Yet, to attract more female recruits, in July 1943, women's basic pay was raised to 80 per cent of the male rate and raises for achieving trade qualifications were provided on an equal basis with men.

For many Canadians, returning to peace and normalcy in mid-1945 also meant getting women out of full-time employment and the military. Mothers were made to feel guilty for not spending more time at home and, after nearly six years of war, many single women worried that time was of the essence if they wanted to avoid spinsterhood. Canada's marriage rate rose from 9 per 1,000 in 1945 to 11 per 1,000 the following year, and the fertility rate per 1,000 women from 24 in 1945 to a post-war peak of 29 in 1947, ushering in a period known as the Baby Boom. No protection was

---

[19]Jeffrey Keshen, *Saints, Sinners, and Soldiers: Canada's Second World War* (Vancouver: University of British Columbia Press, 2006), 159.

extended to women as many employers radically restructured the gender composition of their workforce. In Thunder Bay, the Canadian Car and Foundry Company dismissed all but three of the 3,000 women it had hired to produce aircraft. Also, by the end of 1944, plans were well underway to eliminate the CWAC, the RCAF(WD) and the WRCNS, all of which was completed by 1946.

The popular image remains one of a socially conservative post-war Canada. The overwhelming message to women was that they were to devote themselves to marriage and motherhood. Affordability of home ownership in newly opened suburbs made it possible for more women to stay at home and focus on the household and raising children. It took a generation after the end of the Second World War for Canada's female job participation rate to reach its 1944 wartime peak. Employment of single women was still widely perceived as temporary until marriage, with earnings from wives and mothers seen as supplementing the male 'breadwinner'. Women remained trapped in poorly paid job ghettos. In 1951, 96 per cent of stenographers and typists and 89 per cent of sewing-machine operators were women. A man earned more for doing the same job as a woman. At a time when a male sewing-machine operator made $1.20 an hour, a woman doing the same work received 80 cents an hour.

Still, some progress was evident. The National Council of Women of Canada and the Canadian Federation of Business and Professional Women, largely run by well-to-do women, allied with women trade unionists to campaign for equal pay for equal work. On 5 April 1951, the Ontario government passed the Female Employees Fair Remuneration Act. By the end of that decade, eight other provinces had followed suit, as did the federal government in 1956. The legislation had major gaps, however, particularly in specifying what constituted equal work, thus allowing assumptions about greater male strength and competence to nullify equal pay.

The election of Agnes Macphail to the House of Commons in 1921 was undeniably a critically important moment in the path of progress for women's equality in Canada. In making her mark, Macphail spoke out boldly and courageously and had a sizeable impact in a wide swath of areas, many being well outside what were generally regarded as natural areas for women. Nevertheless, throughout her long political career, at both the federal and provincial levels, she almost always remained the lone female voice in the legislature. Not until 1957 did Ellen Fairclough, a Conservative, become the first female federal Cabinet member, and that was, initially, with the inauspicious title of a Minister without Portfolio. As of 2024, men still held 70 per cent of the seats in the Parliament of Canada but in 2015 Canada had its first gender-equal cabinet in the government of Liberal Prime Minister Justin Trudeau.

In many respects, Agnes Macphail's story symbolizes the broad narrative for the role of women in Canadian society. There were certainly many important steps and much evidence of longer-term trends signifying progress. Today, working women, including as chief executive officers (CEOs), are no longer an anomaly. In the 2024 federal Cabinet, just under half of the members were women. Yet, to this day, the gender pay gap, though narrowed significantly over the decades, still sees Canadian women, on average, earning 15 per cent less than men, and for Indigenous women and for women of colour, this gap is significantly larger. If for Agnes Macphail, and for Canada as a whole, it was and continues to be a long, bumpy, uneven and still incomplete road towards equality, Macphail's triumph in the 1921 general election was a breakthrough achievement that has been built upon by numerous others to bring Canadian women rights, opportunities and success increasingly equal to those of Canadian men.

IMAGE 6 'Windsor, Ontario, November 5th – Barricade by Pickets Creates Traffic Jam.' Image courtesy of AACA Library & Research Center, Hershey, Pennsylvania, USA.

6

The Windsor auto strike, 1945: The rise of social citizenship in Canada

Negotiation and compromise, it might be argued, are essential elements in fashioning the Canada that has emerged since 1867. They were necessary to the nation-building project in 1860s and have continued to influence national life since then and there is no greater evidence of that than 10.00 am on 12 September 1945, when 11,000 workers with the United Automobile Workers of Canada (UAW) Local 200 at a Ford plant in Windsor, Ontario, walked off the job. The union wanted all employees at the plant to be union members (a 'closed shop', meaning that union membership was a requirement for employment) with Ford automatically deducting union fees on each pay day and passing them on to the union in the form of dues. Negotiations between Ford and the union had initially stalled even though it had agreed to a similar arrangement with its American workers. The labour dispute lasted ninety-nine days and spawned sympathetic shutdowns at another twenty-five plants as more than 8,000 auto workers from other plants also participated. Workers walked off the job in solidarity with Ford workers. It also brought hundreds of police officers to Windsor to help break the strike but with Canada coming out of a war that was fought for a new and better world after sacrificing so much after 1939, Windsor proved to be a turning point not only in Canadian labour relations but in the relationship between the Canadian state and its citizens. Mr Justice Ivan Rand, who the two sides agreed would mediate the labour dispute, sought to balance the demands of the two parties and found a compromise. Ford would collect union dues from all workers who benefitted from the collective agreement as the union demanded but it would not require all workers to belong to the union. The 'Rand Formula' brought union security to Canada and established the legitimacy of unions in workplaces across the nation.

Campaigning for the coming June 1945 general election just two months before the strike at Ford, Liberal Joseph James Guillaume Paul Martin promised voters in Windsor, Ontario, that the wartime gains made by labour and farmers would remain secure. There would be no post-war retreat, Martin asserted, as had occurred after the Great War. A year and a half earlier, Prime Minister William Lyon Mackenzie King, in his pivotal January 1944 Speech from the Throne, had unveiled plans for what he had called a 'New Social Order'. Martin reminded audiences of the Liberals' popular family allowances (that would be paid out as of July 1945) and other ambitious post-war reforms that promised Canadians that going forward they need not fear a return to the want and misery experienced during the Great Depression in the 1930s and then through six years of total war from 1939 to 1945. Economic and social security had arrived, Martin assured citizens and he easily won re-election. Although exuberant after receiving news of Victory in Europe (V-E) Day, Canadians were very concerned, even apprehensive about what the post-war period would hold for them. In the election just a month later, on 11 June 1945, they gave the Liberals 41 per cent of the popular vote and 125 of 245 seats for a slim majority in the House of Commons, but the Liberals lost 53 seats, including Mackenzie King's in Prince Albert, Saskatchewan. Little did the elected members of Parliament foresee on the morning after all the votes were counted that, three months later, auto workers in Paul Martin's home town would walk off the job at the Ford Motor Company of Canada plant there, nor that the strike would last a full ninety-nine days, ending, at last, just the week before Christmas nor that it would be one of the most important post-war strikes in Canada and forever change labour relations in Canada.

Paul Martin was a member of Parliament since 1935 and a strong supporter of labour. In 1945, he joined Mackenzie King's Cabinet as secretary of state and from 1946 to 1957 served as minister of Health and Welfare. Canada enjoyed relative economic stability and labour peace in the volatile wartime economy, largely because of its programme of wage stabilization, managed after 1941 by the National War Labour Board. While wages were kept in check to manage inflation, workers were not always happy as they sought both higher pay for themselves and greater security for their unions. Most organized labour had agreed not to strike for the duration of the war. Nonetheless, especially towards the end of the conflict, unions became assertive. Strikes, such as those in 1943 involving 13,000 workers at steel mills in Ontario and Nova Scotia, were becoming more common. Workers were demanding higher wages, the right to strike, and acceptance by employers and the government of the principle of fair collective bargaining. Mackenzie King and his government were generally supportive of labour.

In February 1944, with Order-in-Council PC 1003, Ottawa introduced the Wartime Labour Relations Regulations.[1] Unlike the National Labor

---

[1] Library and Archives Canada (LAC), Records of the Privy Council Office RG2, Minutes of War Cabinet Committee (28 July 1941, 7 C vol. 5, Reel c-4654).

Relations Act (also known as the Wagner Act) in the United States, Canada's PC 1003 did not expressly promote the rights of workers, but it did represent a fundamental and positive change in Canadian labour relations policy. PC 1003 compelled employers to recognize and to bargain with duly elected labour representatives and trade unions. Not intended to radically alter the balance of power between labour and management, PC 1003 neither ensured unions won a better agreement nor did it place strong constraints on managerial prerogatives.[2] Canadian workers had made major gains during the war because of labour shortages and the heightened demand for military products; union membership had more than doubled from 358,967 in 1939 to 724,188 in 1944. With the return of peace, things seemed to be changing back. Companies undertook to limit labour's wartime achievements, with attempts to roll back wage gains and curtail other key accomplishments such as union recognition and job security. Labour unrest and militancy became a big worry for King's government.

In 1935 in Detroit, Michigan, the International Union of United Automobile, Aircraft and Agricultural Implement Workers of America (UAW) was formed. By war's end, this was a large and powerful trade union with more than a million members across North America, including in Detroit's border town neighbour Windsor, Ontario, where membership in UAW Local 200 had grown from 9,000 to 51,000. Windsor workers had built thousands of vehicles, including anti-aircraft gun carriers, for the Canadian war effort. With the war winding down, Local 200 at Ford was facing considerable resistance from management and slow progress in its negotiations for a new contract. The union asked for wage and benefit increases, union recognition and the compulsory check-off or the collection of union dues. Ford refused to recognize the union or its demand for a closed shop that would have required all workers to join the union. After more than a year of negotiations, Local 200 had had enough. On 12 September 1945, when the Ford plant whistle sounded the mid-morning break, 10,000 workers walked off the job. They were later joined by members of UAW Local 195 that held bargaining rights for another approximately 12,000 employees at other Windsor-area automotive industries, including Ford's competitor, Chrysler. Local 195 joined the strike illegally and tensions mounted. Later, Windsor police began escorting Ford security guards across the picket lines. In early November, Ontario Provincial Police (OPP) and RCMP constables were moved to the city. Demonstrating their resolve, the workers stole more than a thousand cars and other vehicles from city streets and parked them near the Ford plant, effectively blocking roads and sidewalks around the plant, making it difficult for law enforcement

---

[2] Judy Fudge and Harry Glasbeek, 'The Legacy of PC 1003', *Canadian Labour and Employment Law Journal* 3 (1995): 357–400.

to move against the strikers as had happened in the case of the Winnipeg General Strike, soon after the armistice on 11 November 1918 ended the First World War. With the fear of looming violence in Windsor, Paul Martin personally intervened to get bargaining going again. The UAW and Ford agreed to return to the bargaining table with the help of a federally appointed mediator, who Martin insisted would have 'progressive ideas'.[3] The appointed mediator was Supreme Court of Canada Justice Ivan Rand, who on 29 January 1946 introduced the eponymous Rand Formula as an arbitration decision ending the Ford Strike of 1945. This would prove to be a historic moment in Canada's labour history.

What a difference this moment was for labour from the First World War. In December 1915, the Imperial Munitions Board (IMB), the Canadian branch of the British Ministry of Munitions, was created by the British Cabinet to oversee Canada's production for the war effort. Joseph Wesley Flavelle, president of the massive William Davies meat-packing company, was appointed to run it, and he did so with an iron fist. Under Flavelle's direction, Canada became a significant arms producer and supplier, eventually producing nearly 30 per cent of the ammunition used by Britain. The IMB extended its reach into some 600 factories and managed more than 25,000 workers, quickly evolving into Canada's largest corporate enterprise. By the time the Great War broke out in 1914, it was standard procedure for the federal government to include a fair wage schedule or a fair wage clause in every government contract awarded.[4] This practice started in 1900 on the initiative of Mackenzie King, who that year became the first deputy minister of Labour. Union leaders assumed this practice would also apply to work in producing armaments which they held to be a type of government-financed public work. Flavelle, characterized by some as 'the virtual czar of Canadian industrial mobilization', adamantly rejected a fair-wage clause for munitions workers, although it had been approved by both the British and Canadian cabinets. He claimed he feared that if it were linked with the IMB, it would become a goal in every labour dispute and the additional costs could jeopardize Canada's war production. When workers withdrew their labour, as machinists did in 1916 at the munition plants in Hamilton, Canada's chief censor ordered newspapers not to report on the strike, and manufacturers in Hamilton united to defeat the union. Such obstinance from management only contributed to the rise of labour militancy.[5] Although

---

[3]Greg Donaghy, *Grit: The Life and Politics of Paul Martin Sr* (Vancouver: University of British Columbia Press, 2015), 72; and William Kaplan, *Canadian Maverick: The Life of Ivan C. Rand* (Toronto: University of Toronto Press, 2009), esp. chapter 5.

[4]David J. Bercuson, 'Organized Labour and the Imperial Munitions Board', *Relations Industrielles / Industrial Relations* 28, no. 3 (1973): 602–16, http://www.jstor.org/stable/23070293.

[5]Michael Bliss, 'A Canadian Businessman and War: The Case of Joseph Flavelle', in J. L. Granatstein and R. D. Cuff, eds., *War and Society in North America* (Toronto: Thomas Nelson, 1971), 20, https://www.jstor.org/stable/23070293?seq=1.

illegal, strikes became common, including in April 1918, when in Winnipeg civic employees walked off the job and letter carriers launched a nationwide strike. Especially as the federal government moved to clamp down on labour activism throughout the First World War, labour became radicalized and more militant. Many workers rejected the conservatism of the Trades and Labour Congress of Canada (TLC), established in Ontario in 1883. On 25 September 1918, an Order in Council PC 2381 banned more than a dozen communist and socialist organizations and stipulated that anyone advocating, teaching, advising or defending 'the use of force, violence, or physical injury to person or property in order to accomplish governmental or economic change' could face five years in jail. Such measures were aimed directly at labour.[6]

When peace came that November, workers were left wondering whether the war had really been fought to defend freedom and advance civilization, since conditions weren't better for them. Another factor stoking anger was growing inflation. Between 1916 and 1918, the cost of living rose by 42 per cent. Labour criticized conscription that the Robert Borden government had introduced in 1917, as well as the continuing absence of legislation guaranteeing collective bargaining rights. In July 1918, the federal government had announced a policy giving workers the right to organize, but at the same time it had outlawed strikes and lockouts for the duration of the war. Across the country, union membership more than doubled during the Great War from 143,000 to 249,000 and peaking at 378,000 in 1919 – with more people employed and labour shortages workers had become less fearful of joining a union. Strikes spread across Canada, totalling a record 3.4 million workdays in 1919. The most celebrated of these labour disturbances at the time was the Winnipeg General Strike.

On Thursday, 1 May 1919, Winnipeg metal trade workers went on strike demanding union recognition, something for which they had battled for more than a decade. The next day, seeking better wages, building and construction trade workers joined them. The following Tuesday, both groups appealed to the Winnipeg Trades and Labour Council (WTLC) for support. Influenced by the success the previous year of sympathy strikes to back Winnipeg municipal workers, the WTLC's members endorsed a general strike by an overwhelming margin of 11,000 to 500. The citywide walkout started at 11.00 am on 15 May. Within twenty-four hours, almost 30,000 men and women working in both the public and private sectors had walked off their jobs. Winnipeg ground to a halt. A Central Strike Committee was organized. With responsibilities for directing the strike and making policy decisions, the committee was made up of 290 members, with three members from each of ninety-five unions and five members of the WTLC. The committee

---

[6]Judy Fudge and Eric Tucker, *Labour before the Law: The Regulation of Workers' Collective Action in Canada, 1900–1948* (Toronto: University of Toronto Press, 2001), 100.

published a daily *Strike Bulletin* to keep strikers informed of developments, and it urged strikers to remain off their jobs and peaceful: 'The only thing the workers have to do to win this strike is to do nothing. Just eat, sleep, play, love, laugh, and look at the sun ... Our fight consists of doing no fighting'.[7]

To show solidarity with Winnipeg's workers and to address their own local labour grievances, walkouts occurred in some twenty-five Canadian communities, including Halifax, Montreal, Toronto, Calgary, Edmonton and Vancouver. In face of these walkouts developing across the country, federal authorities and Winnipeg elites had but little sympathy for the strikers and feared the strike could inspire a revolutionary wave. On 16 May, to help maintain basic services and order, Winnipeg's manufacturers, lawyers and bankers formed the Citizens' Committee of One Thousand. Robert Borden's minister of the Interior and acting minister of Justice, Arthur Meighen, cast the strikers as intent on seizing power and establishing a Bolshevist government akin to what had happened in Russia in the October Revolution of 1917. The *Manitoba Free Press* referred to the strikers as 'bohunks', and the *Winnipeg Tribune* told its readers, 'Remember, behind ... this strike is a group of revolutionaries – its most active followers are undesirable aliens'.[8]

On Tuesday, 17 June, the Royal North-West Mounted Police (RNWMP) arrested eight principal strike leaders, including J. S. Woodsworth, one of the editors of the daily *Strike Bulletin*. Also arrested that day were two members of the One Big Union (OBU) that had just been formed by western Canadian labour leaders (not long after that, the OBU weakened considerably, but it hung on and finally merged with the Canadian Labour Congress in 1956). Four days later, on 21 June, a series of events that became known as 'Bloody Saturday' crushed the strikers and set labour back by more than a decade. The day started as a rally by strikers against the resumption of streetcar service. When the crowds failed to disperse as ordered, the mayor read the 'Riot Act', or more precisely, in accordance with section 64 of the Criminal Code of Canada that defines *riot* as 'an unlawful assembly that has begun to disturb the peace tumultuously', section 67 instructs that such a crowd is to be dispersed by the appropriate authorities, for example, by the mayor when he

> receives notice that ... twelve or more persons are unlawfully and riotously assembled ... command silence and thereupon make or cause to be made ... a proclamation in the following words or to the like effect: His Majesty the King charges and commands all persons being assembled immediately to disperse and peaceably to depart to their habitations or to

---

[7] Quoted by Kenneth McNaught, *A Prophet in Politics: A Biography of J.S. Woodsworth* (Toronto: University of Toronto Press, 1959), 121.
[8] Quoted in Gerald Friesen, *The Canadian Prairies: A History* (Toronto: University of Toronto Press, 1984), 360.

their lawful business on the pain of being guilty of an offence for which, on conviction, they may be sentenced to imprisonment for life.[9]

That is what is meant by reading the Riot Act. The Winnipeg crowd did not disperse. Revolvers drawn, Mounties on horseback charged into it, leaving two strikers dead. Fearing another, and deadlier, confrontation, the Central Strike Committee ended the walkout on 26 June. Seven of the eight arrested leaders were convicted of 'seditious conspiracy' and received jail sentences ranging from six months to six years; Woodsworth was not convicted. The government soon added section 41 to the Immigration Act, making the deportation of radicals easier, and section 98 to the Criminal Code of Canada, establishing a maximum penalty of twenty years' imprisonment for anyone who printed, published, wrote, edited, issued or sold 'any book, newspaper, periodical, pamphlet, picture, paper, circular, card, letter, writing, print, publication, or document of any kind in which it is taught, advocated, advised or defended ... that the use of force, violence, terrorism or physical injury be used as a means of accomplishing any governmental, industrial, or economic change'.[10]

For six weeks in 1919, from 15 May to 26 June, thousands of striking workers brought economic activity to a complete standstill in Winnipeg, Canada's third-largest city at that time. The strike ended in arrests, bloodshed and defeat. The Winnipeg General Strike has come to symbolize the futility of unionism as it met determined resistance from both management and the state. Leaders themselves knew not how to deal with the economic challenges going forward. The next two decades were difficult ones for labour. Employers made concerted efforts to roll back wages, bust unions and blacklist union organizers, often with state support. Strike activity plunged from 3.4 million days in 1919 to 800,000 the following year and bottomed out at 152,000 in 1927. Union membership in Canada similarly plummeted from a high 378,000 in 1919 to 240,000 in 1924, and as a sign of the times, Labour Day parades (once a source of great pride for workers and unions) disappeared from numerous communities. As the Great Depression intensified, by 1931, more than half a million Canadians were looking for work. Unemployment in Canada peaked by 1933, at some 30 per cent. More and more people were losing all hope. Richard B. Bennett, prime minister from 1930 to 1935, feared that the deep economic crisis was threatening the stability, and perhaps even the survival, of the capitalist system and of Canada itself. He expressed concern over the country's growing transient, unemployed and often homeless population of mostly young and single men. With few responsibilities and often feeling themselves unwanted and shunned, it was feared they would come under the influence

---

[9] https://laws-lois.justice.gc.ca/eng/acts/C-46/page-7.html?txthl=riot.
[10] *Revised Statutes of Canada*, 10 George V, Chapter 146, 7 July 1919.

of radical agitators. As an effort to keep such men occupied and under control, Bennett established a nationwide system of work camps. Run by the Department of Defence, the men in these camps cleared bush, planted trees, built and repaired roads that went no where, erected public buildings and rebuilt crumbling military facilities in return for room, board, medical care, 20 cents a day for spending money and 1.3 cents a day for cigarettes.[11] The first such camp opened in October 1932, and by 1934 there were nearly sixty, all of them in remote regions of the country. The camps were nominally voluntary, but those who resisted could be arrested for vagrancy.

Coercion was not Bennett's only way to deal with economic chaos. In January 1935, without consulting or warning his caucus, he went over national radio to outline a Canadian version of US President Franklin D. Roosevelt's New Deal. In five thirty-minute broadcasts, Bennett, who boldly declared to listeners that the 'old order is gone', promised a broad range of reforms, including a national minimum wage, unemployment insurance, maximum hours of work, collective bargaining rights for labour, better pensions for the elderly and public health insurance. Perhaps, it was a last-minute ploy to stave off certain defeat in the election that would be coming soon. At any rate, when Parliament resumed on 17 January, and similar ideas were announced in the Throne Speech, Opposition leader Mackenzie King demanded that the government detail its proposed legislative package. The only specifics the Tories offered was an unemployment insurance plan with the federal government providing one-fifth of the funding, and the rest coming from equal contributions by employers and employees into an unemployment insurance fund. On 14 October 1935, Bennett's party was soundly defeated at the polls.

Canadians in greater numbers were concluding that governments had to do better in addressing their needs and the crippling effects of the Depression. Some began turning to those who were advocating for sweeping change. In 1932, about 100 farmers, workers, academics, socialists and labour representatives gathered in Calgary to establish the Co-operative Commonwealth Federation. The CCF's stated aim was to work towards implementing socialism through democratic means, while in the short term pursuing better social welfare programmes. Committed to respecting parliamentary institutions and peaceful change and rejecting overtures from communists to form a common front, the CCF was nevertheless portrayed as a radical organization. In part, this was its own making. In 1933, J. S. Woodsworth became the first president of the CCF, which later joined forces with the Canadian Labour Congress (CLC) to found the New Democratic Party (NDP), with Tommy Douglas as its first leader. J. S. Woodsworth was a former Methodist minister, a leader in the Winnipeg General Strike, and since 1921 MP for Winnipeg North, a largely working-class and immigrant

---

[11] https://www.albertcountymuseum.com/work-camps.

riding. Tommy Douglas, who went on to become the father of Medicare in Canada (see Chapter 8), witnessed the Winnipeg General Strike first-hand as a teenager and considered it a seminal event in his life.

In 1933, the CCF released what famously came to be called the Regina Manifesto. In setting out the party's purpose and platform, this document not only advocated initiatives such as comprehensive crop insurance and a national labour code, but also ended with the declaration that 'no CCF government will rest content until it has eradicated capitalism and put into operation a full program of socialized planning'.[12] In its first general federal election, on 14 October 1935, the CCF attracted 9.3 per cent of the popular vote and took seven of the 245 seats in the House of Commons. The Liberals won 173 seats in that election, campaigning with the memorable catchphrase of 'King or chaos'.

Mackenzie King who was returned as prime minister in 1935 brought a different philosophy and ideology to the office than he had when defeated by Bennett five years earlier. Now, he was publicly championing the dawn of a new era where 'poverty and adversity, want and misery are the enemies which Liberalism will seek to banish from the land'.[13] Of course, neither Mackenzie King and the Liberals nor the Conservatives, Canada's other dominant political party (but down to 39 MPs elected in 1935), were ready to embrace democratic socialism, as advocated in the Regina Manifesto. Both, however, did share some of its aspirations, especially the hope that the state would intervene in the national economy to provide some measure of protection to workers and ensure stability in the nation.[14]

After a long and difficult decade, there were signs of hope for labour when, in 1937, workers in Oshawa went on strike against General Motors. Historian Irving Abella has described that strike as a landmark in Canadian labour history, because it represented the triumph of industrial unionism over conservative craft unions that comprised the Trades and Labour Congress. The 4,000-strong UAW Local 222 won a 44-hour work week and a seniority system. There was no formal recognition by GM of the UAW, an affiliate of the newly created Committee for Industrial Organization (later Congress of Industrial Organization, CIO), which was organizing industrial workers throughout the United States; yet all in all, it was an important step forward for industrial unionism.[15]

---

[12]'*The Regina Manifesto (1933) Co-operative Commonwealth Federation Programme*', Socialist History Project, http://www.socialisthistory.ca/Docs/CCF/ReginaManifesto.htm; and Raymond B. Blake, *From Rights to Needs: A History of Family Allowances in Canada, 1929–92* (Vancouver: University of British Columbia Press, 2009), 33–7.
[13]Canada, House of Commons, *Debates*, 27 January 1939, 389 (William Lyon Mackenzie King); and William L. M. King, *Industry and Humanity: A Study in the Principles Underlying Industrial Reconstruction* [1918] (Toronto: University of Toronto Press, 1973).
[14]Blake, *From Rights to Needs*, 73–4.
[15]Irving Abella, ed., *On Strike: Six Key Labour Struggles in Canada, 1919–1949* (Toronto: Lorimer, 1975), 93–128.

Canada's politicians were coming to believe that if workers and their families were to be expected to share equally in the burdens and obligations of citizenship, then they deserved a better life than had so far been available to them. This realization was not a matter of political elites simply responding to the economic and political mobilization of workers, but an example of positive statism, an acceptance by politicians, elites and the general public that the state had to respond to new dynamisms emerging throughout society. It was also a common objective coming out of the First World War and in political agendas and widespread thinking in Canada and elsewhere since then even if little progress towards those goals had been made. In 1939, in his federal budget, Mackenzie King suggested that the hold of classical economics – with insistence on balanced budgets as Canadian fiscal policy – was loosening, and a new approach to governing and statecraft was necessary. The government considered deficit financing as a way to spur economic growth, an idea promoted by the now-famous British economist, John Maynard Keynes. The outbreak of the Second World War that September accelerated the movement to deficit financing and a more planned economy, even if privately the prime minister worried about new and aggressive public spending.[16] Mackenzie King was aware that a great 'social revolution' was underway, and he knew, too, that he could not ignore it.

In 1943, an Advisory Committee on Reconstruction appointed in 1939 began to prepare for post-war planning by establishing a subcommittee to examine social security. This subcommittee's research director, Leonard Marsh of McGill University, was widely considered a leading expert on social policy, and a British-trained expert on social security. His *Report on Social Security* adopted many of the recommendations of a similar report published by Lord Beveridge in England. Mackenzie King balked at accepting a sweeping range of proposals. He worried about the price tag and a backlash from provincial governments over excessive centralization. His response was to stake out a middle position. In the January 1944 Throne Speech, the Liberals committed to providing family allowances, a payment graduated from $5 to $8 for each child up to the age of sixteen. When passed by Parliament on 1 August, it became Canada's first universal social programme, slated to begin on 1 July 1945 – and the beginning of a new era perhaps best described as the rise of social citizenship. The country already had a system of unemployment insurance, enacted in 1940, and generous programmes for returning veterans.

Social citizenship addresses the central questions of obligation and entitlement in society. The impetus behind social citizenship policies was the recognition that women, men and their families who had endured, especially, the economic dislocation of the 1930s and deprivation in service of the war

---

[16]Doug Owram, *The Government Generation: Canadian Intellectuals and the State, 1900–1945* (Toronto: University of Toronto Press, 1986), 218–20 and 255–60.

effort expected a post-war world where poverty and adversity, want and misery would be eliminated. From then on, essentially, social programmes became an instrument of statecraft for a new Canada.[17] This new Canada was to be accomplished through an interventionist, activist state coming out of the Second World War, and at its centre was the welfare state. Canadians came to expect their national government to intervene in the job market to protect workers and to provide a decent life for families.[18] It could, of course, be said what Mackenzie King was doing was, in part, a response to 'the times', to the growth of democratic socialist ideas in Canada, especially in the emergence of the CCF as well as to new ideas coming from the venerable old Conservative Party, and not only his own Liberals.

Following their drubbing in the March 1940 election and defeat of their leader, Arthur Meighen, to the CCF, in the February 1942 by-election in the supposedly safe riding of York-South, the Conservatives gathered in Port Hope, Ontario, where they endorsed measures like national collective bargaining legislation, low-cost housing and a national public health insurance scheme. At the Party's convention in Winnipeg that December, John Bracken, Manitoba's premier for the previous twenty years, first elected under the Progressive Party banner, was chosen the new leader. As an overture to Bracken and to reflect his original party's embrace of new approaches to social welfare, and to underline their new direction, the Conservatives rebranded themselves the Progressive Conservative Party of Canada. Canada was not alone and in fact followed other nations such as Australia, Great Britain and the United States which were also engaged in similar debates about new social priorities such as family allowances, veterans' benefits, national health programmes, unemployment insurance and enriched pension plans. Indeed, throughout much of the modern world, but especially in the Allied nations that had participated in total war to defeat the Axis powers of Nazi Germany, Italy and Japan, citizens were demanding a new relationship with the state that would eventually usher in a new form of citizenship. By 1945 such changes were well underway in Canada.

Canada's social programmes were redistributive in nature, and they helped foster a new national identity that would strengthen Canadians' attachment to the nation and to each other. As Janine Brodie points out, the federal government had deliberately and strategically offered the promise of a pan-Canadian social citizenship as a remedy for various challenges to the dilemma of managing a diverse nation.[19] Citizens welcomed such

---

[17]LAC, Mackenzie King Papers, MG26 J5, vol. 99, File General Elections, Speeches Outside Parliament, 'Prime Minister King Speaks on Plans for Postwar', 6 June 1945, and the broadcast 'Government Planning for War and Peace', 30 May 1945.

[18]On this point, see Thomas Humphrey Marshall, *Citizenship and Social Class and Other Essays* (Cambridge: Cambridge University Press, 1950). For differing interpretations of emergence of the welfare state, see Blake, *From Rights to Needs*, 1–16.

[19]Janine Brodie, 'Citizenship and Solidarity: Reflections on the Canadian Way', *Citizenship Studies* 6, no. 4 (2002): 377–94.

developments. When combined with the more traditional and long-standing political and constitutional rights, such as the right to vote, these social rights provided for a full and complete integration of the citizen into the wider social and political order. The citizen was no longer seen as simply the abstract voter but, instead, a flesh-and-blood individual with material needs and with the expectation that the state would consider those needs, not only in circumstances of deprivation or disability but in the normal course of life. Many of Canada's political and economic leaders came to believe that the enactment of social rights was necessary to enable individuals to actually enjoy civic and political rights.

This was the new environment in which workers at the Ford Motor Company in Windsor dropped their tools and walked off the job just days after US General Douglas MacArthur accepted Japan's formal surrender to the Allies on 2 September 1945 aboard the US battleship *Missouri*, anchored in Tokyo Bay. The Second World War, just like the First, witnessed a rapid expansion in union organization. Unlike the period that followed 1918, which was an unmitigated disaster for labour, the years that followed 1945 would be a complete reversal for union and the labour movement. Employers, the state and workers all realized there could be no return to an earlier period. The most significant gains for labour occurred right after the Second World War, as a result of the lengthy Ford strike in Windsor, Ontario. After nearly a hundred days of work stoppage, Ford and its workers agreed to end the dispute on 20 December 1945, when Supreme Court Justice Ivan Rand took up his post as arbitrator. He issued a ruling binding on both the union and the company. It is significant that Paul Martin explicitly recalls that Rand 'was a man who knew the evolution that was taking place in social thinking' in Canada at the time.[20]

After a week of hearings, at the end of January 1946, Rand issued his report and with it changed forever the labour movement in Canada. If Rand did not give the union everything it wished for, one of his recommendations was a major victory for unions that had long fought for recognition and security, and it soon became a defining feature in Canadian labour law along with the wartime gains in PC 1003. The 'Rand Formula', as it became known, meant that all workers within a bargaining unit – whether they were actual union members or not – had to pay union dues that would cover the union's costs of negotiating and administering a labour contract. Prior to Rand's ruling, union officials had to themselves collect dues from its members, and many workers simply did not pay. Rand did not compel workers to join a union; he did, however, insist that if they benefitted from collective bargaining led by the union and other campaigns at the workplace that advanced the interests of their members, and they enjoyed higher wages and improved benefits as a result, then they should share in the cost of the

---

[20]Paul Martin, *A Very Public Life*, vol. 1 (Ottawa: Deneau, 1983), 395.

union's bargaining efforts and companies would be compelled to collect union fees from its workers on behalf of their union.

The Rand Formula was subsequently adopted by other unions and employers and when PC 1003 was later codified in the federal government's revised Industrial Relations and Disputes Investigation Act in 1948, it represented historical accomplishments for labour. Several provinces also gave the Rand Formula legal force in their provincial labour legislation, a development that the Supreme Court of Canada upheld when it ruled more than four decades later that the Rand Formula did not undermine the right of Canadians to freedom of association. It remains in place today.[21]

Justice Ivan Rand was committed to judicial activism in pursuit of social justice, an ideal promoted by US Supreme Court Justice Louis D. Brandeis. For Rand, like for Brandeis, who was also his inspiration, the law was an instrument of social change. Rand was committed to the liberal democratic tradition and 'his fundamental intellectual and working premise placed him in harmonious relations with those strains in Canada society'.[22] His judicial decisions but especially his arbitration report for the Windsor strike captured the *zeitgeist* of the post-war period, bringing the general intellectual, moral and cultural climate of the era to the Ford labour dispute. Like others of the period, Rand had no doubt that labour leaders wished to obtain for workers and their families a secure and self-respecting living which was the objective of all working Canadians – a point that Mackenzie King and other political leaders as well as bureaucrats and others, even business leaders – realized coming out of the Second World War. Justice Rand would certainly have been aware, too, that Canadians from all walks of life wanted to see major change in much of Canada, even in how the nation saw industrial relations and compulsory collective bargaining. Scarred by the Great Depression and turned upside down by the Second World War, the general public had become increasingly sympathetic to the collective action of workers and their unions. Canadians found it hard to accept that their soldiers were fighting for democracy and a better life for people all around the world and yet too many found it difficult to eke out a decent living at home. In early 1943, a Gallup poll revealed that 53 per cent of respondents supported 'compulsory recognition', for labour unions and believed that unions were a legitimate force in society that deserved some legislative protection.[23] In this new era, there would be accommodations with organized labour that included institutionalized collective bargaining, statutory recognition and financial security for labour unions. In exchange, organized labour jettisoned much of

---

[21]E. Marshall Pollack, 'Mr Justice Rand: A Triumph of Principle', *Canadian Bar Review* 53, no. 3 (1975): 519–43.
[22]Ibid., 527.
[23]Taylor Hollander, 'Making Reform Happen: The Passage of Canada's Collective-Bargaining Policy, 1943–1944', *Journal of Policy History* 13, no. 3 (2001): 302–4.

its support for communist-led unionism and committed to the continuation of the free enterprise system and a modified social order. This re-shaping of Canada was an ambitious period of social reconstruction that altered not only the role of the state, but also Canadians' notion of what matters in their own nation. Canada's industrial relations system has remained remarkably consistent since the 1940s, steadfastly centred around the premise of industrial peace. Governments, starting with Mackenzie King's wartime administration, have sought to build labour laws and collective bargaining around what is commonly called a 'peace model' of workplace relations that promotes compulsory collective bargaining if a majority of workers within a workplace have demonstrated majority support for a union. Unions, in return, agree to be responsible economic actors by not spontaneously and hazardously withdrawing their labour to solve common workplace disputes. While there have been refinements and amendments to collective bargaining legislation across Canada since PC 1003 and the Rand Formula that ended the 1945 Ford strike at Windsor, both are essential to the bargaining process as they have provided the basic statutory framework for labour relations in Canada for the past almost eighty years.

IMAGE 7 Lester Pearson, 14th Prime Minister of Canada. https://lop.parl.ca/sites/ParlInfo/default/en_CA/People/Profile?personId=531. Public Domain.

7

Lester Pearson and Suez, 1956: Decolonization and the British world

Canada's Lester B. Pearson was bestowed the 1957 Nobel Peace Prize for his leadership the previous year in bringing the Suez Crisis to a peaceful end. As was customary, the ceremony for this award was held in the Great Hall of the University of Oslo on 10 December. Addressing an audience of more than 700 people, the chairman of the Nobel Committee, Dr Gunnar Jahn, spoke for some time lauding Pearson's extensive career as a diplomat, but especially the work that earned him the prestigious prize he was about to receive:

> Never, since the end of the last war, has the world situation been darker than during the Suez Crisis, and never has the United Nations had a more difficult case to deal with. However, what actually happened has shown that moral force can be a bulwark against aggression and that it is possible to make aggressive forces yield without resorting to power. Therefore, it may well be said that the Suez Crisis was a victory for the United Nations and for the man who contributed more than anyone else to save the world at that time. That man was Lester Pearson.[1]

Canadians expressed great pride in the international recognition showered on Pearson and on their country that December. Yet, just six months earlier, after twenty-two years in power, the Liberal government – in which Pearson had long served as minister of state for External Affairs – had suffered a surprising defeat. Canada's role in the Suez Crisis had, in fact,

---

[1] Gunnar Jahn, speech delivered in Oslo on 10 December 1957, https://www.nobelprize.org/prizes/peace/1957/ceremony-speech/.

generated considerable controversy outside of Quebec, because it turned Canada away from Great Britain in its fight against Egypt to retain control over the canal that Egypt had nationalized. Although Canada had long sought greater independence and recognition for itself, outwardly at least its governments had always expressed strong, loyal connections to what Anglo-Canadians overwhelmingly used to refer to as the Mother Country.

Over the years, however, there had been various instances when Ottawa had not been in full alignment with London. At the turn of the twentieth century, Canada had sent but a modest contingent of troops to side with Britain in its battle against South Africa's Boers and during his years as prime minister, John A. Macdonald made it clear to the British that Canada would not participate in any general system of imperial defence and there would be no automatic Canadian participation in minor imperial conflicts. During the First World War, Ottawa had insisted on greater Canadian control over Canadian military forces and, after that war, demanded for Canada a separate signature on the Treaty of Versailles as well as its own representation at the League of Nations. In 1922, Ottawa had turned down calls from London for assistance against Turkish nationalists at Chanak. Four years later, at the 1926 conference of Great Britain and the Dominions, Canada had pushed for transforming the British Empire into a far less subservient Commonwealth of Nations, in which all were to be equal members. Finally, in 1931, with the Statute of Westminster, Canada at last gained unquestioned political and legal control over its own foreign relations.[2] As just outlined, this realignment was decades in the making, and it would continue to evolve after the Suez Crisis, as Canada's population became ever more diverse, as Quebec nationalism became more pronounced, and as Britain itself, once overseer of the greatest empire ever known, faded in both power and prestige. Canada's major role in the Suez Crisis through Pearson's leadership in creating the United Nations Emergency Force (UNEF), a peacekeeping force that became an important instrument in resolving or at least mitigating conflicts, was a significant inflection point in the story of this relationship. Negotiating the creation of the UNEF brought Canada into the spotlight and on the global stage as an independent actor of consequence.

Lester Bowles Pearson was born not far from Toronto in 1897. In many ways, his life and career reflected as well as shaped Canada's foreign policy. He grew up in a time when the British Empire stretched around the globe, when English-speaking Canadians broadly held that Anglo-Saxon culture was superior and that only through the Empire could Canada attain some measure of international respect and contribute to the advancement of civilization. Pearson's loyalty to England and his strong sense of service led him to volunteer in the Great War. He served with the Medical Corps and then the Royal Flying Corps. While he was overseas, Pearson expressed his

---

[2] Asa McKercher, *Canada and the World since 1867* (London: Bloomsbury Academic, 2019).

deep admiration for British traditions and culture. He expressed distaste, however, for the rigidity and apparent unfairness of the British class system and what he considered to be undeserved British arrogance and haughtiness that extended to include Canadians who, he felt, the British considered to be less refined, less urbane and less intelligent than themselves. Pearson remained an anglophile and an admirer of Britain, but he was not a supplicant.[3]

On leave in London, he was hit by a bus, and the injuries sustained in that accident ended his military service. During a long convalescence, Pearson thought deeply about what he saw as the wastefulness and cruelty of the war, and through that process became more of a conciliator and more of a Canadian nationalist. He felt acutely the immense and unnecessary loss of life which, he came to believe, reasoned diplomacy could have prevented. Following the war, Pearson returned to his studies, taking up a Rhodes Scholarship to attend Oxford University, where in 1923 he was awarded a master's degree. With his easygoing manner, evident charm and superior athletic prowess, he became a leader on campus, where among his many friends were members of the British elite, several of whom went on to political prominence and remained important contacts.

Returning to Canada, Pearson taught for some time, becoming an assistant professor of modern history at the University of Toronto. Before long, his desire to contribute more widely, even internationally, attracted him to the new national foreign service that Prime Minister William Lyon Mackenzie King had assigned Oscar Douglas Skelton to create. Dean of Arts and distinguished professor of political science and economics at Queen's University in Kingston, Ontario, Skelton became undersecretary of state for External Affairs in 1925 and held that position until his death in 1941. He completely transformed the Department of External Affairs (DEA), first established in 1909, from what had been essentially little more than an archive and post office. Skelton was convinced that for Canada to be regarded as an autonomous nation, it required a strong, professional foreign service. He scoured universities for excellent recruits and personally graded aptitude and knowledge-based exams.

In 1928, when he was thirty-one years old, Lester Pearson joined the Department of External Affairs, finishing at the top among those who that year had put their names forward. This step marked the end of his academic career and the beginning of his life as a civil servant. He served as the DEA's first secretary in Ottawa until 1935. At the League of Nations, Pearson, who shone in diplomatic circles, brought a growing respect and presence for Canada internationally. From 1935 to 1941, he was stationed at Canada House in London having been appointed counsellor at the Office of the High Commissioner for Canada. While outwardly offering positive portrayals

---

[3]Lester B. Pearson and Rt. Hon. Jean Chretien, *Mike: The Memoirs of the Rt. Hon. Lester B. Pearson, Volume One: 1897-1948* (Toronto: University of Toronto Press, 2018).

of British policy, he also considered issues through a wider international lens. Canada's tremendous contribution to the Second World War – which included more than a million men in uniform, the Allies' third-largest navy and fourth-largest air force – reinforced both his, and Canada's sense of nationalism, its increasing stature and the conviction that international stability and lasting peace would come through collaboration and not confrontation. He returned to Canada as assistant undersecretary of state at the DEA and in 1942 was appointed Canadian minister in Washington, DC, where he stayed until 1946, for the last two years as ambassador. Then followed two years as undersecretary of state at home until, at the age of fifty-one, in 1948 he left the civil service for partisan politics and was made Canada's secretary of state for External Affairs.

Pearson's Washington posting put him at the diplomatic centre of what was clearly becoming Canada's most important external relationship. One of his principal challenges was to raise awareness of his country, for though geographically connected, there was, in American political circles, little knowledge of and, therefore, little regard for Canadian issues or concerns. Fortunately, this applied less to US President Franklin Delano Roosevelt, who, in earlier days, had visited Canada many times. The FDR administration entered into the Ogdensburg Agreement in 1940, which provided for the collective defence of North America, and the next year the Hyde Park Agreement which bailed out Canada economically now that Britain had become unable to pay for materiel it had ordered from Canada. During the Second World War, Pearson championed Canadian efforts to obtain direct representation on several Allied joint planning boards. In advancing Canada's case, which resulted in several successes, Pearson applied what came to be called the 'functional principal'. Developed by Hume Wrong, Pearson's foreign service colleague, the functional principal made the point that, in certain areas, Canada was a major player and thus warranted commensurate representation.[4]

Pearson was an early champion of the United Nations Organization, formed in 1945, especially for its strong commitment to the principle of collective security. He was Canada's representative on the UN's Relief and Rehabilitation Administration (UNRRA) that focused on humanitarian and refugee assistance and on its Food and Agricultural Organization (FAO). Reflecting his growing stature in diplomatic circles, strong support for the UN and Canada's growing reputation internationally, several high-ranking UN officials advanced Pearson's name to serve as the organization's director-general, a position he said he did not wish to pursue.[5]

---

[4]Adam Chapnick, *The Middle Power Project: Canada and the Founding of the United Nations* (Vancouver: University of British Columbia Press, 2006).
[5]Adam Chapnick, 'Pearson and the United Nations: Tracking the Stoicism of a Frustrated Idealist', in Galen R. Perras and Asa McKercher, eds., *Mike's World: Lester Pearson and Canadian External Affairs* (Vancouver: University of British Columbia Press, 2016), 70–87.

Indeed, historians have described the quarter century or so after the Second World War as a Golden Age for Canadian foreign policy, a period during which Canada came to see and present itself as an independent 'middle power'. As Canada's best-known and experienced diplomat, Lester Pearson was very much in the thick of things, often playing a key role, including in trying to manage the tensions that came with the Cold War that set in between the post-war superpowers, the United States and its Communist wartime ally, the Union of Soviet Socialist Republics (USSR). Mackenzie King retired as prime minister in 1948 and was replaced by Louis St Laurent. In the general election that June, Pearson won a seat in the House of Commons, and immediately was made minister of External Affairs, happy to be reporting to St Laurent. In contrast to Mackenzie King, Pearson found St Laurent less cautious and more visionary in getting Canada engaged internationally.[6]

At the United Nations, Pearson and his foreign service colleagues sought to encourage dialogue between real and potential belligerents. The stark differences between UN member states made common approaches unlikely – especially with the rival superpowers, as permanent members on the UN Security Council, each having a veto over any UN initiative. Canada sought to cultivate other collaborative alliances among states ideologically aligned. Such was the impetus for the North Atlantic Treaty Organization (NATO), founded in April 1949, that joined North American and most non-socialist European countries into a military alliance. Pearson stressed that an advantage of this multilateral structure was that it mitigated more direct control coming from the United States or Great Britain, which were also permanent members of the UN Security Council. Pearson worked hard at establishing compromise language to build support for the creation of NATO, including from his own government. He did this by balancing mutual obligations among member states with respect for their national sovereignty and by encouraging economic cooperation. As Canada's foreign minister, Pearson was a key player in the drafting of Article 2 of the North Atlantic Treaty, known as 'the Canadian clause', which states:

> The Parties will contribute toward the further development of peaceful and friendly international relations by strengthening their free institutions, by bringing about a better understanding of the principles upon which these institutions are founded, and by promoting conditions of stability and well-being. They will seek to eliminate conflict in their international economic policies and will encourage economic collaboration between any or all of them.[7]

---

[6]Galen R. Perras and Asa McKercher, eds., *Mike's World: Lester Pearson and Canadian External Affairs* (Vancouver: University of British Columbia Press, 2016).
[7]https://www.nato.int/cps/en/natohq/official_texts_17120.htm#:~:text=Article%202,of%20stability%20and%20well%2Dbeing.

It cannot be said that Canada determined the outcome of the NATO agreement as, for instance, Article 2 turned out to be largely toothless. But in the negotiations that led to the establishment of the NATO alliance, Pearson enjoyed influence based on his proven skills and experience as a diplomat, and because he knew well (in several cases going back to his days at Oxford) a number of the key players involved.

Canada's presence abroad continued to grow, and by 1948, it had official representation in twenty-nine countries. Canada was involved in the UN negotiations that led to the partition of Palestine and the creation of Israel. Pearson, as foreign minister, played a role in the United Nations establishing in 1949 observers, including for four Canadians, to monitor the new border resulting from the partition of India and Pakistan. Canada participated in developing the Colombo Plan, an intergovernmental organization established to facilitate self-help and mutual assistance in the countries where recent partitions had left political and economic turmoil and that, many feared, made them susceptible to Communist takeover; it began operations in July 1951, and today the Plan's twenty-eight member countries continue to work together in supporting economic and social development in the Asia and Pacific region.[8]

In June 1950, war broke out between the recently divided Communist North Korea and pro-Western South Korea and their allies. This intensified prevailing fears of the 'domino effect', meaning that Communism would spread through one country after another, in this case, throughout Asia. Communists were seen to be gaining power in many places at this time. By 1949, the Soviet Union had acquired the atomic bomb, and the United States was no longer the only country with nuclear capabilities. Also in 1949, the Communist People's Republic of China (PRC) was established, the culmination of the Chinese Revolution of 1911; this led the United States to suspend diplomatic ties with the PRC, for decades. Under the leadership of Chairman Mao Zedong, the PRC supported North Korea, including militarily, when in backing South Korea, US forces approached the Yalu River that separated Korea and China. If South Korea fell to the Communists, many feared that nearby countries, including Japan, might follow. The United States led the charge for military intervention. Canada initially offered a modest pledge of $25 million in military support. Pearson, however, backed a bolder response, convinced that lethargy – or appeasement – risked losing South Korea, and as happened with the Nazis during the 1930s, Communist forces would become more emboldened in their aggression. Pearson wanted a multilateral intervention, to be championed by the United Nations, and for the UN in that way to demonstrate its dedication to applying 'collective security' against aggressors. Maintaining international peace and security was, after all, avowedly the Security Council's primary responsibility. The

---

[8]Ryan Touhey, 'Commonwealth Conundrums: Canada and South Asia during the Pearson Era', in Galen R. Perras and Asa McKercher, eds., *Mike's World: Lester Pearson and Canadian External Affairs* (Vancouver: University of British Columbia Press, 2016), 251–74.

opportunity to do this was, indeed, a viable one because the Soviet Union squandered its veto power in the Security Council. It was boycotting the United Nations because the PRC government was not being officially recognized – rather, and for some decades to come, the UN persisted in according membership status representing all of China to the nationalist forces that the Chinese Communists had defeated and that had retreated to the island of Formosa, renamed Taiwan.

The UN sanctioned a multilateral policing action to contain North Korean forces to the 38th parallel, established after the Second World War as the line dividing Korea into North and South. Following Great Britain, Australia and New Zealand, Canada authorized the despatch of troops. The United States commanded the military operations and provided some 90 per cent of the participating personnel. Nevertheless, that intervention occurred under the auspices of the United Nations – something Lester Pearson led in urging – demonstrated Canada's commitment, as a globally engaged middle power, to establish a more stable international order, in this case, by seeking to apply collective security. Canada put a brigade in the field. By the time the Korean War ended with a ceasefire in 1953, Canada had suffered just over 500 dead and some 1,200 wounded, its greatest military cost outside of the world wars.

Throughout the conflict, behind the scenes Pearson pursued a negotiated settlement. With the PRC's direct involvement, and the Soviets sending military assistance to North Korea, there was grave concern that things could spin out of control by openly and directly pitting the nuclear superpowers against each other. Although not driving the talks, Canada remained a voice at the table and may indeed have tempered more extreme positions. Pearson dealt directly with the PRC government's representatives and assisted in reaching an agreement to end the fighting. Personally, Pearson favoured officially recognizing the PRC and approved of ongoing dialogue with it. The Canadian government, in standing with the United States, its key ally by now, and in light of strong domestic anti-Communist public opinion, chose – unlike Great Britain, Denmark, the Netherlands and Norway – to close its diplomatic offices in Nanjing in 1951, and did not establish official ties with the mainland Chinese government until 1970.[9]

Not but a year after a ceasefire was obtained in Korea, Canada became very much involved in trying to reach accords to end fighting in Indochina between Communist rebels and French colonial forces. A guerrilla war – encompassing present-day Laos, Cambodia and Vietnam – started in 1946 with the Communist Vietminh uprising led by Ho Chi Minh. The United States had been assisting France, especially as its occupational forces faltered. Lester Pearson spoke of the uprising as grounded more in anti-colonialism than in communism. In 1954, there were 140,000 French troops

---

[9] John English, *The Worldly Years: The Life of Lester B. Pearson, 1949-1972* (Toronto: Lester & Orpen Dennys, 1989).

in the area, many of them in desperate straits, surrounded at Dien Bien Phu in Vietnam's north. Pearson recommended a ceasefire, balanced with halting the spread of Communist insurgents. Canada refrained from direct military involvement but did contribute to the 1954 Geneva Accords, a settlement that temporarily divided Indochina along the 17th parallel and included the promise of a future election with the winner to govern a united country, a contest Ho Chi Minh was confident of winning.

Canada, along with India and Poland, became part of the International Control Commission (ICC) to monitor the Geneva settlement that divided Vietnam into North and South, provided for French withdrawal, and would have instituted elections for reunification by 1956. It soon became clear that US troops were not going to withdraw, and that the election would not take place, as worry grew that the Communists would prevail. Although from some quarters frustration was expressed with the Americans, Pearson would not openly criticize the US government, as he was sure that would hobble Canada's influence and its quiet diplomatic effect, thereby serving Communist interests. Canada maintained its involvement on the ICC for nearly two decades, seeking to make the United Nations work, and to counterbalance Poland's presence on the Commission – given overt Soviet control of Poland, and Poland's unrelenting criticism of the United States while ignoring any Vietminh violation of the peace terms.

Leveraging its close ties to Washington, Ottawa sought to mitigate the global threat posed by nuclear weapons. Pearson expressed concern over Canadian facilities, for example, at Goose Bay, in Labrador, being used to house US aircraft and most components of atomic bombs. While neither Canada nor any other country could control US management of nuclear weapons, Ottawa did obtain a commitment to be informed and consulted with respect to 'storage, overflight and strikes'[10] if involving Canadian territory. Pearson also led negotiations with the Americans to establish radar stations in Canada's north to monitor against a potential Soviet aerial attack. Ottawa worked to keep NATO strong, including by improving means of consultation between member states, and helped set the terms under which, in 1954, the Federal Republic of Germany (West Germany) became part of the alliance.

Canada made its most significant mark in demonstrating its independence as a country and its international importance as a middle power in the Middle East, particularly with Lester Pearson's leadership in defusing the Suez Crisis in 1956. The 193-kilometre Suez Canal was completed in 1869, connecting the Mediterranean and the Red seas and making that the most direct shipping route between Europe and Asia. Owned and managed by the Franco-British Suez Canal Company, with French and British shareholders, the Suez Canal was, in fact, on Egyptian property. With the rise of anti-colonial Arab

---

[10]Geoffrey A. H. Pearson, *Seize the Day: Lester B. Pearson and Crisis Diplomacy* (Ottawa: Carleton University Press, 1993), 111.

nationalism and with the European powers profoundly weakened by the Second World War, it became far more challenging for the Europeans to retain control over the canal. Canada, among others, had seen the writing on the wall. In 1951, Pearson had offered Britain only moral support as Iran reclaimed its oil fields from the Anglo-Iranian Oil Company and expelled 4,500 foreign workers from its lands.

Initial uprisings by Egyptians to take over the Suez Canal meant that, by 1952, there were 80,000 British troops safeguarding it, at times faced by gunfire. Prime Minister Winston Churchill, well-known champion of the then-disintegrating British Empire, refused to negotiate with the Egyptians. Things grew increasingly tense with Gamal Nasser, riding a wave of Arab nationalism and anti-colonialism, coming to lead Egypt in 1952, initially through a military coup and then making himself prime minister two years later. Britain's Foreign Secretary, Anthony Eden, was willing to negotiate, but Churchill maintained this was tantamount to a shameful withdrawal and humiliation for Britain. By1954, however, Churchill, then approaching eighty years of age, was in declining health and influence. Britain concluded it could not afford to indefinitely keep its current military commitment in the area and commenced talks. Nasser signed a treaty with the British that would see the troops withdrawn but left open for negotiation the matter of canal ownership. In Egypt, this 1954 compromise sowed discord, especially from the more radical Muslim Brotherhood, which then tried to assassinate Nasser who, in turn, launched a brutal reprisal.

Intensifying worry among Western governments was Nasser's decision to strike a stance of neutrality in the Cold War and his leadership in what became the Non-Aligned Movement, formerly established in 1961 and now comprising 120 member countries. Concerning, too, was the growing tension between Egypt and Israel, involving raids along their common border that worsened over the course of 1955 with Egypt deploying Russian-supplied weapons. Nasser fumed about the West arming Israel, while Egypt was criticized for doing the same with Palestinian insurgents. Pearson met with Egyptian officials, including in Cairo, to encourage moderation. He then met with Eden who, in 1955, replaced Churchill as Britain's prime minister. Pearson suggested a UN force (replacing a small number of observers) to keep the peace along the border; the British rejected this suggestion, claiming that it would further escalate tensions by bringing in a larger military presence.

Egypt, at this time, was also pursuing construction of the Aswan High Dam, a massive engineering project that would expand irrigated land and offer better protection from floods. This undertaking generated concern in the West, especially in the United States: the apparently forthcoming Soviet assistance for the dam's construction was being assessed as a way for the Communists to increase their influence in this critically important region.

British leaders portrayed Nasser as a megalomaniac and dictator who, as recent history with the Nazis had shown, should not be appeased. Canada's Foreign Minister Lester Pearson put forward a different, more nuanced view.

He submitted that anti-colonial struggles, such as he judged to be unfolding in Egypt, were not the same as a brutal grab for power. He refrained from open condemnation of the Egyptian leader, seeking to keep open the paths for negotiation.[11]

Things, however, worsened. On 26 July 1956, Nasser unilaterally declared Egypt's nationalization of the Suez Canal and at the same time offered financial compensation at fair market price to shareholders and promises of reasonable charges for shipping through the waterway. Those working at the canal were informed that they now answered to the Egyptian government. Revenue that came from the canal, Nasser announced, would be used to fund construction of the Aswan Dam. Nasser's plan was premised on a smooth transition, one that would ostensibly protect existing financial interests. But his announcement became a lightning rod – a rallying cry for Arab nationalists – while in Britain and France it was portrayed as a brazen, illegal attack on what they deemed to be their lawful assets. There was also grave concern that if Nasser moved to shut down the Suez Canal to achieve his goals, Britain's economy, and indeed, much of Europe's, would be devastated.[12]

Canada encouraged dialogue and did not automatically back Great Britain. This was Pearson's aim, both at the United Nations and in the 'shuttle diplomacy' that brought him into direct contact with the major stakeholders. Canada sought recognition as a trusted 'honest' broker that, despite its long-standing and loyal connections to England, close ties to the United States and membership in NATO, was to be seen as a fair and reliable participant on the international stage. Indeed, as the crisis played out, Prime Minister St Laurent infuriated many Canadian anglophiles by declaring that England, as well as France, had to stop behaving as if they were supermen.[13]

Within forty-eight hours of the canal being nationalized, Britain and France froze Egyptian assets. Both nations expressed frustration with Washington as the United States offered only tepid criticisms of Egypt. Britain began mobilizing for an attack on the canal area, planned for mid-September. Pearson pushed for immediate UN control of the canal, a position that Canada's new federal Conservative leader, John Diefenbaker, condemned on the ground that this would be abandoning Britain and rewarding aggression. Pearson fretted not only over potential British military action, and the pressures it might produce in Canada to back England, including, perhaps, militarily. He was concerned that conflict in the region might draw in the Israelis to settle tensions with Egypt, tensions that dated back to the Arab-Israeli War of 1948. He also worried about a split between Washington and London. Although the United States denounced Nasser's actions, it wanted things settled through diplomacy, and not with a conflict

---

[11]Greg Donaghy, 'The Politics of Accommodation: Canada, the Middle East, and the Suez Crisis, 1950–1956', *International Journal* 71, no. 2 (2016): 313–27.
[12]John Melady, *Pearson's Prize* (Toronto: Dundurn Press, 2006).
[13]Raymond B. Blake, *Canada's Prime Ministers and the Shaping of a National Identity* (Vancouver: University of British Columbia Press, 2004), 68–71.

that could get out of control, potentially pitting the United States against a USSR allied with Egypt.

In October, world peace seemed about to unravel. On Tuesday, the 23rd, a countrywide uprising broke out in Hungary against Soviet control of that country. The major Western powers were completely focused on the Suez situation, enabling Soviet forces to quickly and brutally put down the Hungarian Revolt by 11 November; thousands were killed and wounded and nearly a quarter of a million Hungarians fled their country, many to Canada. On the 29th of October, Israeli forces, as prearranged with Britain and France, crossed into the Sinai Peninsula. Their stated purpose was to neutralize Palestinian guerrilla fighters that Nasser was accused of supporting. Quickly the Israelis defeated the inferior Egyptian military and then moved towards the Suez Canal. In response, the following day, the British and French governments, utilizing a UN resolution calling for an immediate ceasefire, announced that they would occupy a zone around the canal and establish a 15-kilometre buffer between the Israelis and Egyptians. As expected, Nasser rejected this. On Wednesday, the 31st, the British and French units responded by attacking Egyptian forces by air. The Soviet Union, upping the ante, threatened to intervene to protect Egypt. Meanwhile, American President Dwight D. Eisenhower was incensed that the Europeans had planned their intervention in secret without his knowledge. The US presidential election was on Tuesday, 6 November, not even a week away. Eisenhower, in making a re-election bid against Democrat Adlai Stevenson, would have preferred to have attention focused on the Soviet intervention in Hungary and not on any divisions among the Western allies.[14]

Australia and New Zealand supported Great Britain. This put pressure from some in Canada to follow suit. Pearson, however, remained focused on building support for a UN peacekeeping force. In early November, the Suez debate moved to the UN General Assembly. There, diplomats from many countries turned to Canada's well-known, experienced and highly respected Lester Pearson to establish a breakthrough. Pearson worked with the US delegates to get them to back the idea of a UN peacekeeping force and indicated that Canada would contribute military personnel to ensure its viability and success. Although gaining traction, including in Washington, London and Paris resisted the proposal. As the UN session continued, a British armada moved closer to Egypt. Tensions were peaking. Pearson continued to work tirelessly to obtain support for the multilateral UN-comprised and -commanded force, to be named the United Nations Emergency Force (UNEF), in which no national flags were to be flown, and which would answer to the UN Security Council – unlike the UN police action in Korea that was essentially US-commanded. When at last, on 4 November, a Canadian-led resolution was brought before the UN General

---

[14]Geoffrey Arthur Holland Pearson, *Seize the Day: Lester B. Person and Crisis Diplomacy* (Montreal and Kingston: McGill-Queen's University Press, 1993), 156–76.

Assembly to establish the UNEF, fifty-seven member states agreed, well surpassing the required two-thirds support. Indeed, no country recorded opposition, although nineteen abstained, including Egypt, Israel, Great Britain and France. This was an incredible accomplishment that averted what could have been a catastrophic conflict bringing the two nuclear superpowers into direct armed conflict against one another.[15]

The precise composition of the peacekeeping force had yet to be set. Here, too, Pearson played an important role, successfully proposing Canada's General E. L. M. Burns to assume its command, as he had effectively led Canadian troops in Europe in the Second World War and had headed up the small UN observer force between Israel and Egypt. Pearson also worked to have British and French military personnel included in the UNEF. Initially, however, Canada was embarrassed when Egypt rejected its participation because those who were initially selected for it came from the Queen's Own Rifles, whose name, traditions and dress were decidedly British. Ultimately, a face-saving compromise was reached whereby Canada's contribution of 1,000 soldiers, which made up one-sixth of the UNEF, were assigned to background roles in communications and logistics.

Many Anglo-Canadians accused Pearson of deserting the Mother Country to do Washington's bidding by helping to push Britain out of Egypt. One poll showed that 43 per cent of Canadians supported Britain's actions in Suez compared with 40 per cent who were opposed. In the House of Commons, Opposition leader Diefenbaker unsuccessfully tried to move a motion regretting that the government had followed 'a course of gratuitous condemnation of the action of the UK and France' and 'encouraged a truculent and defiant attitude on the part of the Egyptian dictator'.[16] Quebec generally supported the government. In English-speaking Canada, Conservative-minded newspapers such as the *Globe and Mail* and the *Calgary Herald* said Canada had acted 'shamefully',[17] but the *Toronto Star*, known as supporting the Liberals, declared Canada's leading role in resolving the Suez Crisis to be a proud moment for the country. Many saw it as emblematic of Canada coming into its own as a truly independent middle power with an internationalist outlook grounded in the pursuit of peace and global stability.

Canada's part in the Suez Crisis symbolized a larger transition that had been developing for some time. Its actions in defusing the crisis allowed Canada to be seen definitively and very publicly as separate from Great Britain. Canada presented itself as a middle power, certainly aligned with the West, but also pursuing a global agenda to safeguard world peace, which included preventing a split in the North Atlantic alliance that it had done much to help establish.

---

[15] Michael K. Carroll, *Pearson's Peacekeepers: Canada and the United Nations Emergency Force, 1956–67* (Vancouver: University of British Columbia Press, 2009).

[16] Andrew Cohen, *Lester B. Pearson* (Toronto: Penguin, 2008), 154.

[17] Antony Anderson, *The Diplomat: Lester Pearson and the Suez Crisis* (Fredericton: Goose Lane Editions, 2015), 259.

Lester Pearson's leadership in shaping this national course was long and well established before the Suez Crisis. He continued transitioning Canada from its imperial past when he became prime minister, elected in 1963, following a Diefenbaker government that unsuccessfully sought to turn Canada back to tighter ties with Britain, both on economic trade and defence policy. In 1965, the Pearson government in demonstrating its nationalism and Canada as a completely independent entity, in the face of well-organized and intense opposition, changed Canada's official flag from the Red Ensign to the current red-and-white flag featuring a maple leaf in its centre.

Following Pearson's diplomatic successes, and more specifically flowing from the accolades leading to the Nobel Peace Prize he received, for many years, Canadian participation in international peacekeeping continued to grow, often under Pearson's leadership. For some time following the Suez Crisis, Canada supplied about 10 per cent of troops for such UN initiatives around the globe. Indeed, it was not until 1989 that for the first time Canada refused a UN request to contribute to a peacekeeping force, and recent decades have seen a dramatic decline in such activity, to the point where Canada stood lower than fifty other countries among UN member states who contributed to peacekeeping operations.

More recently, Canadian participation and support for overseas involvement remain mixed. Some 4,500 Canadian troops participated in the 1991 Gulf War; yet, in 2003, Canada refused the US administration of George W. Bush to commit service personnel to support the invasion of Iraq. On the other hand, starting two months after the attack on the Twin Towers in New York City on 11 September 2001, and over the course of some thirteen years, over 40,000 Canadian troops deployed to Afghanistan to support the American-led coalition to topple the Taliban and to root out the terrorist network known as Al-Qaeda, at a cost of 165 dead and some 2,000 wounded. Currently, in 2025, more than 60 per cent of Canadians polled said they would support sending Canadian peacekeepers to Ukraine to help enforce an agreement between that country and its Russian military opponent. Also telling, however, is that Conservative Party of Canada, which received over 40 per cent of the popular vote in the 29 April 2025 federal election, only 1.5 per cent less than the Liberals, who formed a minority government, stressed in their platform that they would slash some $10 billion from government foreign aid and divert much of those funds to strengthening Canada's military.[18] Still, despite the contradictions, which appear more manifest in current times, Canada's historic and leading role in peacekeeping for several decades became – and, in fact, remains – a notable part of its image, or at least one that many Canadians like to emphasize.

---

[18] angusreid.org/ukraine-canada-us-support-russia-putin-trump-carney-trudeau-canadian-peacekeepers/; www.cips-cepi.ca/2025/04/23/election-2025-what-are-the-parties-saying-about-foreign-aid/.

IMAGE 8 Tommy Douglas being named as the first leader of the federal New Democratic Party, 4 August 1961. Vern Kent, Saskatchewan Film Board.

8

Saskatchewan doctors' strike, 1962: Universal health care for Canada

Who is the greatest Canadian? In fall 2004, the Canadian Broadcasting Corporation asked that question for a thirteen-week TV series. More than 10,000 names were submitted by mail, phone and online. The list – naming military figures, athletes, revolutionaries, politicians, entertainers, astronauts, inventors, scientists, medical pioneers and various others – was whittled down to ten by a panel of experts. More than a half million people tuned in weekly to consider the candidates, many of whom had a celebrity advocate. Canadians were then invited to vote. On 28 November, with an estimated 1.2 million people watching, the winner was announced: it was Tommy Douglas, the founder of Medicare in Canada. Although controversial, even revolutionary, for its time, Medicare has become entrenched and over the years, as a defining feature, not just of Canada's social welfare apparatus, but, in the minds of many Canadians, of the country's character. In 2007, American filmmaker Michael Moore made a documentary called 'Sicko' in which he looked at various countries' health care systems, starting with Canada's, about which he was very complimentary. From his research for the film, Moore was somewhat surprised to find himself concluding that no political party in Canada could or would even attempt to recommend backtracking on universal public health insurance. Yet, currently, surveys, such as one of 10,000 Canadians in early 2024, showed that while most expressed pride in the country's commitment to universal health care, there was also vast frustration, with more than 30 per cent reporting they had no family physician nor same or next day access to a doctor, and, for several procedures, excruciatingly long wait times, prompting increasing numbers with the financial means to pay for services themselves outside the country.[1] It was in Saskatchewan, where the social democratic Co-operative Commonwealth Federation established its strongest roots, that the battle over Medicare was fought, the outcome of which ultimately committed Canada to universal health care, a principle that, despite its growing strains and gaps, as well as ever-rising health care costs, most Canadians still look upon with pride.

Millions of Canadians used to live in fear of serious illness because they had no means to afford medical care. Private medical insurance policies provided very different levels and scope of coverage, depending on how much one paid. Out of compassion, doctors often offered care to patients who could not afford their fees, or accepted items such as food for payment. Tommy Douglas' dream and crusade for medicare started to take shape in Saskatchewan in the early 1960s.[2] In the province where he had been the Co-operative Commonwealth Federation (CCF) premier since 1944, lots of people were against these measures at first. This was especially the case among doctors who went on strike on 1 July 1962. They were protesting implementation of the Saskatchewan Medical Care Insurance Act, which came into force that day, as well as the provincial government that promulgated it. This unprecedented standoff attracted press coverage across North America. On the first day of the strike, headlines, even in the *New York Times*, covered the death of nine-month-old Carl Derhousoff, the youngest child of a Hutterite family from the small Saskatchewan community of Usherville. It was reported that the baby would have survived had he received prompt medical care. Later, a coroner's jury, looking into the cause of the baby's death – meningitis – did not support that conclusion, although this point received little public attention. The story told at the time was that the parents, realizing their baby was terribly ill, drove more than 120 kilometres, desperately trying to find emergency medical assistance, but they had no success. Many people blamed the striking doctors for being greedy, uncaring and unprofessional. To the doctors and their supporters, however, this was a crisis foisted upon the province by an ideologically driven socialist government and its long-time leader who remained headstrong no matter the costs, even in human life.

Concepts of publicly supported health care in Canada had several earlier manifestations, but they were all limited in scope. In 1883, St Joseph's hospital in Victoria, British Columbia, offered a plan under which, for the payment of a dollar monthly, participants could see a doctor, be admitted to hospital and have the costs of medicine covered, assuming that the number of participants maintained the plan as financially feasible. Also in

---

[1] 'Massive New Survey Finds Widespread Frustration with Access to Primary Health Care', *CBC News*, 27 February 2024, https://www.cbc.ca/news/politics/primary-care-canada-10-000-canadians-report-1.7125990.

[2] Gregory Marchildon, *Tommy Douglas and the Quest for Medicare in Canada* (Toronto: University of Toronto Press, 2024).

the late nineteenth century, some hospitals in New Brunswick and what became Alberta offered pre-payment plans to obtain timely medical care. The federal Liberals had talked about public health insurance in their 1919 party platform, that made William Lyon Mackenzie King leader, but like so many other circumstances with King, little or nothing happened until it became politically necessary/expedient. Indeed, only a weak and unclear expression from King was made to support public health care in the 1921 federal election campaign. As with many other social programmes, the tendency was for both the federal and provincial governments to claim that, financially and constitutionally, it was primarily the other's responsibility. British Columbia's provincial government held a plebiscite in the mid-1930s on implementing a publicly funded health care system. Fifty-nine per cent of voters expressed support, but strong opposition from doctors and their many allies convinced the government to quietly back down.

The federal government began to roll out significant social programmes during the Second World War. As the last major Western country to adopt an unemployment insurance system, Canada's Parliament passed the Unemployment Insurance Act in August 1940; premiums to fund the programme began to be collected in 1941, and the first benefit payments were made in 1942. Two summers later, Parliament passed the Family Allowances Act, widely known as the 'baby bonus'; this was Canada's first universal welfare programme, and it came into effect on Dominion Day in 1945.[3]

There was widespread suffering through the Great Depression of the 1930s, and many Canadians also remembered the sharp economic downturn that had followed the Great War. There were extensive fears this would happen again. A September 1943 public opinion poll showed a plurality of Canadian voters leaning towards the social democratic Co-operative Commonwealth Federation (CCF). A federal government report on social security was published that same year. Taking inspiration from the widely acclaimed Beveridge Report that came out in England in 1942, this was the *Report on Social Security for Canada*, also known as the Marsh Report, for its author, Leonard Marsh, a McGill University economist. Marsh submitted a sweeping array of federal social welfare initiatives, including publicly funded health insurance. Although the Mackenzie King government moved more slowly than Marsh recommended, and balked at any talk of health insurance, it was clear that the political mood in the country had become far more amenable to, even openly supportive of broad government intervention to guarantee a decent minimal standard of living for all Canadians.[4]

---

[3]Raymond B. Blake, *From Rights to Needs: A History of Family Allowances in Canada, 1929–92* (Vancouver: University of British Columbia Press, 2009).
[4]Leonard Marsh, *Report on Social Security for Canada* (Toronto: University of Toronto Press, 1975).

This mood was strikingly evident in Saskatchewan, with its harsh climate, the uncertainty from its boom-and-bust agricultural economy and the relative isolation in which so many of its people lived. Its population had long been disposed to 'collectivist efforts'.[5] The cooperative movement, which originated in Europe in the nineteenth century, had by the early twentieth strongly taken root there. Arguably, among Canada's provinces, Saskatchewan was the hardest hit by the Great Depression: its Gross Provincial Product dropped by almost three-quarters between 1928 and 1933. The policy manifesto founding the Co-operative Commonwealth Federation as a political party was announced in Regina in 1933, with J. S. Woodsworth as its first leader.

Tommy Douglas was born in Scotland in 1904. About six years later, his family emigrated to Canada, to Winnipeg, a centre of labour activism and political radicalism. A knee injury he suffered when he was seven became osteomyelitis. The family was told that amputation would be necessary. Then, Dr Stanley Alwyn Smith, an orthopaedic surgeon at Winnipeg's Children's Hospital, offered to perform expensive and complicated corrective surgery for free as part of a clinical experiment for educational purposes on condition that his students could observe all the procedures. This offer saved not only the child's leg, but also the family from bankruptcy. The experience left a deep impression, making Tommy Douglas a lifelong champion of publicly funded medical care. This conviction was reinforced later in his life, when the effects of the leg injury kept him from going into action during the Second World War; however, he did make plans to go overseas to visit troops. On a train heading east, he became very ill and was forced to recuperate in an Ottawa hospital. 'When I was ready to come out of hospital, my hospital bill was just under a thousand dollars', Douglas later recalled. 'This gives you some idea of why hospital insurance certainly appealed to me. I didn't have a thousand dollars. I had to borrow the money'.[6]

In Winnipeg, Douglas was witness to the often-violent ways that labour and political activism, especially when involving socialists, was brutally crushed. He served a five-year apprenticeship as a printer, acquired his journeyman's license, but decided to return to school. He became a Baptist minister, one fully ensconced in the message of the Social Gospel movement, a movement with wide working-class appeal. Social Gospellers were active on a range of issues, fighting addiction, poverty, the ill-effects of industrialization and urbanization, as well as other social and economic issues with the Christian message and Christian good deeds – as well as high-level political deeds. Winnipeg was the centre for much of the movement's development in Canada, and it is where Douglas first met J. S. Woodsworth.

---

[5]Robin F. Badgley and Samuel Wolfe, *Doctors' Strike: Medical Care and Conflict in Saskatchewan* (Toronto: Macmillan, 1967), 3.
[6]Thomas H. McLeod and Ian McLeod, *Tommy Douglas: The Road to Jerusalem* (Edmonton: Hurtig Publishers, 1987), 188.

After his ordination as a minister, Douglas and his wife Irma (nee Dempsey) moved to Saskatchewan.

Weyburn, Saskatchewan, is where Tommy Douglas first rose to political prominence. Starting in 1935, he represented that community in the House of Commons, until he shifted to provincial politics after becoming leader of the Saskatchewan CCF in 1942. Publicly funded health care was cited as a priority in the CCF's founding document, the 1933 Regina Manifesto, and was a goal to which Douglas declared his intent to achieve from his earliest political days. He spoke of his 'pledge that if I ever have anything to do with it, people would be able to get health services just as they are able to get educational services, as an inalienable right of being a citizen'.[7]

The CCF was clearly on the rise. In 1943, it finished a close second to the Conservatives in Ontario's provincial election. The next year, Saskatchewan voters went to the polls. Douglas's rival, Liberal William Patterson, had been premier since 1935. In the 1944 campaign, Douglas pushed home the point that compared with most other provinces, Saskatchewan fell behind 'in almost every field of welfare, education, roads, industrial development, and farm security'.[8] Effectively, he cast the Patterson government as spent when it came to new ideas to build a better future for Saskatchewan after the war.

The Liberals tried to scare voters, telling farmers that the CCF would foreclose on their debts, which for many people in Saskatchewan had grown during the Depression, and seize their property. They accused Douglas of being a Communist. Douglas' response was his insistence that 'the only freedom we were taking away was the freedom to exploit someone else'.[9] Voters were hungry for significant change, particularly for fulfilment of the CCF's promise to pursue social reforms, including publicly funded health care. Turnout was massive for the Saskatchewan election held on 15 June 1944, and the result was decisive. The CCF took just over 53 per cent of the popular vote – 18 per cent more than the Liberals – and received a massive majority in the Legislative Assembly, winning forty-seven of the fifty-two seats.

Douglas immediately signalled major change with health care, serving not only as premier, but also, initially, by assuming the public health portfolio. He was not introducing the goal of publicly funded health care into a vacuum. For decades, there had been municipally based plans, not only in Saskatchewan, but also in Manitoba and Newfoundland (although it was not a province until 1949), as well as parts of the United States, under which residents agreed to pay a tax to support a doctor to provide them with services for which they would not be charged additional costs. Indeed,

---

[7]Dave Margoshes, *Tommy Douglas: Building the New Society* (Lantzville, BC: XYZ Publishing, 1999), 130.
[8]McLeod and McLeod, *Tommy Douglas*, 178.
[9]Lewis Thomas, ed., *The Making of a Socialist: The Recollections of T.C. Douglas* (Edmonton: University of Alberta Press, 1982), 168.

by the early 1940s, in Saskatchewan, 107 municipalities, 59 villages and 14 towns were paying 180 doctors, both full- and part-time, to offer health care. Such action depended on local support, and the arrangements often lacked stability and sustainability because of the unpredictability of farm incomes. Saskatchewan had also seen cooperative health insurance plans and health insurance associations, but even when operated on a not-for-profit basis, for many people the premiums could be too high for them to participate.

In 1944, Saskatchewan's newly elected CCF government initiated several reforms. One was passage of the Trade Union Act to enshrine the right of labour – including provincial government employees – to organize and bargain collectively. Government Crown companies were established, actions were taken to weed out partisanship in the hiring of civil servants, and measures were introduced to halt foreclosures on mortgages. Then came the first salvos to grant publicly funded access to health care. The CCF government established a commission under Dr Henry E. Sigerist that, in 1946, resulted in a pilot programme in Swift Current and vicinity, encompassing some 50,000 people, that provided medical coverage from taxes collected. It seemed to work well and enjoyed good support. When, however, Premier Douglas talked of extending these arrangements provincewide, he was faced with major pushbacks, especially from doctors. Moving more slowly, early in 1945, the provincial government introduced legislation that would issue 'old age pensioners, blind pensioners, mother's allowances cases, and all wards of the government' cards entitling them to 'medical care, hospital care, dental care, eye care, glasses, and drugs'; the CCF government also put into practice a measure that the previous Liberal government had passed, but not implemented, 'providing for free care and treatment for all cancer patients'.[10] This was covered by a 1 per cent sales tax and small increases in provincial income tax that, together, covered about 60 per cent of costs; the rest the province funded from other revenue. When it started, this level of public health care cost $7.5 million, equating to 15 per cent of the provincial budget; by 1955, those figures had climbed to $49 million and 20 per cent.

When the Saskatchewan government proceeded to cover hospital care for all its residents, it had the fewest hospital beds per 1,000 people in Canada. By 1954, it had gone to the very top in this category. Still, by the end of the 1950s, only half of Saskatchewan's population was covered by private medical insurance plans, and they were of varying scope and quality. Getting sick could mean personal bankruptcy. People without medical insurance still could receive treatment, but were expected to pay back the costs, and often faced collection agencies. Doctors could appeal to the provincial government

---

[10] Ibid., 169; and C. Stuart Houston and Merle Massie, 'Four Precursors of Medicare in Saskatchewan', in Gregory P. Marchildon, ed., *Making Medicare: New Perspectives on the History of Medicare in Canada* (Toronto: University of Toronto Press, 2012), 137–50.

for reimbursement for treating those who could not pay, but by no means was repayment guaranteed.

It took some fifteen years for the CCF to move towards its second, and far more significant innovation: publicly financed universal comprehensive health coverage. During this period, Saskatchewan's CCF earned people's trust by introducing steady, progressive, but not radical, changes, and by not threatening either the market economy or private land ownership. The CCF demonstrated its commitment to helping farmers when crop prices or a poor harvest shook their economic survival. By the end of the 1950s, several other provinces had joined Saskatchewan in covering the costs of hospital care. In Ottawa, the Progressive Conservative government, elected in 1957 under John Diefenbaker, who represented the constituency of Prince Albert, Saskatchewan, introduced the Hospital Insurance and Diagnostic Services Act, a shared-cost initiative with the provinces to cover patient costs for several hospital procedures, an agreement that by the end of 1960 every provincial government had joined.

Revenues for the Saskatchewan government increased dramatically in the late 1950s, from oil and minerals, providing the financial basis for Saskatchewan to consider Medicare. However, in mid-1950s, voters in Regina and Assiniboia – with strong pressure from the province's College of Physicians and Surgeons – rejected a proposed adoption of the regional health care scheme introduced in Swift Current in 1946. Many of Saskatchewan's doctors had migrated to the province after the Second World War; they had left the constraints of Britain's National Health Service, that was introduced in 1948, and did not want it replicated in their new home. The stage was now set for a battle.

In a now-famous speech at Birch Hills, in April 1959, during a by-election campaign, Douglas proclaimed his government's intent to move forward on creating publicly financed medical insurance. 'There are many people who cannot avail themselves of the voluntary plans, either because they cannot afford the premiums or because they have congenital conditions, which are not covered by them', he announced. 'It is for these reasons that the government has come to the conclusion it should embark upon a comprehensive medical care program that will cover all our people'.[11] This was an alarming situation for doctors. A government-managed payment system was viewed as setting a ceiling on their income, an arrangement that did not exist anywhere else in North America.

Just before the Birch Hills speech, Douglas and his Cabinet established the Interdepartmental Committee to Study a Medical Care Program and look at various models and costs. Opposition from doctors was predicted, but no recommendations were forthcoming on how that should be managed. The proposed plan promised that no patient would ever see a medical bill

---

[11] Badgley and Wolfe, *Doctors' Strike*, 22.

presented to them. Saskatchewan's doctors were incensed, stating they had not been consulted, and insisting that any plan that had the government setting fee schedules for medical services interfered with their doctor-patient relationships, including, they claimed, by potentially determining what treatments would be covered. Premier Douglas rejected the doctors' arguments. Later in 1959, Saskatchewan's CCF announced its intention to extend public medical insurance to include not only hospital care but also doctors' visits. Physicians were to be paid a specified amount by the provincial government and not the rates doctors could decide to charge their patients or private insurers. In the early days of working out his thoughts on Medicare, Douglas had suggested putting doctors on a provincially paid salary, but he soon backed away from that idea in favour of a fee-for-service schedule, thus leaving it up to doctors to determine – through patient visits – the scope of their annual income.

Douglas believed that public opinion would sway doctors into accepting Medicare. He promised there'd be no fees or premiums. Slightly increased provincial taxes would cover one-third of anticipated costs; the government would pay for the rest. The provincial government stipulated that it would only act to implement this initiative if re-elected. A provincial election was scheduled for June 1960. During that campaign, the Canadian Medical Association (CMA) spent $100,000 on advertising, warning that re-electing the CCF would see doctors, especially talented ones, flee the province. The CMA's campaign included outrageous claims such as 'Medicare bureaucrats … might commit women with menopausal problems to insane asylums',[12] or warnings to Catholics that a government-controlled health care system would mandate birth control.

Saskatchewan's voters were not swayed. Although dropping 4 per cent in the popular vote in the 1960 election, the CCF won only one fewer seat than in the previous, 1956 election, retaining a majority, thirty-six of fifty-five seats. The Interdepartmental Committee forged ahead with its work under Woodrow Lloyd, a former teacher who had served as education minister and treasurer before he succeeded Tommy Douglas as premier. It was tough going. Only a small number of doctors were willing to engage with the government. As the Committee completed its work, Ross Thatcher, the provincial Liberal leader, demanded that voters be offered the opportunity to decide directly on the proposed measure, though he was unclear of how that would proceed. Soon after his 1960 electoral success, however, and before getting things underway, Douglas shifted his political sights back to Ottawa. In 1961, the CCF in alliance with the Canadian Labour Congress (CLC) reinvented itself as the New Democratic Party (NDP), with Tommy Douglas as its first leader, a position he held for the next ten years.

---

[12]McLeod and McLeod, *Tommy Douglas*, 199.

Opening the new legislative session in Regina, which was Douglas's farewell to the provincial legislature, he spoke of his pride in Saskatchewan leading the way, predicted that Medicare would become a national programme, and expressed his hope that with time it would extend from physician services to cover areas like vision and dental care. The plan that was introduced in Saskatchewan did not require any premiums from people; its costs would be entirely covered through provincial revenues. With the passing of the Saskatchewan Medical Care Insurance Act that took effect on Dominion Day in 1962, Saskatchewan became the first Canadian province to introduce universal public health insurance.

Things had become polarized that spring. The College of Physicians and Surgeons of Saskatchewan voted 295 to 5 against cooperating with the government in implementing the Act. Initially, 1 April 1962 was set for the programme going into force. Virtually no doctors would work with the government on its implementation; some quietly admitted that if they did, they would be vilified and ostracized by their colleagues. Doctors threatened to walk off the job if the measure went ahead. Seeking to offer every opportunity to reach an accord, Premier Lloyd set a revised, though final date for implementation of 1 July. The extension solved nothing, except to give more time for opposition forces to mobilize. At the outset of May, some 600 doctors gathered in Regina. The premier, while attempting to address the boisterous crowd, was met with jeers, boos and hisses. Then, to loud cheers, a full 99 per cent of the physicians in attendance voted to reject Medicare and said they would not abide by its provisions. They portrayed the proposed scheme as a socialist attack on their autonomy, and as making them employees of the state.

In communities across the province, patients formed scores of Keep Our Doctors committees, drawing support from 'opposition politicians, druggists, dentists, conservative businessmen, some clergymen, the medical profession, and everyone with a grievance against the government'.[13] Started by four mothers who, over coffee, determined they had to take action to protect their children, Keep Our Doctors portrayed itself as a grassroots organization. With considerable funding, these committees distributed alarmist material, including through newspapers, making claims, for instance, that pregnant women would be unable to get help to ensure safe deliveries. Keep Our Doctors supplied physicians with placards to place in their office windows explaining that they had closed because of their opposition to the Saskatchewan Medical Care Insurance Act. The committees supplied form letters to doctors for distribution to patients, stating: 'I cannot, in all conscience, provide services under the Act and thus my office will be closed on July 1st. It will stay closed until the Government will allow me to treat

---

[13]Badgley and Wolfe, *Doctors' Strike*, 52.

you, as I have in the past, without political interference or control'.[14] Many pharmacists warned that prescription drugs would become less available or not be refilled. Allies of Keep Our Doctors at rallies portrayed the CCF as communists. These activists even turned to racist stereotypes to further stoke opposition. At one event, for example, 'a caricature' was featured of a doctor supposed to have been imported by the Saskatchewan government, 'with a large Semitic nose, a Chinese pigtail, and a Middle East style of clothing, and bearing a large sign reading "Sask Gov't Medicare Imports"'. Reports foretold of people who, once a doctors' strike began, would need to travel hundreds of kilometres to get treatment for medical emergencies. On 29 June, Saskatchewan's medical society put out a communiqué, explaining to the public that '1. All doctors' offices will be closed to patients. 2. No doctors will be available for home visits, except in the "direst emergencies." 3. No telephone advice will be available from doctors. 4. There will be no prescription services. ... The patient will have no choice of doctor ... and ... it is likely the emergency services will become "more and more limited" as the days progress'.[15]

Warnings were issued about skyrocketing medical costs, coupled with rising taxes, to support a public health insurance system. The argument was advanced that it was patently unfair to make everyone's health coverage the same, not to say, for many with private insurance, inferior, to help what was purported to be a small number of people without health insurance and who could be assisted through other means. Fearmongering included the claim that, to save costs, the government would control what doctors could prescribe or the proper course of care, thus resulting in people not receiving optimum appropriate medical attention.

The anger of many descended not only on Premier Lloyd but also on Tommy Douglas, who, as the new federal NDP leader, lost a June 1962 by-election in Regina by some 10,000 votes for a seat in the House of Commons, a campaign in which he faced threats of violence. Still, in the belief that compromise with doctors was not possible, the Lloyd government moved ahead with its plans, setting up the machinery to implement the Medicare programme. The government insisted that the plan was eminently fair to doctors, pointing out that the fee schedule was based on norms currently charged. As a doctors' strike became more imminent, the province began recruiting replacement physicians. On 17 June, following up on a trip by Saskatchewan government officials to Great Britain, the Reuters news agency carried notices of opportunities to relocate to the province. With financial and logistical assistance from the provincial government, nearly a dozen physicians arrived in Saskatchewan just before 1 July.

---

[14]Ibid., 53.
[15]Ibid., 55.

Saskatchewan's doctors made good on their threat. Their strike was the most substantial, organized and potentially serious threat to the expansion of government social services to date, leaving Canadians more exposed than ever to medical catastrophe. Ninety per cent of doctors' offices in Saskatchewan closed on 1 July 1962. Across North America, news sources reported this unprecedented action. Reactions were mixed. Portrayed as a socialist intrusion into the relationship between doctor and patient, as well as a flagrant attack on personal choice and freedoms, pressure from several sources, particularly the medical establishment, mounted on the provincial government to back away from the plan. Many among the public, however, characterized the striking doctors as unprofessional, uncaring and driven by greed. One letter signed by members of what was called the Swift Current Citizens Safety Committee asserted that doctors were 'rebelling against the people'.[16]

The provincial government responded by opening several regional emergency centres, at which some 200 medical personnel were made available. Striking doctors worked with local committees to organize a rally for 11 July in front of the provincial legislative building in Regina, hoping to attract 40,000 people to the event as a show of solidarity. After more than a week out of their offices, facing mixed public opinion and a provincial government unwilling to back down, opposition began to fizzle. Only 4,000 turned up for the rally. By mid-July, about half of the province's doctors had returned to work, many in communities where they were well known and friends with locals, making it personally awkward, not to say draining to deny help. The strike ended in twenty-three days, and in contrast to the hysteria, no one died.

In mid-July, the government brought in a mediator, the British physician, Lord Taylor, who, in 1948, had helped to implement Britain's National Health Service. On 23 July 1962, the Saskatchewan doctors' strike officially was over. A final agreement made a few changes, enabling doctors, under a narrow set of circumstances, to opt out of the plan, provided for future fee increases, and made room for more physicians to sit on the province's Medical Care Insurance Commission. With that, all of Saskatchewan's 928,000 citizens could now acquire public health insurance. To help pay for Medicare, the Saskatchewan sales tax was hiked from 3 to 5 per cent, provincial corporate and income tax by 22 per cent, and an annual levy of $12 for an individual and $24 for a family was introduced

Most doctors quickly accepted the terms and grew accustomed to the new system. Moreover, many soon expressed a preference for it, because they no longer had to deal with patients or even private insurance companies regarding payments. There continued to be push and pull on the level of services that the government could provide, the remuneration doctors

---

[16]https://en.wikipedia.org/wiki/Saskatchewan_doctors%27_strike.

received and what many physicians claimed was excessive bureaucracy to obtain payments. Still, within a very few years, anger within the medical profession had died down. By 1965, 72 per cent of Saskatchewan's doctors believed the new government medical insurance system should remain in place, especially since, by that time, other provinces, and the federal government on a shared-cost basis with the provinces, were moving in the same direction. The quality of health care did not collapse as some had predicted, and rather than witnessing an exodus of doctors from Saskatchewan, things improved: between January 1962 and June 1964, the number of physicians in the province grew from one per 1,037 to one per 980 people. In addition, the bureaucracy supporting Medicare in Saskatchewan became more efficient, meaning that the costs of administering the system declined from 5.71 per cent of provincial government health expenditures in 1963 to 5.39 per cent just two years later.

The Co-operative Commonwealth Federation of Saskatchewan delivered a hallmark achievement by implementing the first universal health insurance system in North America; however, the battle left much bitterness. Medicare continued under Saskatchewan's next provincial government, but when voters went to the polls in 1964, they were ready for a change. This was also because Lloyd was far less charismatic than Douglas, many opposed new provincial funding for Catholic schools, there was a lack of population and employment growth, and an increasing belief that the CCF, after twenty years in power, no longer seemed fresh and lacked vision. Though the CCF tied with Ross Thatcher's Liberals in the popular vote, with each receiving just over 40 per cent, the Liberals emerged with a narrow majority government, winning thirty-two of the fifty-eight seats. However, if the CCF had received a mere 240 more votes distributed in the right ridings, it would have won the most seats. Likely given the razor thin margin of victory, Thatcher, though having cast himself as an opponent of Medicare during the campaign, opted not to touch the system once elected.

The CCF lost the Saskatchewan election in 1964, but by persisting in the face of strident protest from doctors and their many powerful allies, and the fears they raised, it established a monumental legacy. Though Woodrow Lloyd carried much of the weight during the heat of battle, it was Tommy Douglas who was the architect and instigator of public health insurance, starting in 1947, and most significantly in 1962. By getting it done, and then by normalizing Medicare among doctors, others began to quickly jump on board across Canada.

Indeed, that process began just as Douglas committed to creating a public health care system in Saskatchewan. In 1961, Prime Minister John Diefenbaker established a Royal Commission on Health Services under the direction of Supreme Court Justice Emmett Hall. It reported three years later, after Saskatchewan's system was fully entrenched. The Hall Commission, which included two physicians, one being the former president of the Canadian Medical Association, unanimously agreed that a national tax-supported public health insurance system should be established guaranteeing quality medical care without direct billing to citizens. The Hall Commission report went even further, recommending that coverage include dental care, home care, optical services and certain prescription drugs; however, as in Saskatchewan, beyond physician services, these other areas were considered too costly to include.

Under Diefenbaker's successor, Liberal Prime Minister Lester Pearson, shared-cost arrangements with provincial governments were implemented, thus applying the Saskatchewan model to every Canadian. Pearson's initial inclinations were more cautious. In the 1963 general election campaign, the Liberals received a strong minority government with 128 of 265 seats in the House of Commons. Pearson had initially promised to provide free medical services to those under sixteen and older than sixty-five; all others would be required to pay a $25 user fee to see a doctor. In need of NDP support to get the legislation passed, Pearson was forced to broaden his view. What resulted brought remarkable change, and much-needed protection to people all across the country. In 1961, only 42.6 per cent of medical costs incurred by Canadians were paid through private insurance. Working with all the provinces to arrive at this unprecedented and very expensive shared-cost national health insurance plan took three years. Symbolically, as happened six years earlier in Saskatchewan, universal health insurance for all Canadians was unveiled on Dominion Day 1968, with Ottawa making funds available to all the provinces to join. It wasn't easy or straightforward to get to the finish line. Quebec, British Columbia, Manitoba and Ontario preferred a direct transfer of funds without any federal oversight, while Alberta sought an arrangement allowing for user fees and retaining a role for private insurance companies. Atlantic Canada was most amenable; being poorer, these provinces desperately needed federal support for any type of health care initiative. By the end of 1970, all the provinces and Canada's two territorial governments had agreed to a common set of standards that included universality and portability of coverage across Canada, no user fees and comprehensive coverage of physician services. With Ottawa paying half the costs, this soon became governments' largest expenditure, but also, before long, was held up as a defining feature of Canadian values.[17]

With the national health insurance programme in place, the mould was set for other major breakthroughs on social welfare on a shared-cost basis. The most significant to follow was the Canada Pension Plan (CPP). In 1966, the CPP completely rehauled a federal initiative started in 1927 that provided meagre funds to indigent people aged seventy years and older, and whatever funds were distributed had to be repaid to the government

---

[17]P. E. Bryden, 'The Liberal Party and the Achievement of National Medicare', in Gregory P. Marchildon, ed., *Making Medicare: New Perspectives on the History of Medicare in Canada* (Toronto: University of Toronto Press, 2012), 71–88.

from the recipient's estate after death and, in some cases, by their children no matter what they may have inherited. The new Canada Pension Plan was made available to everyone sixty-five years of age or older and was financed through specified payments from employers and employees, with substantial federal government contributions.

In standing up to doctors, the fears their strike evoked and the powerful allies they had, Saskatchewan led the way in transforming the social benefits Canadians received. Arguably, the outcome of this battle, and the legacy it established, changed the way Canadians wanted (and many still want) to see their country, namely, as a nation embracing a commitment to care for the welfare of all. In 1984, with passage of the Canada Health Act, extra medical billing remained prohibited. One poll, taken in 2024, showed 90 per cent of Canadians as taking pride in the country providing health care to all its citizens. Yet, it is also the case that with rising costs of health care, and the increasing inability of governments to provide quick and comprehensive service, confidence in the publicly funded system has waned. Overcrowded hospitals and ever-longer wait times to receive procedures have prompted increasing numbers of Canadians – especially those with the financial means – to seek care elsewhere, namely in private facilities in the United States. Currently, many Canadians would have likely sided with striking Saskatchewan doctors, claiming that Medicare, though demonstrating compassion and care, has denied them choice of treatment and reduced medical service to a low bar. Indeed, an April 2024 national survey revealed that only 48 per cent of Canadians indicated satisfaction with their health care. Still, around the same time, another survey said that rather than jettisoning public health care, 83 per cent wanted further investments into the system.[18] And it remains the case that Tommy Douglas who, over the course of more than twenty years and in the face of sometimes intense opposition, in championing and symbolizing the crusade that brought Medicare to the forefront in Canada, has remained, decades later, the choice of so many Canadians as their country's greatest person.

---

[18]Danielle Martin, et al., 'Canada's Universal Health-Care System: Achieving Its Potential', 391, no. 10131 (2018): 1718–35, https://www.thelancet.com/journals/lancet/article/PIIS0140-6736(18)30181-8/fulltext; www.ipsos.com/en-ca/less-half-of-canadians-are-satisfied-their-provincial-healthcare-system; https://www.healthcoalition.ca/voters-want-premiers-to-take-action-on-health-care-crisis-new-poll/.

IMAGE 9 Thirty-five Yukon Indian teenagers brought to Toronto as a centennial project. Mario Geo/Toronto Star via Getty Images.

9

Canada, 1967: The centennial and searching for a better Canada

Canada's Centennial was celebrated in all possible large- and small-scale ways across the country throughout 1967. Preparations started early. In 1959 Progressive Conservative Prime Minister John G. Diefenbaker made known that official planning for the 100th anniversary of Confederation was under way. In 1960, the Canadian Centennial Council, representing more than 100 non-governmental organizations, was established in Ottawa. In 1961 Diefenbaker announced that the federal government would be funding the construction of upwards of 900 'centennial buildings' throughout Canada, an undertaking of such enormous significance that even half a century later it was characterized as 'a major step in national unity'.[1] In April 1963, Liberal leader Lester B. Pearson succeeded Diefenbaker as prime minister. Shortly after, Parliament renamed the National Centennial Act passed in September 1961 the Centennial of Confederation Act in 1963. Within its amended terms, the Centennial Commission, a Crown corporation, was established. Well-known journalist John Fisher, dubbed 'Mr. Canada', was made its head. The Canadian Centennial Council and the Commission collaborated with each other closely. A main goal of the Commission was to encourage widespread participation in celebrations at all levels, with a mandate 'to promote interest in the Centennial and to plan programmes and projects related to the Centennial's historical significance'.[2] Its work

---

[1] '50 years on, centennial buildings still important symbols',
https://www.cbc.ca/news/canada/centennial-buildings-50th-anniversary-1.3654283.
[2] House of Commons Standing *Committee* on Canadian Heritage, section 2.3 Canada's Centennial (1967), 21, in *Canada's 150th Anniversary in 2017, Chapter 1: Introduction*; hereafter, CHPC report, 21.
https://www.ourcommons.ca/documentviewer/en/41-1/CHPC/report-4/page-21#:~:text=In%201961%2C%20Parliament%20passed%20the%20National%20Centennial,administrative%20framework%20for%20the%20federal%20government%27-s%20involvement.

was assisted by a National Committee comprising federal and provincial ministers responsible for the Centennial and a National Conference made up of Judy LaMarsh, Canada's secretary of state, and sixty people appointed by her; there was also a Centennial organization in each province. The Royal Canadian Mint produced a set of commemorative Centennial coins, designed by war artist and well-known realist painter, Alex Colville; the Centennial Medal, designed by Bruce W. Beatty; and 5.5 million Centennial medallions that in 1967 were distributed to all schoolchildren in Canada. All of these were funded by the Centennial Commission.

National symbols were important to Pearson. He was sure they inspired deep emotional meaning and help nourish loyalty, patriotism and devotion to the nation. A new definition of Canadian identity, he believed – with new national symbols – would help foster a greater sense of unity. He felt that every Canadian, of whatever origin, should be able to take pride in the nation, its citizenship and its national symbols. The most important national symbol to Pearson was to be a new truly distinctive flag, truly national in character and easily identifiable as Canadian. Since 1868 Canada's national flag had been the British Union Jack or some version of it, namely, the Red Ensign. 'The question of a new national flag was an important part of the question of national unity and, let there be no mistake', Pearson insisted, 'there are serious divisions in Canada that have to be reconciled'.[3] The Red Ensign was simply too British, held Pearson, a First World War veteran. He understood that it was difficult for those who were not of British heritage to rally around it as a symbol of Canada.[4] In the House of Commons, on 15 June 1964, Pearson introduced his resolution for a new Canadian flag. The ensuing debate was both acrimonious and lengthy, but ultimately successful. On 15 February 1965, Canada's new flag was flown for the first time. Pearson declared this represented 'a new stage in Canada's forward march from a group of separate and scattered and dependent colonies to a great and sovereign Confederation stretching from sea to sea and from our Southern border to the North Pole'. It was, he hoped, 'to become a symbol of Canada, a symbol of the equal partnership of Canada's two founding peoples, and a recognition of the contributions and the cultures of many other groups then living in Canada'.[5] Many times Pearson promised to change other symbols as well, but with less success. Only in 1982 was the designation for 1 July officially changed from Dominion Day to Canada Day, and that same year 'O Canada' became the country's official national anthem while 'God Save the Queen' was retained as the royal anthem. In 1965, the Centennial

---

[3] *Winnipeg Tribune*, 18 May 1964.
[4] Canada, House of Commons, *Debates*, 6 April 1965, 39–42 [Lester B. Pearson].
[5] 'Text of the Address by the Rt. Hon. Lester B. Pearson, PM of Canada, on the Occasion of the Inauguration of the National Flag of Canada, 15 February 1965', PMO, press release, Diefenbaker Papers, MG01/VII/A/1722.12, vol. 184; 'Pearson's Address on Maple Leaf Flag', *Globe and Mail*, 16 February 1965, 4.

Commission introduced the Centennial Symbol, a stylized maple leaf and 'encouraged people to use it in any way they liked'.[6] Created by graphic designer Stuart Ash, this symbol, the Centennial logo, was put in the public domain so it could be used free of charge. Used extensively, the Centennial logo 'served as a unifying element of the celebration'.[7]

Canada's 100th anniversary had its own, catchy and hugely popular song that is enjoyed by Canadians to this day. Orchestra leader, trumpeter, singer-songwriter and member of the long-running radio programme *Happy Gang*, Bobby Gimby, heralded as the 'Pied Piper of Canada', composed 'Ca-na-da!' It is also known by its formal title, 'Canada: A Centennial Song', while in French it is called 'Une chanson du centenaire'. With lyrics in both languages, it was written as a children's marching song. It became an immediate hit, using children's voices to sing the chorus. Gimby would invite local school children up on stage to sing it with him wherever he performed it.[8] The CBC-TV used it for its documentary, 'Preview '67'. The Centennial Commission quickly adopted it as a theme song for the country's big anniversary. In April 1967, 'Ca-na-da!' was 'no. 1 for 2 weeks on the RPM Top 100 Singles in Canada'.[9] More than half a million recorded copies were sold over the years.

Always mindful of strengthening Canadians' national identity and unity, Pearson saw Dominion Day events in Ottawa 'as a way to ramp up enthusiasm for the 1967 Centennial'. Budgets for these events were increased for an annual 'televised variety show on Parliament Hill' every Dominion Day. These shows featured performers from across the country, 'selected with an eye to emphasizing a new conception of Canadian identity that was more explicitly multicultural and bilingual'.[10]

To mark the 100th anniversary of Canada, the Centennial Flame was added to Parliament Hill. It was supposed to be dismantled after a year, but Canadians loved it so much that the monument became a permanent feature. The flame sits on top of a special fountain surrounding it, into which people (these days) throw coins. 'To symbolize Canada's unity', on each side of the fountain is a bronze shield with the coat of arms of a province or territory with the year it joined Confederation carved into the granite in front of it; the granite is also carved with the provincial or territorial floral emblem.[11] Celebrating 150 years of Confederation, the monument was deconstructed

---

[6]CHPC, 21.
[7]'Federal Projects for Canada's 1967 Centennial', https://www.edmonton.ca/city_government/edmonton_archives/1967-exhibit-federal-projects.
[8]"Catchy Song Still Echoes for Ca-na-da's Pied Piper Gimby', *Toronto Globe & Mail*, 24 July 1987, A2.
[9]"Canada (song)', https://en.wikipedia.org/wiki/Canada_(song).
[10]"Canada Day', https://www.thecanadianencyclopedia.ca/en/article/canada-day.
[11]"Centennial Flame', https://www.canada.ca/en/public-services-procurement/services/infrastructure-buildings/parliamentary-precinct/discover/grounds.html.

and rebuilt in 2017 to add a thirteenth side with Nunavut's coat of arms, territorial flower and the date it officially became a territory.

The Centennial was a moment when the tensions that existed across the country in the years leading up to it – and that became ever more pressing issues in the years that immediately followed – were by and large set aside. Perhaps 'a good party would make all things right in the nation'.[12] And what a party it was. Canadians marked the Centennial year with all manner of special events and activities, and 'partied extra hard on Dominion Day'.[13] Provinces, municipalities, businesses and individuals mounted thousands of events that all contributed to a national mood of excitement and optimism. Every possible field of endeavour, from the creative and performing arts to sports teams, businesses, cultural organizations and schools, became involved in special Centennial productions and projects, 'mobilizing all facets of Canadian society to an unprecedented degree'. There were bathtub races, parades, period costume parties and the town of St Paul, Alberta, 'even built a landing pad for UFOs'.[14] Each province and territory received Centennial funding 'for one marquee structure'.[15] Examples of these are the Arts and Culture Centre in St John's, NL, the Fathers of Confederation Memorial Building in Charlottetown (now called the Confederation Centre of the Arts), the National Arts Centre in Ottawa, the Ontario Science Centre in Toronto and the Centennial Concert Hall in Winnipeg. Children born in Canada in 1967, and especially those born on that Dominion Day, were declared 'Centennial babies': Kara ffolliott (née Kara Marie Ott) was officially declared Canada's 'first "Centennial baby" – born at 12:18 a.m. on 1 July 1967 in Regina'. Her family was 'awarded the Centennial Medallion by Secretary of State Judy LaMarsh', as well as a set of Centennial coins and an engraved plaque from the Saskatchewan Centennial Association.[16] Many, many projects were funded by the $25 million provided to the Centennial Commission. Each dollar spent by a municipality on a centennial event was further matched by $1 from the federal government and $1 from most provincial governments. Those funds and an additional $90 million from Ottawa resulted in new facilities such as hockey rinks, community centres, libraries, art galleries and theatres, as well as national tours for the Anne of Green Gables theatrical production, Les Feux-Follets, Don Messer and His

---

[12] Gillian Michael, '100th Birthday Party Begins', *Globe and Mail*, 2 January 1967, 1–2.
[13] "Canada Day used to be called Dominion Day – wait, what?"
https://www.cbc.ca/archives/canada-day-used-to-be-called-dominion-day-wait-what-1.4728333.
[14] "Canada's Centennial Celebrations, 1967",
https://www.thecanadianencyclopedia.ca/en/article/1967-centennial-celebrations-emc.
[15] '50 years on, centennial buildings still important symbols',
https://www.cbc.ca/news/canada/centennial-buildings-50th-anniversary-1.3654283.
[16] 'Taking the title from Pam Anderson: 1st "Centennial baby" was born in Regina',
https://www.cbc.ca/news/canada/saskatchewan/centennial-baby-kara-ffolliott-1.4186991.

Islanders, the Montreal Symphony Orchestra, the National Ballet of Canada and many others.

The federal government funded a special Confederation Train, which began its cross-country journey in Victoria, British Columbia, on 9 January 1967. Whenever it arrived and departed, its horn sounded out the first four notes of 'O Canada'. In October, it arrived in Nova Scotia, and on 5 December it made its final stop, in Montreal. Along its journey, the train had 'awed 2.5 million visitors in 63 cities across the country'.[17] Also known as the Centennial Train, it had a diesel locomotive emblazoned with the Centennial logo on its nose, and specially designed coach cars loaned by the Canadian National Railway (CNR) and filled with exhibits showcasing Canadian history and culture. In places the train could not reach, Ottawa sent Centennial Caravan tractor-trailers, carrying similar exhibits, reaching another 6.5 million people in more than 650 smaller communities. Both were very popular attractions.

The year's biggest attraction by far was the hugely successful International and Universal Exposition known as Expo 67, which ran from April to October. Themed 'Man and His World', Expo 67 attracted more than 50 million visitors to Montreal, including Her Majesty Queen Elizabeth II, just before she attended Dominion Day celebrations on Parliament Hill, and later in the summer, French President and Second World War hero, General Charles de Gaulle.

The festivities celebrating a hundred years of Confederation began at midnight on New Year's Eve 1966. On Parliament Hill, Prime Minister Lester Pearson lit the Centennial Flame for this first time, with Judy LaMarsh (the minister responsible for the Centennial Commission), Opposition Leader John Diefenbaker and thousands of others in attendance. Cities and towns everywhere in Canada held fireworks, parades, bell-ringing and lighting ceremonies. In provincial capitals, premiers of all political stripes – with the exception of the premier of Quebec – lit centennial flames and bonfires and watched fireworks as they lauded Canada's accomplishments. In Toronto, more than 40,000 people showed up at Queen's Park for a torchlight parade and fireworks, prompting Ontario Conservative Premier John Robarts to remark that interest in the centennial had been seriously underestimated. On New Year's Day 1967, the CBC started its first broadcast of the year with Gordon Lightfoot's song 'Canadian Railway Trilogy'. The song had been commissioned by the CBC to mark the Centennial, and Lightfoot's ode to the building of the transcontinental railway, what he called the 'life blood' of the country, became 'one of his signature songs'.[18]

On Saturday, Dominion Day 1967, the grounds of Parliament Hill were covered with deep crowds of enthusiastic revellers. Queen Elizabeth was there

---

[17]'Canada's Centennial Celebrations, 1967'.
[18]'Re-examining Gordon Lightfoot's "Canadian Railroad Trilogy"', https://www.cbc.ca/music/re-examining-gordon-lightfoot-s-canadian-railroad-trilogy-1.6066106.

to extend her congratulations, but first she cut a massive birthday cake made for the occasion. Pearson spoke of the beginnings of a new chapter in the nation's story: 'Let the record of that chapter be one of co-operation and not conflict; of dedication and not division; of service, not self; of what we can give, not what we can get'. History and geography, he boasted, have made Canada 'a particular kind of community to display the unity in diversity that all mankind must find if it is to survive the perils of the nuclear age'.[19] In her message delivered on Parliament Hill and televised, Queen Elizabeth outdid the prime minister in her praise of Canada. The Centennial, she said, was a moment for Canadians 'to reflect upon the nation's history and consider how unique and splendid it has been'. 'Too often', she lamented, 'Canadians do not always realize how much their achievements have made them the envy of others who watch and admire them'.[20] That same day, under the Queen's authority, the Order of Canada, one of Canada's highest civilian honours, was established. The moment was one to celebrate and cheer the nation, not to dwell on its misdeeds and troubles. Noted Canadian author Pierre Berton called 1967, 'the last good year' that marked the emergence of Canada as a mature and self-confident nation.[21]

Such joy and solidarity were not, however, universally shared at this time. By far the most troubling event that year, with far-reverberating consequences, was the visit to Montreal of French President Charles de Gaulle. He came to Canada to see Expo 67 and to join the Centennial celebrations. From the get-go, his visit spelled trouble. de Gaulle started by breaking diplomatic protocol that required him to land in Ottawa. He chose, instead, to disembark in Quebec City from the French warship *Colbert*, named for Jean-Baptiste Colbert who worked tirelessly to promote New France during the reign of Louis XIV and make France a world power. As his motorcade made its way to Montreal along the Chemin du Roy, de Gaulle made several stops, always relentlessly mobbed by enthusiastic crowds and people waving placards with the separatist slogan 'Vive le Québec libre!' This was the rallying cry of the Rassemblement pour l'Indépendance Nationale (RIN), founded in 1960 to promote Quebec's independence. In Montreal, on 24 July, de Gaulle made a public speech. From the balcony of City Hall, before a 'large throng waving fleur de lys flags and a sovereigntist banner and chanting his name', he proclaimed, '"Vive le Canada. Vive Montréal. Vive le Québec ... " and then a pause, "libre"'. When he shouted, 'Vive le Québec libre!' the crowd of about 20,000 'went wild'.[22] The president of France had thereby given

---

[19] Quoted in Jennifer Ditchburn, 'Policy Thinking for the Next 50 Years', *Policy Options*, 2 January 2017, https://policyoptions.irpp.org/magazines/january-2016/policy-thinking-for-the-next-50-years/.
[20] Lewis Seale, 'Queen Urges Understanding and Goodwill', *The Globe and Mail*, 3 July 1967, 8.
[21] Pierre Berton, *The Last Good Year* (Toronto: Doubleday Canada, 1997).
[22] Marian Scott, 'De Gaulle's "Vive le Québec libre" Speech Rocked the Country', *Montreal Gazette*, 25 July 2017, https://www.montrealgazette.com/news/article488176.html#storylink=cpyhttps://www.montrealgazette.com/news/article488176.html.

credence to the demand for Quebec's independence from Canada. de Gaulle's agenda for that day had not included a speech. de Gaulle was supposed to just wave at the crowd and then attend a ceremony for dignitaries on the rear terrace of City Hall. But on hearing the people chanting 'we want de Gaulle', he told Montreal's Mayor Jean Drapeau, 'I have to speak to those people who are calling for me'.[23]

Pearson was outraged. In an official statement delivered to the French Embassy the next day and read on national television that evening, Pearson rebuked the French president, who abruptly cut his visit short. de Gaulle's remarks were 'unacceptable to the Canadian people and their government', declared the prime minister, adding, 'The people of Canada are free. Every province in Canada is free. Canadians do not need to be liberated'.[24] de Gaulle's 1967 speech from the balcony at Montreal's City Hall had not helped Quebec become independent. Nevertheless, the speech became a symbol of the rise of Quebec nationalism in the years around Canada's Centennial and resonates to this day in Quebec, with tributes to the general's visit still to be 'found in the province's place names, various commemorative events, and monuments erected in his honour'.[25]

The 1960s and early 1970s represented a time in the history of Canada that was anything but tension-free even if the Centennial was all about national unity and Canada's accomplishments since 1867. The de Gaulle incident was emblematic of that discord. Beginning in the late 1950s, Quebec had begun a period of intense social, political, economic and cultural change. This was the beginnings of the Quiet Revolution. It was characterized by the rise of francophone nationalism, rapid modernization and a sweeping secularization that had the state replacing many of the responsibilities previously borne by the Church, it would run through to at least the early 1970s. Critical in this process was a new middle class of technocrats, academics, intellectuals and bureaucrats that had emerged in the 1950s to impose their version of modernity on Quebec society by the early 1960s. Mounting pressure from the Province of Quebec for greater autonomy within Canada was, indeed, becoming a great threat to national unity. The election of Jean Lesage and the Quebec Liberal Party, which after a generation, mostly under authoritarian Premier Maurice Duplessis, unseated the Union Nationale in 1960, winning fifty-one of ninety-five seats and 51 per cent of the popular vote, is seen by many as the springboard to the Quiet Revolution. In a snap election held in 1962, Lesage sought a mandate for the nationalization of the electricity industry in Quebec, with

---

[23]"General De Gaulle and "Vive le Québec libre"', https://www.thecanadianencyclopedia.ca/en/article/de-gaulle-and-vive-le-quebec-libre-feature.

[24]Michael Gillan, 'Words Unacceptable to Canadians: De Gaulle Rebuked by Pearson', *Globe and Mail*, 26 July 1956, 1, 4.

[25]"General De Gaulle and "Vive le Québec libre"', https://www.thecanadianencyclopedia.ca/en/article/de-gaulle-and-vive-le-quebec-libre-feature.

the slogan *maîtres chez nous* (masters in our own house); his party won even more seats and an even larger percentage of the popular vote than two years earlier. The nationalization programme was carried out. In 1964, the Parti libéral du Québec cut all ties with the Liberal Party of Canada to become an entirely provincial party.

This was also a period of replacing anglophone dominance in the political and economic sphere of Quebec with a Québécois middle class, ending the colonization, as some described it, that they had endured since the Conquest on the Plains of Abraham in 1759. There were protests in Quebec in 1962 over job discrimination against Quebeckers who did not have English fluency. In 1963, a militant, revolutionary independence group, the Front de libération du Québec (FLQ) was formed.[26] On 31 May 1963, with the headline 'Bombs in a Quiet Land', *Time* magazine reported that a growing reign of terror was engulfing the province, attributed to the FLQ. Between 1963 and 1970, the FLQ was responsible for more than 200 bombings and dozens of robberies that killed six people and injured many more.[27] Queen Elizabeth was in Canada in 1964 to commemorate the centennial of the historic 1864 Charlottetown and Quebec conferences that led to Confederation in 1867. Large and violent demonstrations greeted her in Quebec City. Even so, she visited the Citadelle and addressed Quebec's Legislative Assembly, renamed in 1968 the National Assembly, in both English and French. Most in Quebec held no such radical views. Some Quebeckers feared that those who were promoting a particular brand of ethnic nationalism would hurt French-speaking Quebeckers by isolating them from the rest of Canada. Some people believed that the development and protection of French were a responsibility of the federal government, and that French-speaking Canadians should and could be at home in any part of Canada; prominent among that group was Pierre Elliott Trudeau (see Chapter 10).

Well before the Centennial year, Pearson had become very worried about Quebec and the threats to national unity. He took as his first task, therefore, the issue of national unity and the need to address and improve French-English relations. He saw Quebec as a province like the other nine, but also as 'a motherland' to French-speaking Canadians – and in a very real sense a nation within a nation. He did not, however, see Quebec with its predominately French language and distinctive culture as a separate political unit, but more akin to what the Scots, Irish and Welsh experienced in the United Kingdom: nations could have their own language, traditions, culture and customs but have no desire for political sovereignty and independence. That would describe the French-Canadian nationality, he insisted, reminding Canadians that Confederation was a partnership of two nationalities or

---

[26]https://www.ojp.gov/ncjrs/virtual-library/abstracts/terror-quebec-case-studies-flq-front-de-liberation-quebecois.
[27]'Bombs in the Quiet Land', *Time*, 31 May 1963.

two nations in the ethnic and sociological sense, but it was one nation politically, legally and constitutionally.²⁸ He repeatedly encouraged the anglophone majority of English-speaking Canadians to become 'more conscious' of the aspirations of French-speaking Canadians. Quebec might consider separation, said Pearson, if English-speaking Canadians allowed themselves to forget 'the rules of the game which were established by the Fathers of Confederation'.²⁹ Too often, Canadians failed to understand that the French-English partnership established in 1867 had become unequal and less productive than it was at Confederation and that this was a major domestic problem. Quebec, on the other hand, he advised should not be 'too impatient if it finds that this consciousness seems slow to express itself'.³⁰ Quebec must find its destiny within Canada, not outside of it, although making progress would take time. For Pearson, it was about 'setting our house in order, without pulling it down', and he asked Canadians to work to bring together all the 'diverse elements in our national life, all the people whose variety of culture and creed and tongue and viewpoint contributes so much to the richness of our heritage and the uniqueness of the Canadian identity which we have built and will continue to develop'.³¹

For more than a generation, Quebec's place in Canada would dominate the national political agenda. Although it could be said that Lester Pearson did not always understand what was happening in Quebec and that he wondered as did many in English-speaking Canada what did the province really want, he fully understood that the changes there were a threat to national stability. His first response was to appoint the Royal Commission on Bilingualism and Biculturalism on 19 July 1963, just after his first Dominion Day (later renamed to Canada Day) as prime minister. Known as the B&B Commission, it was to study and report on the existing state of bilingualism and biculturalism in Canada and 'recommend what steps should be taken to develop the Canadian Confederation on the basis of an equal partnership between the two founding races' of French and English.³² Ironically, multiculturalism soon replaced biculturalism as the national mantra. Nevertheless, in 1964, the B&B Commission noted that 'Canada, without being fully conscious of the fact, is passing through the greatest crisis in its history, [and] the source of the crisis lies in the Province of Quebec'. Quebec

---

²⁸Canada, House of Commons, *Debates*, 6 April 1965, 43–4.
²⁹'Excerpts from Address by the PM, the Rt. Hon. Lester B. Pearson, at the Founding Convention, Liberal Federation of Canada (Quebec), Quebec City, 26 March 1966', Prime Minister's Office (PMO), press release, Diefenbaker Papers, MG01/VII/A/1722.13, vol. 184.
³⁰'Biggest Problem Unity, Strength, Pearson Says', *Globe and Mail*, 14 October 1965, 10.
³¹'Address by the Rt. Hon. Lester B. Pearson, PM of Canada, at a Dinner of the National Centennial Administration, First National Conference on Canada's Centennial', Ottawa, 15 October 1963, Lester B. Pearson Fonds, MG26 N6, vol. 22, file General – Speeches, 1963–8, LAC.
³²Canada, House of Commons, *Debates*, Speech from the Throne, 16 May 1963, 7–8.

was frustrated with its place in Confederation, worried that its language and culture were threatened by the growth of English-speaking Canada, but it was also concerned with the increasing centralization of power in Ottawa, particularly since the Second World War, and how in Quebec the English-speaking minority dominated the French-speaking majority in so many areas, nowhere more so than in economic affairs.

One of the relatively easy steps for Pearson was to address the state of the French language: it had to be made more accessible throughout Canada and especially within the federal government. He expressed the hope that bilingualism would become the norm rather than the exception among civil servants and help answer the question of what does Quebec want. On 17 October 1968, on recommendations from the B&B Commission, legislation was tabled in the House of Commons to make English and French the official languages of Canada and to confirm the equal status, rights and privileges regarding their use in all institutions of Parliament and the Government of Canada. The Official Languages Act came into force on 7 September 1969.[33]

In the meantime, Quebec became more assertive in how federal dollars were spent in that province, and it frequently spoke of 'repatriating' control of social spending. Pearson was accommodating and embarked on what became known as cooperative federalism. One might argue that this was a concept of Canadian federalism that extended back to 1867, as it was an approach to governing based on the federal and provincial governments working together to achieve mutual goals. Pearson agreed that Quebec could opt out of several federal-provincial initiatives to create its own programmes that it believed better met the priorities of Quebec; the best known of these is the Quebec Pension Plan (QPP). Within months of becoming prime minister in 1963, Pearson set to work establishing the contributory Canada Pension Plan (CPP), with the proviso that provinces could withdraw from it if they established a comparable programme of their own. Quebec did so and established its QPP. While the pension arrangement worked well, there were major disputes between Quebec and the federal government over other policies, notably, on family allowances, labour mobility, immigration and others that worried some, even in Quebec, who feared that it was a step towards independence.

Among Pearson's most celebrated initiatives as prime minister leading to the Centennial were his efforts to improve conditions for Canada's Indigenous peoples and for Canadian women. In 1964 he invited anthropologist Howard B. Hawthorn to study and prepare a report on the lives and circumstances of Indigenous peoples so that the government might consider ways to redress the persistent disadvantages they faced. In his 1966 report, Hawthorn concluded that Indigenous peoples were Canada's most

---

[33]Official Languages Act of 1969, R.S.C. 1970, c. O2, s.2.

disadvantaged and marginalized citizens. He argued for the elimination of the assimilationist policies and recommended against ending separate status for those recognized as 'Indians' under the Indian Act. He suggested a permanent special recognition of Indigenous people and facilitating their becoming self-determining, 'Citizens Plus'.[34] In addition to the normal rights and duties of citizenship, Indigenous peoples also possessed rights through a variety of treaties.[35] Pearson began consultations with First Nations organizations across the country, and in the 1965 Speech from the Throne promised to reorganize certain government departments to provide for the special needs of Indigenous people and the development of Northern Canada.[36] In his centennial year Throne Speech, Pearson acknowledged that Ottawa had a responsibility to those who 'face grave problems in their attempts to share the benefits and opportunities of Canadian society'.[37] Amendments to the Indian Act were planned that would encourage community development for the benefit of Indigenous peoples, although little progress in that regard had been made before Pearson retired from politics in April 1968.

On 16 February 1967, Pearson created the Royal Commission on the Status of Women with the mandate to 'inquire into and report upon the status of women in Canada, and to recommend what steps might be taken by the federal government to ensure equal opportunities for women in all aspects of the Canadian society'.[38] The Commission was not able to table its report in Parliament before Pearson resigned. Nevertheless, while he was prime minister, in fourteen cities across the country, it held thirty-seven days of public hearings, many of which were specifically held at times convenient to women with children; nearly 900 witnesses appeared, and 468 briefs and more than 1,000 letters were received, reflecting a growing desire among women for a different Canada than had existed for much of the period since 1867. Pearson's decision to appoint the Commission – the first chaired by a woman, Florence Bird – showed his and the Government of Canada's recognition (finally) that women had legitimate grievances.

Canada's Centennial year was a transformational moment for Canada. At the National Centennial Conference's meeting in Quebec City in April 1967,

---

[34]Harry Bertram Hawthorn, ed., *A Survey of the Contemporary Indians of Canada: A Report on Economic, Political, Educational Needs and Policies*, vol. 1 (Ottawa: Indian Affairs Branch, Department of Indian Affairs and Northern Development, 1966).
[35]See Hawthorn, *A Survey of the Contemporary Indians*, 12; and 'The White Paper 1969', Indigenous Foundations, https://indigenousfoundations.arts.ubc.ca/the_white_paper_1969/50/.
[36]Speech from the Throne, 18 January 1965, 8.
[37]Canada, House of Commons, *Debates*, Speech from the Throne, 8 May 1967, 3.
[38]Royal Commission on the Status of Women in Canada (RCSW), https://www.canada.ca/en/women-gender-equality/commemorations-celebrations/royal-commission-status-women-canada.html.

Prime Minister Pearson expressed praise for the many centennial projects accomplished and underway as 'tangible evidence of our success in pursuing the Canadian dream'. Yet, he reminded delegates that the Centennial's most significant legacy was not going to be buildings and cultural events but things immaterial and not easily discernible. 'Let us remember', he said,

> that the better part of any nation is not tangible, but it is that part which lives in the hearts of people. So, it is for us to ensure that that national purpose we pursue ... is founded upon human principles that have universal and permanent value. Then we can be as certain as any people that our nation will endure because it deserves to endure.[39]

Not on that occasion, but many times elsewhere, Pearson declared that a nation can survive only when it finds accommodation for all its ethnic, linguistic, diverse and regional communities. It is surprising then that Pearson and Pierre Trudeau, his minister of justice, refused to attend the 'Confederation of Tomorrow' conference that was hosted by Ontario Premier John Robarts in Toronto between 27 and 30 November 1967 in the top floor of the brand-new Toronto-Dominion Centre where the carpeting had not yet been installed. Roberts wanted his fellow premiers to hear directly from Daniel Johnson about the changes that were transforming Quebec society and what he saw as Quebec's place in Canada. With the exception of British Columbia's W. A. C. Bennett who told Robarts 'I'm lost on these issues once I cross the Rockies', they all came as much to listen to each other as well as to engage in a conversation about a vision of Canada for the future.[40] Robarts understood that Canada was then – and remains – a work in progress that can thrive when its leaders and its citizens understand its constituent parts and are willing to compromise to make it a better place. The nationwide euphoria of 1967, especially the overwhelming success of Expo 67, despite the very best efforts made by the federal, provincial and municipal governments, could not mask the divisions and discontent that existed in various parts of Canada, especially Quebec, before and after the Centennial. These remained to be tackled and perhaps resolved in the coming decades.

---

[39] Quoted in Meaghan Beaton, *The Centennial Cure: Commemoration, Identity, and Cultural Capital in Nova Scotia during Canada's 1967 Centennial Celebrations* (Toronto: University of Toronto Press, 2017), 189.

[40] Andrew Parkin and Steve Paikin, 'Robarts' Leadership in Unifying the Country 50 Years Ago Should Be Celebrated', *Toronto Star*, 27 November 2017, https://www.thestar.com/opinion/contributors/robarts-leadership-in-unifying-the-country-50-years-ago-should-be-celebrated/article_19f8c238-6e20-5111-8952-4f4c535c88bc.html.

IMAGE 10 Despite the rain, the Queen and Prime Minister Trudeau walked amongst the spectators on Parliament Hill in Ottawa, on 17 April 1982 as they sign into law the new constitution of Canada. The Canadian Press/Tim Clark, CP212661177.

10

The charter of rights and freedoms, 1982: Remaking the nation

From the country's earliest days, Canada's highest law, its constitution, in effect, was the British North America (BNA) Act, a piece of legislation housed at Westminster after 1867. One hundred and fifteen years after Confederation, Canada finally patriated its constitution, transferring it from the authority of the British Parliament to Canada's own federal and provincial legislatures. This step made Canada a completely sovereign country. The Constitution Act, 1982, updates the BNA Act, now called the Constitution Act, 1867, articulates an amending formula and opens with the new, nationally transformative Canadian Charter of Rights and Freedoms/Charte canadienne des droits et libertés as Part 1 of the constitution.

The road to Canada's complete sovereignty and to a rights-based nation was a long, evolutionary process. Initial steps were taken by Prime Ministers Wilfrid Laurier and Robert Borden, moved further along by William Lyon Mackenzie King and Louis St Laurent, and then their successors, and finally by Prime Minister Pierre Elliott Trudeau. Incrementally, over the years from the late nineteenth century when Laurier refused to participate automatically in British Imperial initiatives around the world, Canada had made more and more of its own decisions. Robert Borden, known for his leadership in the Great War, insisted that Canada would decide how it would participate in it, even if it was legally automatically party to that momentous conflagration from the moment in 1914 when Great Britain declared war on Germany. Borden demanded, and secured, a voice for Canada in the War Cabinet in London, at the Paris Peace Conference after the armistice ending the war, and at the founding of the League of Nations in 1919. With the return to peace, Canada continued to expand its role in international affairs and ending the embarrassing and awkward process of having its external relations conducted through the British Foreign Office. At the Imperial

Conference in London in 1926, Canada was formally recognized as the constitutional equal of Great Britain, an accomplishment formalized five years later in the Statute of Westminster. Numerous attempts after that to bring the constitution to Canada collapsed, often in federal-provincial squabbling, with the main stumbling block usually being the inability of the first ministers to agree on an amending formula. Nevertheless, more steps did get taken. Demonstrations of the dominion's sovereignty included Canada's own declaration of war against Nazi Germany in 1939, its formal creation of Canadian citizenship separate from British subjecthood in 1947 and St Laurent's accomplishment in 1949 of ending appeals to the Judicial Committee of the Privy Council in London, when he made the Supreme Court of Canada the final instance of judicial appeal for Canadians.

St Laurent would have liked the next step to full independence for Canada to be patriating the constitution. He found little agreement, however, on just how to do that or how the constitution might be amended once it came to Canada. He enacted legislation allowing Canada's Parliament to amend items in the BNA Act that were within the exclusive jurisdiction of Ottawa, and he held discussions with the provinces about how best to proceed with constitutional change. Nevertheless, St Laurent was no more successful than others before him in removing what he referred to as 'the last traces of our former colonial status'.[1] Until 1949, the constitution could only be changed by a further act at Westminster. The British North America (No. 2) Act, 1949, confirmed the Terms of Union between Canada and Newfoundland and also granted Canada's Parliament limited power to amend the constitution in many areas of its own jurisdiction, without involvement of the United Kingdom; after that, the constitution was amended in this manner several times until 1975.

Progressive Conservative John George Diefenbaker and Liberal Lester B. Pearson had little more success than their predecessors in dealing with the constitution conundrum. Diefenbaker, who became prime minister in 1957, made great strides, however, in launching a formal protection of rights and freedoms, a process that would be strengthened and completed only some twenty-two years later by Pierre Trudeau, with the Charter of Rights and Freedoms. Although Diefenbaker never created a brand like Trudeau's famous 'Just Society', social justice and the promotion of fundamental rights and freedoms were animating issues for him. His commitment to social justice took many forms, including changes to the rules around less restrictive immigration and supports to address regional disparity. None were more important, however, than his bill of rights, introduced in Parliament on 5 September 1958, as Bill C-60 for the Recognition and Protection of

---

[1]'Full Nationhood for Canada', National Broadcast by the Rt Hon. Louis S. St Laurent, 22 November 1949, Louis St Laurent Papers, MG26-L, vol. 265, file PM-1949 Full Nationhood for Canada-Broadcasts, 22 November 1949, Library and Archives Canada (LAC).

Human Rights and Fundamental Freedoms. Bill C-60 promised to redefine the 'landmarks of liberty' and give 'positive evidence that when Canada accepted the [United Nations] Universal Declaration of Human Rights her acceptance was a dedication to the people of Canada'. As Diefenbaker put it, Bill C-60 'would make Parliament freedom-conscious ... It would act as a landmark by means of which Canadians, through Parliament, would have redeclared those things which have made Canada great ... It would give to Canadians the realization that wherever a Canadian may live, whatever his race, his religion or his colour, the Parliament of Canada would be jealous of his rights'. The bill was limited to areas within federal jurisdiction and did not infringe on provincial prerogatives, but when it came into effect on 10 August 1960, it offered Canadians some protections from their own federal government. Such protections were critical to national unity which was only possible, Diefenbaker said, when Canada accepted 'the principle that every individual, whatever his colour, race or religion, shall be free from discrimination and will have guaranteed equality under the law'.[2] He hoped Canadians would collectively acknowledge, and work to remove, the bigotry and racism that then existed.

Pearson, who became prime minister in April 1963, shared those views and promoted a thriving multi-ethnic Canada within a two-language paradigm: two founding races and many cultures becoming one nation functioning in French and English. For Pearson, unity in diversity was an essential characteristic of the Canadian polity. He hoped to extend diversity beyond the political to the constitutional, strengthening the nation's cultural framework and linking the past with the future. In a conference called 'Federalism for the Future', held in Ottawa with Canada's first ministers in early February 1968, Pearson described what he wanted to see in a new constitution for Canada: recognition of the two official languages to ensure cultural and linguistic equality; a constitutional charter of rights for all Canadians that would cover a wide range of political, legal, egalitarian and linguistic rights and modernization of the BNA Act and, with it, the institutions of federalism, including the Supreme Court, the Senate and the division of powers and jurisdictions between the federal and provincial governments. Pearson had no intention of weakening the federal government or of limiting its authority and responsibilities in mitigating the effects of economic fluctuations on Canadians and in promoting growth and economic equality in all parts of the country.[3] Pearson retired from politics that April, but many of his hopes would be fulfilled by his Minister

---

[2]John G. Diefenbaker, *One Canada: Memoirs of the Right Honourable John G. Diefenbaker*, vol. 2, *The Years of Achievement, 1956–1962* (Toronto: Macmillan, 1975), 257–9.

[3]'Constitutional Conference, Federalism for the Future (5–7 February 1968)', https://primarydocuments.ca/federalism-for-the-future-a-statement-of-policy-by-the-government-of-canada/.

of Justice and Attorney General, Pierre Trudeau, who had been appointed to the portfolio on 4 April 1967. It was at that February 1968 conference that many Canadians began to understand (and even appreciate) Trudeau, as he vociferously challenged Quebec Premier and leader of the Union Nationale, Daniel Johnson, who was calling for a radical restructuring of Canada. Trudeau stood for Canada, and he reminded Johnson that Quebec could satisfy its aspirations within Confederation to the delight of English-speaking audiences, who thought they had found a politician to stand up to Quebec. They had early glimpses of Trudeau, too, when in 1965, he interviewed René Lévesque, then a Quebec politician and minister of the Crown, on a seven-minute segment (Are you a Separatist Mr Lévesque) on CBC-TV's *This Hour Has Seven Days* and pushed him aggressively on how far he would go to advance Quebec's demands.

One of Trudeau's first legislative acts as prime minister was to follow through on the decision made by Pearson and his Cabinet on 26 March 1968, to introduce legislation in Parliament to make Canada officially bilingual. Canada's Official Languages Act came into effect on 7 September 1969, making French and English the country's official languages. A second early legislative initiative was his embrace of official multiculturalism. On 8 October 1971, Trudeau announced 'a policy of multiculturalism within a bilingual framework [as it is] the most suitable means of assuring the cultural freedom of Canadians'. Multiculturalism, said Trudeau, would safeguard freedom and break down discriminatory attitudes and cultural jealousies. Speaking in the House of Commons, he called on all Canadians to 'support and encourage the various cultures and ethnic groups that give structure and vitality to our society' and 'to share their cultural expression and values with other Canadians and so contribute to a rich life for us all'.[4]

Quebec did not see things that way, and in the following years severely tested Canada's national unity. Led by René Lévesque, the Parti Québécois (PQ) assumed power in 1976 on a campaign of independence for Quebec, including the promise of a referendum as part of the party's election platform. Lévesque claimed that the current federal arrangements prevented the province from reaching its full economic, social and cultural potential, and he dismissed the attempts by the Government of Canada to accommodate Quebec through its language and multicultural policies. In 1980 he announced that the province would be holding a referendum on sovereignty-association. Had the referendum been successful, Quebec would have negotiated a new arrangement with Canada making it politically independent while retaining economic ties with Canada through a mutual trade agreement and the sharing of Canada's monetary system.

While Quebec was by no means the sole driver of Trudeau's desire for a new, made-in-Canada constitution, the situation emerging there definitely

---

[4]Canada, House of Commons, *Debates*, 8 October 1971, 8545–6.

lent urgency to the impetus to make that a reality. But Trudeau's dreams for this change and renewal appeared to end abruptly when in 1979 the Liberals lost a general election to the Progressive Conservatives. The new Prime Minister, Joe Clark, however, miscalculated on a crucial confidence vote, which brought down his minority government after just 273 days. The general election that followed returned the Liberals. Trudeau was sworn back in as prime minister on 3 March 1980 and remained in that position until 30 June 1984, when he retired from politics for good.

On 20 May 1980, Quebec held what became its first referendum on sovereignty-association. Trudeau made several appearances in the province on behalf of the 'non' side and played a significant role in the federalist victory. Six days before the vote was held, he addressed an audience in the Paul Sauvé Arena in Montreal. Invoking the memory of Wilfrid Laurier and other great Canadians, he declared, 'My countrymen are not only those in whose veins runs the blood of France. My countrymen are all those people – no matter what their race or their language – whom the fortunes of war, the twists and turns of fate, or their own choice, have brought among us'. Trudeau dismissed the PQ as 'hucksters' who lacked the courage to ask a simple question: Independence, yes or no? A no vote, Trudeau promised, was, nonetheless, a vote to renew federalism and a mandate to renew the constitution.[5]

Constitutional renewal took on new vigour, and from that moment on turned into 'a fierce, 18-month political and legal struggle that dominated headlines and the agendas of every government in the country'.[6] On 6 June 1980, in 'A Statement of Principles for a New Constitution', Trudeau outlined his constitutional goals: recognize Canadians as a free and self-governing people; acknowledge that Canada emerged from the English and French presence on North American soil which had long been the home of Indigenous peoples; accept Canada as a multicultural society made up of different cultures from around the world; promote Canada as a sovereign, constitutional monarchy and a federation founded on democratic principles; recognize French and English as the country's official languages; and embrace and enshrine in the constitution a list of fundamental freedoms, including basic human and language rights that could not be bartered away. He pointed out that he regretted and found it particularly 'distressing and very distasteful', that any premier would say, 'Look, I'll give you freedom of religion or of linguistic equality: I'll give you that, in exchange for the offshore or for fishing rights'. Rights are not negotiable, Trudeau affirmed.[7]

---

[5] 'Transcript of a Speech Given by the Rt Hon. Pierre Elliott Trudeau at the Paul Sauvé Arena in Montreal, 14 May 1980', Prime Minister's Office, Press Release, PETF, MG26 013, vol. 51, S/D, 14 May 1980, Montreal 1980, LAC.

[6] 'Patriation of the Constitution', https://www.thecanadianencyclopedia.ca/en/article/patriation-of-the-constitution.

[7] PET, 'A Statement of Principles for a New Constitution', 6 June 1980, PETF, MG26 014, vol. 4, OSSM, 9 June 1980, Statement of Principles, 1980, LAC.

The tenth round since 1927 of negotiations on the reform of Canada's constitution opened on Monday, 8 September 1980. Attended by the prime minister and all ten provincial premiers, that nationally televised meeting gave Canadians far more than a glimpse of Trudeau's vision for their country. The premiers outlined their objectives, essentially holding that Canada and its peoples would be better served under devolution to the provinces of a long list of federal powers. Then the prime minister spoke up and gave what is widely seen as one of the most important political speeches in Canadian history. 'What we are fighting for here', said Trudeau, 'is a renewed federalism, an improved division of powers and a few other things'. He noted in this thirty-minute speech that there were two competing views of Canada. The first, held by the premiers, he explained, was that the common good could best emerge through 'each province acting with greater independence and greater ability to maximize its own self-interest'. The second view, Trudeau pointed out, was that there was a national interest, which, when pursued nationally, made Canada more than the sum of its parts, more than the sum of ten provinces. Canadians, he argued, want national institutions and a national government capable 'of acting on behalf of all of them ... with the power to speak for all Canadian people'. Trudeau then turned to what really mattered to him, to what he considered to be the essential responsibility of the Government of Canada: the ability to protect the fundamental rights of all of Canada's people. He pointed out that 'basic fundamental rights of the people are so sacred that none of us should have jurisdiction in order to infringe those rights'. In explaining the importance of the constitution, Trudeau said,

> Now I don't cringe at using the word "people." ... the people are the basic authority which we all obey ... but why must the constitution be obeyed? Because it expresses the will of the people, not the parliament in Westminster, not even the Queen, certainly not the Canadian government or the ten provincial governments acting in unison on a declaration or a press release. The people are the basic authority in this country and in some way the constitution must say that and in some way our actions must reflect that.[8]

Trudeau added, echoing St Laurent, that the process whereby Canada must go 'cap in hand, to England to amend its constitution' was not only an 'embarrassment [but] a national disgrace'. It was time to end such an embarrassment and exercise 'the most basic, the most elementary acts of national will', and have 'a Canadian constitution made in Canada by Canadians'. Looking straight into the television camera and ignoring

---

[8]'Transcript of the Prime Minister's Statement at the First Ministers Conference on 8 September 1980', https://primarydocuments.ca/first-ministers-conference-prime-ministers-statement/.

everyone in the room, he said that if the premiers refused to cooperate, they should at least agree to bring the constitution home and

> 'then continue our haggling if we have to in Canada'. 'Well, patriation as we know has been on the agenda of First Ministers conferences since 1927, under six different Prime Ministers but over this long period of 53 years we have miserably failed, we, the politicians, to patriate the constitution and this again has nothing to do with powers. ... It is merely saying that this vestige of colonialism ... has become something of a national disgrace because we have proved that we couldn't exercise the most basic, the most elementary act of national will of saying 'Okay, let's bring the constitution back and have the same constitution here and then continue our haggling if we have to in Canada'. ... It is interesting to note why we have failed. ... between 1927 and 1971 all these attempts failed because there couldn't be agreement on amending formula and heaven knows that many and every variation was looked at. ... if we don't want to continue to fail again ... we must either agree in the next three or four days or we must agree to change the rules of the game and what were the rules of the game was that we couldn't patriate without unanimity ... unless we are prepared to change that rule there will always be some province and probably many which will say "I will be the one that doesn't join the unanimous agreement because ... I will use this as leverage for me to increase my powers as a provincial government" and that is what has happened in the last nine years.

In concluding, Trudeau said,

> I can't believe that after hearing speeches made this morning, I can't believe that we wouldn't all agree ... that there will be no bargaining between packages, that we won't trade powers for us governments or politicians against something that the people really want, the right to have a Canadian constitution made in Canada and which protects all their fundamental rights.[9]

Trudeau demanded that the constitution be patriated and that it include a charter of rights and freedoms guaranteeing fundamental freedoms and the full protection of the law for every Canadian, regardless of origin, race, colour or sex.[10]

---

[9] "Transcript of the Prime Minister's Statement at the First Ministers Conference on 8 September 1980', https://primarydocuments.ca/first-ministers-conference-prime-ministers-statement/.

[10] "Transcript of the Prime Minister's Statement at the First Ministers Conference on 8 September 1980', https://primarydocuments.ca/first-ministers-conference-prime-ministers-statement/ and see Raymond B. Blake and John D. Whyte, '40 Years Later: A Look Back at the Pierre Trudeau Speech That Defined Canada', *The Conversation*, 2 September 2020, https://theconversation.com/40-years-later-a-look-back-at-the-pierre-trudeau-speech-that-defined-canada-143983.

This conference on amending and patriating the constitution was a failure, too. Trudeau lost patience with the premiers. Having consulted with his caucus and Cabinet, on 2 October – as he had forewarned in this speech at the previous constitutional conference – Trudeau announced that the federal government would act unilaterally, that Ottawa would make a unilateral request to the British Parliament to patriate Canada's constitution. The Conservatives and Opposition Leader Joe Clark strongly opposed the plan and used every possible procedural device to halt this resolution. It was contested in the courts, right up to the Supreme Court of Canada, as *Reference Re Resolution to amend the Constitution* – also known as the Patriation Reference – in late spring 1981. The courts ruled that Ottawa had the constitutional authority to proceed unilaterally, but doing so contravened Canadian legislative and constitutional convention. The Supreme Court issued its decision on 28 September 1981 and stated, 'Constitutional convention plus constitutional law equal the total constitution of the country'.[11]

Negotiations resumed, and after another difficult and fractious year, Trudeau's 'one last time' federal-provincial conference on constitutional reform began in Ottawa on 2 November 1981. Three days later, 'the constitutional fight was essentially over'.[12] Quebec was not part of the deal. The English-speaking premiers broke with Lévesque, and on the evening of 5 November, in his absence, agreed to arrangements with the federal government. Quebec saw this step as an abject betrayal and called it the 'Night of the Long Knives'/*Nuit des longs couteaux*. Despite Trudeau's insistence on a 'people's' constitution, Canada's constitutional odyssey came to an end through elite accommodation.

More contentious since that date have been aspects of Part 1 of the Constitution Act, 1982, the Canadian Charter of Rights and Freedoms. According to the Government of Canada,

> since 1982, the Charter has been an essential part of Canada's democracy, and it will continue to shape our identity as a nation. The Charter affirms that we are a multicultural society and that it must be read and understood with this in mind. The rights and freedoms guaranteed in the Charter govern how governments act, including the right to equality, freedom of expression and the right not to be deprived of life, liberty or security of the person, except in accordance with the principles of fundamental justice. It also protects the rights of First Nations, Inuit, and Métis in Canada.[13]

---

[11]'Patriation Reference', https://www.thecanadianencyclopedia.ca/en/article/constitution-reference.

[12]'Patriation of the Constitution', https://www.thecanadianencyclopedia.ca/en/article/patriation-of-the-constitution.

[13]'Learn about the Charter', https://www.justice.gc.ca/eng/csj-sjc/rfc-dlc/ccrf-ccdl/learn-apprend.html.

Several provincial leaders were concerned during the constitutional negotiations that a charter of rights and freedoms would give courts and judges too much power and restrict the right of provincial governments to make laws as they saw fit. A solution was section 33, the notwithstanding clause, which allows a federal, provincial or territorial government to temporarily override certain Charter rights for periods of five years. While the federal government to date has never used section 33, several provinces have done so to restrict, for example, linguistic rights and gender expression for students under sixteen while at school. Some of those who participated in the constitutional negotiations have argued that section 33 was never intended for such issues.[14] The fact remains, however, that in November 1981 – in the rush to secure a deal – little consideration was given to the wider impact and implications of the notwithstanding clause. For Trudeau, constitutional renewal had reached a successful conclusion, though later, he, too, recognized the problem with section 33.

Saturday, 17 April 1982, was a windy, rainy and otherwise miserable day in Ottawa, but the prime minister was radiant and celebratory, as Queen Elizabeth II proclaimed the country's new constitution. Canada had severed its last colonial link: its constitution was finally an act of the Canadian Parliament. With the Constitution Act, 1982, the nation had acquired full and complete national sovereignty. This document, proclaimed Trudeau, embodied the Canadian ideal 'where men and women of Aboriginal ancestry, of French and British heritage, of the diverse cultures of the world, demonstrated the will to share this land in peace, in justice, and with mutual respect'. Canada was now a nation 'where every person is free to fulfill himself or herself to the utmost, unhindered by the arbitrary actions of government'. In Trudeau's idea of Canada, it was not ethnic particularisms that would be privileged but the rights of the individual. Canada had achieved political solidarity, he hoped, by building a national identity that made space for, and accepted, the legitimacy and diversity of every member in all the communities coexisting within a bilingual nation. Equally important for national unity, the principle of equalization – the sharing of wealth between the more and less fortunate provinces that began in 1957 – was included in the constitution so that the poorer provinces could discharge their obligations without excessive taxation.[15]

This moment also meant that Trudeau had created a Canada where there was no single or dual ethnicity, only citizens bound together by their

---

[14]"Democracy's Sledgehammer: The Use of the Notwithstanding Clause for Saskatchewan's Bill 137, "The Parent's Bill of Rights"', 26 September 2024, https://www.schoolofpublicpolicy.sk.ca/research-ideas/publications-and-policy-insight/policy-brief/bill-137.php.

[15]'Remarks by the PM at the Proclamation of the Constitution Ceremony, 17 April 1982', PETF, MG26 014, vol. 6, Original Speeches, Statements, and Messages, 17 April 1982, Proclamation Ceremony 1982, LAC.

collective belief in the equality of all through a set of shared values and rights. The rights philosophy created a new form of identity and attachment to the nation-state. As had George-Étienne Cartier in the 1860s, Trudeau explained to Canadians that diversity was not a problem but a strength to be celebrated.[16] The national narrative was redefined and strengthened by Trudeau, creating a civic nationalism that replaced ethnicity as the defining national characteristic with a new political society based on a philosophical vision around liberal individualism as the organizing principle for the nation-state. For Trudeau, the constitution entrenched cultural diversity and multiculturalism, which was a reversal of early government policies to assimilate immigrants and Indigenous peoples. Trudeau's policy of official multiculturalism ensured that all Canadians could keep their particular identity and take pride in their particular heritage, but they had to do so through either the English or French language and accepting what he considered core values of being a Canadian. Multiculturalism asked Canadians to accept all cultures and to recognize that pluralism and ethnic diversity would strengthen, not threaten, the Canadian nation. Culture was now an individual matter, while the state's responsibility was to protect individual rights. Under this new form of citizenship and attachment to the nation-state, rights became the basis of the political community.[17]

With the Constitution Act, 1982, the Charter of Rights and Freedoms came into force. Section 27 explicitly identifies multiculturalism as a characteristic of the nation, in that it reads, 'This Charter shall be interpreted in a manner consistent with the preservation and enhancement of the multicultural heritage of Canadians'. Section 15 came into effect three years after the rest of the Charter, on 17 April 1985, to give governments time to bring their laws into line with the equality rights that section guarantees. With special reference to New Brunswick, section 16.1(1) was added to the Charter in 1993, and it states: 'The English linguistic community and the French linguistic community in New Brunswick have equality of status and equal rights and privileges, including the right to distinct educational institutions and such distinct cultural institutions as are necessary for the preservation and promotion of those communities'.[18]

Liberal individualism, individual rights and freedoms, civic nationalism, and the promotion of diversity and multiculturalism became celebrated as Canadian ideals, as the normative approach to fostering a sense of belonging. Even so, many Canadians regretted what had been lost in this new national narrative. Quebec insisted that Canada was neither a collection of individuals nor a multicultural nation; it was two nations, one francophone

---

[16]PM's July 1st Message 1972, PETF, MG 26 Series 011, vol. 67, file PM's Speeches 1972 67–4, PM's July 1st Message, 1972, LAC.
[17]See Will Kymlicka and Wayne Norman, 'Return of the Citizen: A Survey of Recent Work on Citizenship Theory', *Ethics* 104, no. 2 (1994): 352–81.
[18]https://www.justice.gc.ca/eng/csj-sjc/rfc-dlc/ccrf-ccdl/check/art16.html.

and one anglophone, even if Quebecers clearly embraced the rights regime being promoted by Trudeau. First Nations and other Indigenous peoples, who experienced their own renaissance in the 1950s and 1960s, could never accept that they were part of a multicultural (immigrant) community and fumed that under the rights paradigm their grievances were neither recognized nor settled (discussed later in this volume). Apart from Quebec and Indigenous peoples, there were also those who complained about 'hyphenated Canadians'. Especially after the passage of the Canadian Multiculturalism Act, in 1988 by Brian Mulroney, an accepted critique of the policy of multiculturalism and diversity emerged and an increasing demand by the late 1990s and beyond for the restoration of citizenship education in the public education system and elsewhere to create a shared sense of belonging. Prime Ministers Jean Chrétien, Paul Martin and Stephen Harper shared such views.

Notable among such critics were Trinidadian-Canadian author, Neil Bissoondath, and former British Columbia premier and later Liberal MP and federal minister of health, Ujjal Dosanjh who had been born in Kalan, a village in Jalandhar, in 1947 shortly after the end of British rule in India. In 1994 Neil Bissoondath published his widely acclaimed and controversial book, *Selling Illusions: The Cult of Multiculturalism in Canada*. He asserted that multiculturalism made newcomers think more about where they came from than about where they were, namely, in Canada. He vehemently contradicted the contention that Trudeau's aspirations in this regard had any positive effect, stating that 'the multicultural society has tended to diminish the role and autonomy of the individual by insisting on placing individuals within preconceived, highly stereotypical confines'.[19] BC's Ujjal Dosanjh, too, has harboured and expressed his profound concerns about a 'blind devotion to multiculturalism'. He explained his views like this:

> What you want is creative multiculturalism, generous multiculturalism, but not unthinking or mindless multiculturalism where everything anybody brings to this country is acceptable … Diversity is great if we can begin to live with each other in equality, in understanding … but we also understand our collective obligations to building a better society. If we can't live together with each other properly and make concessions to each other, then this phrase that politicians use – that diversity is a strength – is nonsensical.[20]

---

[19] Neil Bissoondath, *Selling Illusions: The Cult of Multiculturalism in Canada* (Toronto: Penguin Books, 1994), 224.
[20] Jason Proctor quoting Ujjal Dosanjh in 'Angus Reid Institute Poll: Canadians Want Minorities to Do More to "Fit In,"' CBC News, 3 October 2016, https://www.cbc.ca/news/canada/british-columbia/poll-canadians-multiculturalism-immigrants-1.3784194.

Questions have also been raised about 'reasonable accommodation', concerning, for example, what levels of accommodation should be provided for new immigrant communities or for religious communities (specifically in Quebec). Section 15(1) of the Charter states: 'Every individual is equal before and under the law and has the right to the equal protection and equal benefit of the law without discrimination and, in particular, without discrimination based on race, national or ethnic origin, colour, religion, sex, age or mental or physical disability'. Although not a term expressly used in the Charter, 'reasonable accommodation' may involve adapting a practice or general operating rule or granting an exemption to someone facing discrimination. This would be in accordance with section 15(2) of the Charter, which states: 'At the same time as it protects equality, the Charter also allows for certain laws or programs that aim to improve the conditions of disadvantaged individuals or groups. For example, programs aimed at improving employment opportunities for women, Indigenous peoples, visible minorities, or those with mental or physical disabilities are allowed under subsection 15(2)'.[21]

Some Canadians have insisted that the Charter of Rights and Freedoms, which brought in its train judicial activism and a preoccupation on rights, has led to a clear imbalance between rights and responsibilities and undermined Canadian democracy, as Ujjal Dosanjh argued, for example.[22] There emerged a 'civic deficit', some maintained, characterized by disputes by particular groups to defend their specific interests and by a lack of knowledge of democratic values, of civic responsibility and of the responsibilities of citizenship.[23] These and similar criticisms led to and are exemplified by the new Canadian citizenship guide, to be used by newcomers studying for their citizenship test. Issued by Conservative Prime Minister Stephen Harper's government in 2009, revised in 2012 and entitled *Discover Canada: The Rights and Responsibilities of Citizenship*, its contents represent what 'might be considered a fundamental shift in Canadian citizenship from one emphasising multiculturalism, rights and diversity to one that encourages the integration of newcomers into Canadian society'.[24] The political right has been particularly critical of multiculturalism, lamenting the breakdown of social cohesion and the weakening of traditional values, and characterizing the Canadian state as being in perpetual crisis divided by a collection of rival

---

[21] https://www.justice.gc.ca/eng/csj-sjc/rfc-dlc/ccrf-ccdl/check/art15.html.

[22] Frederick Lee Morton and Rainer Knopff, *The Charter Revolution and the Court Party* (Peterborough: Broadview, 2000); and William Gairdner, *The Trouble with Canada* (Toronto: Stoddart, 1990).

[23] William Galston, *Liberal Purposes: Goods, Virtues and Duties in the Liberal State* (Cambridge: Cambridge University Press, 1991).

[24] Raymond B. Blake, 'A New Canadian Dynamism? From Multiculturalism and Diversity to History and Heritage. Canadian Citizenship under Stephen Harper', *British Journal of Canadian Studies* 26, no. 1 (2013): 80.

rights groups (LGBTQIA2S+ versus heterosexual, Indigenous peoples versus non-Indigenous, French-speakers versus English-speakers, immigrants versus native-born, rural versus urban and other points of cleavage) accentuated by the rejection of traditions and a national history, and government failure to defend traditional institutions and values they believe necessary for stability and bolstering a national community. Recent observers have suggested that the promotion of multiculturalism provides 'a tacit basis for discrimination and racial violence' long existing and still evident in Canada. They contend that multiculturalism allowed Canadians 'to ignore the harsh lived reality of many minorities and to refute the claim that racism is alive and well in Canada'.[25]

If today multiculturalism is criticized for its failure to significantly address long-standing racism against ethno-cultural communities, many Canadians still see Canada's Constitution Act, 1982 – the patriated constitution, which begins with the Canadian Charter of Rights and Freedoms – to be among Trudeau's most laudable accomplishments and key to his shaping the nation in positive ways. Trudeau worked determinedly to save Canada from its particularisms, which he believed threatened to destroy it. The challenge was to mould Canada's diversity into a unique identity that could sustain the nation through minimizing differences and accentuating points of commonality to thereby achieve enough social cohesion to keep the disparate elements united. For Trudeau, a constitution made in Canada by Canadians, codified rights and cultural pluralism would be the markers of a strong national Canadian identity and true cohesion.

---

[25] Cary Wu et al., 'As Asian Canadian Scholars, We Must #StopAsianHate by Fighting All Forms of Racism', *The Conversation*, 15 April 2021, https://theconversation.com/as-asian-canadian-scholars-we-must-stopasianhate-by-fighting-all-forms-of-racism-157743.

IMAGE 11 Signing of Mexican president Carlos Salinas, US president George H.W. Bush and Canadian prime minister Brian Mulroney participate in the signing of the North American Free Trade Agreement in October 1992. Unknown Author, George Bush President Library and Museum. Public Domain, https://commons.wikimedia.org/wiki/File:Nafta.jpg.

11

The free trade election, 1988: Towards a new nationalism for Canadians

For a very long period of Canada's history, protectionism and economic nationalism were standard policy features defining Canada's identity. With the general election of 21 November 1988, Progressive Conservative Prime Minister Brian Mulroney put that well-established Canadian narrative on trial and made voters the jury. Mulroney's free trade initiative articulated a new, confident and mature Canadian nationalism. After nearly a century of protectionism, however, it was no surprise that many Canadians were worried. Up to this moment in time, few issues had agitated voters like Canada's relationship with the United States, and most especially the issue of free trade.

In the mid-nineteenth century, British North America (BNA) prospered under the 1854 Reciprocity Treaty between the United Kingdom and the United States. Although this free exchange of natural resources was at times controversial on both sides of the border, there was dismay and anger when the United States cancelled the treaty and from 1866 it was no longer operative. This was one of the concerns that propelled politicians in the BNA colonies towards Confederation, with hopes of creating a single Canadian market to replace the American one. Canada's nation-building Prime Minister, John A. Macdonald, implemented the protectionist National Policy in 1879, imposing high tariffs on imported goods. Its purpose was to counter the growing wave of protectionism in the United States and shield Canadian manufacturers from American competition. The Liberal Party of Canada headed into the 1891 general election under Wilfrid Laurier, their leader since 1887, with unrestricted reciprocity – complete free trade – with the United States as their major campaign promise. The Conservatives, still led by Macdonald, were completely opposed to this idea. They called the Liberal plan 'veiled treason' that would lead to the destruction of Canada and its annexation to the United States, even though just three years earlier

Macdonald himself had attempted to secure a trade deal with the United States. The Conservatives won. As the campaign got underway, Macdonald's uttered one of his most famous lines, 'A British subject I was born, a British subject I will die', although it should be noted that notions of identity were then complex, as neither Scotland (Macdonald's birthplace) nor Canada (his home since the age of five) possessed their own citizenship or, indeed, technically speaking, any citizenship at all as, until 1946, all Canadians were British subjects. Elaborating on his position, he added, 'With my utmost effort, with my latest breath, will I oppose the "veiled treason" which attempts by sordid means and mercenary proffers to lure our people from their allegiance'. Macdonald made opposition to the Liberals' free trade policy a question of national survival.[1]

Shortly after losing that election, the Liberals quietly dropped their commitment to free trade for a generation. Then, in 1911, with the US Congress under pressure to bring down consumer prices, Wilfrid Laurier, prime minister of Canada since 1896, managed to negotiate a reciprocity pact with the US President William Howard Taft. The arrangement was an attractive one for Canada. But industrial and manufacturing interests mobilized opposition. They claimed that before long the United States would be demanding that Canada also lower its tariffs with the result being American domination of Canada, followed thereafter by Canada's complete political absorption into the United States. Prominent American politicians only heightened that fear by uttering predictions that Canada would soon become part of their country. Champ Clark, speaker of the US House of Representatives from 1911 to 1919, said he looked forward to the day when 'the American flag will float over every square foot of the British North American possessions, clear to the North Pole'. In the general election held on 21 September 1911, Canadian voters soundly rejected Laurier's reciprocity pact and ousted the Liberals. 'We must decide', Opposition Leader Robert Borden had declared, 'whether the spirit of Canadianism or Continentalism shall prevail on the northern half of the continent'.[2] Although Borden himself was not an opponent of free trade, the Conservatives had discovered that their mixing of British imperialism (which Quebec very much opposed) and Canadian nationalism worked well with voters. For at that time, as historian Carl Berger famously put it, 'imperialism was one form of Canadian nationalism'.[3] Continentalism was another. Among those

---

[1]'Election 1891: A Question of Loyalty', https://www.thecanadianencyclopedia.ca/en/article/election-1891-a-question-of-loyalty-feature.
[2]'Canada and the World: A History – 1896–1914: The Laurier Era, section: Reciprocity and the Fall of Laurier', https://epe.lac-bac.gc.ca/100/206/301/faitc-aecic/history/2013-05-03/www.international.gc.ca/history-histoire/world-monde/1896-1914-1.aspx@lang=eng#reciprocity. See Robert Craig Brown, *Robert Laird Borden: A Biography* (Toronto: Macmillan, 1975).
[3]Carl Berger, *Sense of Power: Studies in the Ideas of Canadian Imperialism, 1864–1914* (Toronto: University of Toronto Press, 1970), 2.

in Canada who advocated this path for Canada and the United States were Goldwin Smith and Erastus Wiman, who believed the dismantling of tariff between the two nations would foster economic growth and prosperity for both and help unite the British world.[4]

William Lyon Mackenzie King also spurned free trade, perhaps because he feared a repeat of the Laurier debacle. Some of his influential ministers and various other officials assured him, however, that free trade would be good for Canada and Canada's prosperity. In November 1935 King and President Franklin D. Roosevelt signed the Canada-US Reciprocal trade agreement which reduced tariffs between the two countries, although it was much narrower than the 1854 treaty on reciprocity. It was expanded in 1938 and the outbreak of war a year later encouraged, even necessitated further continental integration as Canada and the United States saw a significant increase in military and economic integration. This included establishing a permanent alliance for continental defence, integrating defence production and coordinating economic efforts through agreements like the Ogdensburg Agreement and the Hyde Park Agreement. Nevertheless, the 1938 bilateral agreement on trade was suspended in 1948, after both countries signed the General Agreement on Tariffs and Trade (GATT). Evidently, this last step pleased the prime minister, for on 24 March 1948, just two months before his retirement from politics, Mackenzie King confided to his now-famous diary, 'I would no more think of at my time of life and at this stage of my career attempting any movement of the kind [free trade with the US] than I would of flying to the South pole'.[5] As prime minister, John G. Diefenbaker worried mightily about Canada's dependence on trade with the United States and attempted to divert at least 15 per cent of trade away from the United States to the Commonwealth and Europe.

At least as part of a larger system of multilateral trade, with time freer trade with the United States did find its way back onto the Canadian agenda. In January 1965, Prime Minister Lester Pearson and US President Lyndon Johnson signed the Canada–US Automotive Products Trade Agreement (APTA, or more commonly, the Auto Pact), a limited form of free trade in the automotive sector. One of the first groups to float expanding this idea was the Economic Council of Canada, as in its 1975 report, *Looking Outward: A New Trade Strategy for Canada*. Like earlier proponents, the Council linked free trade with increased productivity and economic prosperity. 'Canadians are, in general', these economists reported, 'relatively complacent about the future of the country's economy, [convinced that] Canada's economic outlook is that of a bountiful land growing ever more prosperous'. That was not the

---

[4]Gary Pennanen, 'Goldwin Smith, Wharton Barker, and Erastus Wiman: Architects of Commercial Union', *Journal of Canadian Studies/Revue d'études canadiennes*, 14, no. 3 (1979): 50–62.
[5]Quoted in Jack Lawrence Granatstein, *Yankee Go Home? Canadians and Anti-Americanism* (Toronto: Harper Collins 1996), 92–3.

case, however. Given Canada's low productivity, its small internal market, inadequate industrial plant size and high tariffs, there was, in fact, little reason for such optimism. The Council even rejected concern that freer trade would weaken Canadian sovereignty.[6] In 1983, the Department of External Affairs (DEA) published *A Review of Canadian Trade Policy: A Background Document to Canadian Trade Policy for the 1980s*. According to the DEA, the situation was not good. Instead, it was clear that Trudeau's nationalist policies, that had resulted in the creation of the Canada Development Corporation (CDC) in 1971, the Foreign Investment Review Agency (FIRA) in 1973 and the National Energy Program (NEP) in 1980, as well as his much-vaunted 'Third Option' to reduce Canada's dependence on trade with the United States in favour of enhanced economic links with Asia Pacific and the European Community, were all pretty much failures.[7]

In June 1983, Brian Mulroney became leader of the Progressive Conservative Party of Canada, replacing Joe Clark, who had led the party since 1976 and was prime minister from 4 June 1979 to 13 December 1980. During the 1983 leadership campaign, Mulroney was pro-business, but against free trade. Yet, soon after that, he started talking about Canada as a North American nation, one that must have a good relationship with the powerful neighbour to its south. Canada, he argued, had to reject the inward and interventionist policies pursued for most of its history. Mulroney found Pierre Trudeau's economic nationalism to be particularly misguided. Like his predecessors, Mulroney saw trade as the life blood of the nation. He pointed out, however, that Canadians to their detriment were ignoring the fact that the United States was the largest market for their goods, services and investment, and that they were America's leading trading partner, while trade between the two nations was being impeded by significant barriers and an array of non-tariff measures. Mulroney told Canadians on many occasions that if they just wished to do so, they could do things differently. By the mid-1980s, many of them were precisely thinking that.

With the NEP and rising American protectionism adding increasing harm to Canada's trading relations, even the Liberal Party began to consider the prospects of more sectoral free trade with the United States. In 1982 Trudeau appointed his former Finance Minister Donald S. Macdonald to head the Royal Commission on the Economic Union and Development Prospects for Canada. This has been characterized as 'probably one of the most important Royal Commissions in Canadian history', with Mulroney using its 1985 report 'to justify his about-face on free trade'. The Macdonald Commission came out in favour of free trade with the United States, giving that debate renewed energy and bolstering free trade's legitimacy. But before the Commission had even

---

[6] Economic Council of Canada, *Looking Outward: A New Trade Strategy for Canada* (Ottawa: Information Canada, 1975), 26.
[7] Canada, DEA, *A Review of Canadian Trade Policy: A Background Document to Canadian Trade Policy for the 1980s* (Ottawa: Supply and Services Canada, 1983), 223–24.

finished its work, in a statement made on 19 November 1984, Macdonald advised that 'Canada should take a "leap of faith" into a comprehensive free trade agreement with the United States'.[8]

Just weeks earlier, on 4 September, in the largest landslide victory in Canadian political history, the Progressive Conservatives were swept to power, soundly defeating the Liberals, led at this time by John Turner. Almost immediately after being sworn in as prime minister, Mulroney began trade negotiations with the US administration. On 26 September, he met with President Ronald Reagan, who he knew favoured free trade with Canada. Lest there be any confusion – perhaps more to reassure Canadians than Americans – at that meeting in Washington, DC, Mulroney insisted that once the historic Canada-US relations had been 'refurbished', it would not mean Canadian 'subservience', but would signal 'a degree of maturity and understanding that our trade and our technological advances hinge upon an excellent relationship [and] there would be no "erosion of Canadian identity, or integrity or sovereignty"'.[9] He presented Canada as a loyal friend, one that was willing to give the United States 'the benefit of the doubt', as with any great friend.[10]

Increasingly, after being opposed for decades, Canada's business community started to come out in support free trade. In 1984 the Canadian Manufacturers Association reversed its long-standing opposition as did several provinces, including Alberta and Quebec, the two most disaffected and alienated – but also two of the wealthiest and most powerful – in Confederation. Government and the private sector both had come to see that Canada could not guarantee access to markets through a continued reliance on the 1947 multilateral General Agreement on Tariffs and Trade. The public, too, was supportive: in 1985 an Environics Research survey found that two-thirds of Canadians favoured a free trade deal with the United States, even though polls also warned that Canadians continued to worry about the loss of sovereignty in a trade deal with the Americans.

Mulroney was in the United States once again that December to address the Economic Club of New York. Speaking to an enthusiastic audience, he proclaimed that Canada was open for business, and then he announced that between Canada and United Sates, the 'most noteworthy measure of our relations is in our economic ties'. Canada's motives were 'noble and our course clear', he asserted, as 'two sovereign democracies, sharing the same continent, have much that will benefit each other and even more that will enhance the cause of a durable peace in the world'. He did concede

---

[8]'Continentalizing Canada: The Politics and Legacy of the Macdonald Royal Commission', https://cbra.library.utoronto.ca/items/show/16538.
[9]Quoted in William Johnson, in 'Good "Chemistry" Hailed: Mulroney-Reagan Talks Yield Hope for Close Ties', *Globe and Mail*, 26 September 1984, 1.
[10]Quoted in Lawrence Martin, 'Cozying-Up to Reagan Full of Pitfalls for Mulroney', *Globe and Mail*, 25 September 1984, 7.

that 'in the minds of some Canadians, such statements are tantamount to servility [where] simple acts of friendship are ridiculed because they are instantly equated with a loss of sovereignty'. All the same, many Canadians, he said, were 'unimpressed and unmoved' by such misguided reactions, as they had gained a 'renewed sense of confidence in themselves as a nation'.[11]

A few months later, Ronald Reagan had a very charming and very busy brief visit with Brian Mulroney in Quebec City. Because the President arrived there on St Patrick's Day, 17 March, and both leaders were of Irish ancestry, the event was dubbed the 'Shamrock Summit'. The two discussed numerous issues, including military planning, upgrading the North's 1957 Distant Early Warning Line (DEW Line), acid rain reduction, and the management, research and enhancement of Pacific salmon stocks of mutual concern. Most significant, however, for the moment examined in this chapter, was a statement they signed the next day. Entitled 'Declaration by the Prime Minister of Canada and the President of the United States of America Regarding Trade in Goods and Services', it states,

> We believe that the challenge to our two countries is to invigorate our unique economic relationship ... We have today agreed to give the highest priority to finding mutually-acceptable means to reduce and eliminate existing barriers to trade in order to secure and facilitate trade and investment flows ... As a first step, we commit ourselves to halt protectionism in cross-border trade in goods and services.[12]

Months later, on 26 September 1985, Mulroney announced in the House of Commons that Canada would be seeking a bilateral trade agreement with the United States. 'For half a century', he declared, 'Canada has pursued a policy of trade liberalization. Today, more than ever, our prosperity and that of our partners depends on an expanding world trade and a growing world economy'.[13] He informed Parliament that he had notified President Reagan of his interest in pursuing a trade agreement between the two countries, as trade was 'critical to Canada's livelihood'. Mulroney went on to assert, 'No responsible person anywhere today advocates protectionism as a national economic strategy', because a strong protectionist impulse, even in Canada, was 'always self-defeating'. The path to free trade with the United States would be difficult, he admitted, but 'to shrink from this challenge and

---

[11]'New Climate for Investment in Canada', notes for a speech by the Rt. Hon. Brian Mulroney, PM, to the members of the Economic Club of New York, NY, 10 December 1984, Statements and Speeches, 84/18, Cultural and Public Affairs Information Bureau (CPAIB), Department of External Affairs (DEA).
[12]'Joint Canada-United States Declarations on Trade and International Security, 18 March 1985', https://www.reaganlibrary.gov/archives/speech/joint-canada-united-states-declarations-trade-and-international-security.
[13]'Canada/US Trade Negotiations', statement by the Rt. Hon. Brian Mulroney, PM, to the House of Commons, 26 September 1985, Statements and Speeches, 85/11, CPAIB, DEA.

opportunity would be an act of timidity unworthy of Canada. It would be contrary to our national interest'. Mulroney insisted that any trade deal would be purely commercial: 'Our political sovereignty, our system of social programs, our commitments to fight regional disparities, our unique cultural identity, our special linguistic character – the essence of Canada are not at issue in these negotiations'.[14]

In enumerating the benefits of free trade, Mulroney made clear that the cultural and social features that defined Canada 'are not at issue in those negotiations'. During a visit to the University of Chicago in December 1985, in a speech entitled 'On Being Good Neighbours: Canada and the United States', he pointed out a distinction between Canada and the United States: 'In the United States you cast the net of national security more widely than we do; in Canada we cast the net of cultural sovereignty more widely than you'. Cultural sovereignty was as important as political sovereignty, and neither was negotiable.[15]

The free trade issue in the next few years would continue to be as contentious as it was enduring. Mulroney's House of Commons announcement stirred up old shibboleths and the anti-American sentiment that had marked earlier attempts towards such a trade deal. As Mulroney would explain, however, his free trade initiative did not run counter to the major currents of Canadian history. Indeed, it was ingrained in the Canadian story: free trade had been the goal for both Macdonald and Laurier; even Mackenzie King and Pierre Trudeau towards the end of their tenure had toyed with sectoral free trade. All the same, Canadians had been conditioned to fear for their cultural industries, social programmes and sovereignty if continental free trade became a reality. Against this deeply ingrained view, Mulroney asked Canadians to be confident that they could thrive in a new economic relationship. He spoke directly to Canadians about free trade over the CBC network on 16 June 1986, where he outlined his rationale for the change in Canadian policy. The new trade initiative would 'create new wealth and new jobs', he promised. He was aware that his enemies and 'neo-reactionaries, the prophets of protectionism, the apostles of the status quo' would attempt to stall the economic opportunities ahead. He called on Canadians to have faith in themselves and their nation. Free trade negotiations would 'represent an important turning point in the life of our country', even if 'the road ahead will not be easy, nor without risks'.[16]

---

[14]'Canada/US Trade Negotiations', statement by the Rt. Hon. Brian Mulroney, PM, to the House of Commons, 26 September 1985, Statements and Speeches, 85/11, CPAIB, DEA.
[15]'On Being Good Neighbours: Canada and the United States', notes for an address by the Rt. Hon. Brian Mulroney, PM, to the University of Chicago and the Time Speakers Forum, 4 December 1985, 15, Statements and Speeches, 85/28, Cultural and Public Affairs Information Bureau (CPAIB), DEA.
[16]Quoted in Hugh Winsor, 'Mulroney's TV Speech Imitates Trudeau Style in Appeal to Emotions', *Globe and Mail*, 17 June 1986, 4.

In a major Cabinet shuffle on 30 June 1986, Mulroney moved British Columbia MP Pat Carney from energy, mines and resources, where she'd been instrumental in dismantling Trudeau's unpopular NEP, to international trade, where she would be involved in negotiating the Canada-US Free Trade Agreement that came into force on 1 January 1989. Carney told conference delegates at Dalhousie University in Halifax in 1987 that the federal government's stand on free trade 'represents a new vision of Canada, a strong, vibrant economy with a leading role to play internationally. What greater aspiration for those of us who love this country and believe fully in its potential', she asked. 'What greater demonstration of Canadian nationalism than supporting a free trade agreement that will open up new economic opportunities and help us make the most of them'.[17]

In his Leaders' Day address after the 1986 Throne Speech, Mulroney encouraged Canadians to be confident that their 'culture and dignity [are] strong enough to stand up in international trading blocs, create jobs at home and strengthen our culture and identity'. In addressing the issue of free trade with the United States, he spoke almost as a visionary:

> We say we can make a good deal for Canada which will bring benefits to Canada and provide new opportunities for growth and jobs for Canadian youth. Let the timorous and the fearful fret. Let them say that Canada cannot compete internationally. Let them talk about the protectionism they want here. "Protect us," they say, "we are not big enough. Protect us against les méchants de l'exterieur. Give us the protection. Build tariff walls." This is for the weak and for those who care not about Canada. I tell you, Mr. Speaker, that Canadians are competitive. Canadians are courageous. Canadians are daring, and I tell you, Mr. Speaker, that when the history of this day is written, it shall be recorded who the daring were, and the daring were those who had confidence in Canada and in themselves.[18]

To Mulroney, Canadian competitiveness in the North American market and globally were all second nature. He was from a community in Quebec that depended on aluminium, as well as pulp and paper, for the export market. He had been president of the Iron Ore Company of Canada, which exported much of its product. 'We have always known the importance of international markets', he said at the 1987 Canada Day celebrations in his

---

[17] Pat Carney, 'Canadian Trade at a Cross Roads', in M. Smith and F. Stone, eds., *Assessing the Canada-U.S. Free Trade Agreement* (Halifax: Institute for Research on Public Policy/Institut de recherches politiques, 1987), 157.
[18] Canada, House of Commons, *Debates*, Leaders' Day Address, 3 October 1986, 51; Brian Mulroney, Address to the House of Commons, 3 October 1986, https://lipad.ca/full/1986/10/03/15/; and in Michael Rose, 'Free from the Start', *Maclean's*, 13 October 1986, 22–3.

native Baie-Comeau. 'We lived by them; we saw it in our jobs and in our very lives. We saw the importance of securing those markets and securing new ones, and we have never feared for our sovereignty or our identity'.[19] Free trade, the way he framed it, could heal the national fissures he had inherited. It would bring greater wealth to less-advantaged regions and would give the Western provinces 'the degree of prosperity, regional equity and justice that has been too long denied. We can't have two Canadas, one rich and one poor', he said, echoing words that Trudeau had spoken so frequently. In Mulroney's formula, free trade would be the great equalizer.[20] Mulroney's story of Canada pitted a market-oriented internationalist vision against a government-centred nationalist one. 'To build requires vision and courage, to destroy requires neither', Mulroney declared to Albertans in early August 1988: 'Nation building is not for the fearful or the faint of heart. Great challenges require bold responses and firm direction'.[21]

In the House of Commons, on 30 August 1988, Mulroney introduced the enabling legislation for the Canada-US Free Trade Agreement. 'It will bring an era of prosperity, creating opportunities for all Canadians and for all regions. It will also sustain Canada's much valued social programs and allow the government to continue to support cultural initiatives as well as embark on a series of national policies ranging from environmental protection to regional development to childcare'. Canada would become a global 'beacon of hope for the forces of more open trade'. The main achievement, though, he rejoiced in pointing out, was not so much the removal of tariffs or new rules of trade, but Canadians' new national identity: 'Canada is surer of its identity today than it ever was before throughout its history'. Trade with the United States had grown after 1945, and as it did, Canada had become stronger, not weaker, Mulroney asserted. As evidence, he cited its expanded international role, the flowering of its artistic and cultural communities, the strengthening of its political and territorial sovereignty, and its unique social programmes. He also mentioned the 1965 Auto Pact and the pivotal role it had played in the prosperity of Ontario. 'If there is a link between increased trade with the United States and our quintessential Canadianness', he told the House, 'it is that free trade enhances Canadian vitality and ensures the expression of our nationhood'. Mulroney was convinced that Canada could become truly prosperous only by looking forward with confidence and pride.[22]

---

[19]Quoted in Graham Fraser, 'His Town Is a Symbol of the Nation, PM Says', *Globe and Mail*, 2 July 1987, 1.
[20]Kevin Cox, 'PM Promises Wealth to Western Canadians with Free Trade Deal', *Globe and Mail*, 16 November 1987, 1.
[21]Quoted in Matthew Fisher, 'Mulroney Pitches Free-Trade Deal during Blitz of Alberta', *Globe and Mail*, 1 August 1988, 1.
[22]Canada, House of Commons, *Debates*, 30 August 1988.

The Opposition parties disagreed. Both the Liberals and New Democrats unleashed an impassioned attack on Mulroney's free trade proposal. On 4 October, for instance, NDP leader Ed Broadbent told an Edmonton audience that free trade would undermine Medicare and open the door to American management firms in search of profits in the health care industry. He also went to Ontario's wine district and said that the free trade agreement was a 'betrayal of Canada's grape growers'. In Windsor, a city that benefitted tremendously from the Auto Pact, he told auto workers that their jobs were threatened with free trade.[23]

Leader of the Official Opposition John Turner spearheaded the Liberal assault. Free trade 'will finish Canada as we know it' and reduce it to its old status of colony, he charged. 'The price [for free trade] is our sovereignty, our freedom to make our own choices, to decide what is right for us, to go on building the kind of country we want ... We do not want to become Americans'. Turner challenged Mulroney to settle the debate by calling an election, and on 1 October Mulroney did precisely that.[24]

At Rideau Hall, after Governor General Jeanne Sauvé had dissolved Parliament, Mulroney said, 'Our view of Canada is confident and outward looking. We see a country and world changing before us and we are determined to respond positively and aggressively to that change'. He offered a vision of 'one Canada, united, progressive, prosperous, and strong. We have a dream', he said, that 'together we can build a better Canada'. Mulroney was offering a new vision of Canada's future, not a nostalgic vision of the past.[25] He told the Golden Age Club of Baie-Comeau that 'this country is entitled to its visions, and this country is entitled to its great dreams'.[26]

The situation for the Liberals was not looking good. Then, midway through the campaign for the election held that November, a televised English-language leaders' debate was held. Under the bright lights of the TV cameras and before an estimated viewing audience of some 5 million voters, in an instant Turner resuscitated his party and galvanized the public's attention. What did Turner do to alter his political fortunes? He told Mulroney, 'I happen to believe you sold us out'. Mulroney had 'mentioned 120 years of history'. Turner responded to this unequivocally, starting with, 'We built a country east and west and north. We built it on an infrastructure that deliberately resisted the continental pressure of the United States. For 120 years we've done it'. And then came Turner's most biting accusation: 'With one signature of a pen, you've reversed that, thrown us into the north-

---

[23]See *Maclean's*, 24 October 1988.
[24]Peter C. Newman, 'The Big Decision', *Maclean's*, 10 October 1988.
[25]Ross Howard, 'Mulroney Hoping to "Heal Divisions" after Winning His Second Majority', *Globe and Mail*, 22 November 1988, 1.
[26]'Mulroney Makes Last Appeal in Quebec', *Globe and Mail*, 21 November 1998, 10.

south influence of the United States and will reduce us, I am sure, to a colony of the United States because when the economic levers go, the political independence is sure to follow'.[27] Turner, wearing the mantle of Canadian nationalist, accused Mulroney of selling out the country to the Americans. The Liberal campaign was rejuvenated and, momentarily at least, it looked like Turner stood a chance of heading back to the prime minister's office – as the great defender of the Canadian nation.

Nearing the end of the campaign, Mulroney would begin every speech with 'John Turner says that the cause of his life is to tear up a treaty; the cause of my life is to build a nation'. He even referred to himself as 'Brian the Builder' and Turner as 'John the Ripper'.[28] In the debate that brought such attention to Turner, Mulroney argued that he, too, was a nationalist: 'I today, sir, as a Canadian, believe genuinely in what I am doing. I believe it is right for Canada. I believe that in my own modest way I am nation-building. Because I believe this benefits Canada and I love Canada'. As the *Winnipeg Free Press* had observed during the campaign, Mulroney had to prove above all that the free trade agreement was a nationalist pact that put Canada and not just economics first.[29] At the end of the campaign, Mulroney believed that he had done that, and he told *Maclean's* in an exclusive interview that the free trade agreement 'is an important act of nation-building'.[30]

Mulroney's narrative and his brand of nationalism prevailed at the polls and won him a second consecutive majority government with 43 per cent of the popular vote. Atlantic Canada, Toronto, and parts of Manitoba and Saskatchewan voted against the Conservatives, but by the end of 1988, polls revealed that most Canadians did, indeed, favour free trade. Mulroney told Canadians the victory showed their desire to create a new national story of a mature and united nation, not one that was timid and insular. 'This was an election in which Canadians in all parts of the country said yes, the U.S. is a big country. But so what? Our own country, this Canada of ours, is not defined by the size or the might of our neighbour, the United States'.[31] Later, in the coming months, Mulroney participated in talks with Mexican President Carlos Salinas de Gortar and US President George H. W. Bush that resulted in the North American Free Trade Agreement (NAFTA), which came into effect after Mulroney left office.[32]

---

[27]'John Turner, Brian Mulroney, debate free trade, Oct. 1988', https://greatcanadianspeeches.ca/2019/09/18/john-turner-brian-mulroney-debate-free-trade-oct-1988/.
[28]'Stung Mulroney Asserts Own Patriotism', *Globe and Mail*, 14 November 1988, 9.
[29]*Winnipeg Free Press*, 6 November 1988.
[30]*Maclean's*, 21 November 1988.
[31]Hugh Winsor, 'Sound and Fury on Free Trade May Leave Many in the Dark', *Globe and Mail*, 25 November 1988, 1.
[32]'Official Signing of NAFTA – 17 December 1992', Brian Mulroney Institute of Government, https://www.mulroneyinstitute.ca/mulroney/video-library?field_video_library_category_target_id=All.

On 24 February 1993, Mulroney resigned as prime minister and was succeeded by Kim Campbell. A general election was held on 25 October. The Conservatives won only two seats – the worst defeat for a governing party at the federal level in Canada's history. Liberal Jean Chrétien became the new prime minister. He was opposed to free trade. Chrétien declared that Mulroney had destroyed the 'national community that feels distinctively ours', adding Canada was founded, not by market-oriented reform policies, deregulation or smaller governments, as he said Mulroney believed, but by citizens who hold that 'government can be a force for good in society'. Chrétien pledged to immediately cancel many of Mulroney's policies, notably, the Goods and Services Tax (GST), which had spawned great anger, as well as NAFTA – if within six months of his taking office, Canada could not renegotiate better terms with the United States and Mexico. In fact, Chrétien did neither.[33] On becoming prime minister, he quickly changed his position on the Canada-US Free Trade Agreement and on NAFTA. Even more, he promoted a free trade area of the Americas (which did not come to fruition) and accepted the growing influence of the World Trade Organization (WTO), which in 1995 replaced GATT. As was so often the case with him, Chrétien read Canadian attitudes correctly, and he did so with NAFTA and international trade more generally. At one point, he told a student protesting NAFTA that 'you cannot build a wall around Canada as the New Democrats are proposing. It's not very realistic and it will be self-defeating'.[34] While publicly Chrétien continued to insist that Canada would not sign the deal, he privately instructed his officials to 'find ways for us to agree to ratify NAFTA'. Speaking to Canadian reporters at the Asia Pacific Economic Co-operation (APEC) forum in Seattle, he presented himself as the defender of Canadian sovereignty and Canadian interests. He told a news conference that he had reminded President Bill Clinton that 'Canada must be independent – not the 51st state' and that its wishes regarding trade must be accepted.[35] This was good rhetoric for Canadians at home, and the American and Mexican leaders even signed a three-page memorandum to discuss subsidies, anti-dumping measures and the export of water; however, they refused to address Chrétien's main concern, which was a common energy market. On 2 December 1993, Chrétien ratified NAFTA, claiming that he had achieved everything he promised in the federal campaign, although commentators observed that he had achieved little in his attempt to renegotiate that agreement.[36]

---

[33] Liberal Party of Canada, *Creating Opportunity: The Liberal Plan for Canada* (Ottawa: Liberal Party of Canada, 1993), 105; Paul Martin, *Hell or High Water: My Life in and out of Politics* (Toronto: Douglas Gibson Books, 2008), 96–104.

[34] Edward Greenspon and Anthony Wilson-Smith, *Double Vision: The Inside Story of the Liberals in Power* (Toronto: Doubleday, 1996), 38.

[35] Jeff Sallot, 'Chrétien's Style Impresses Clinton', *Globe and Mail*, 22 November 1993, A1.

[36] Barrie McKenna, 'Liberals Concede NAFTA Fight', *Globe and Mail*, 3 December 1993, A1.

A Maclean's-CBC annual poll for 1999, a decade after the Canada-US trade agreement, found that Canadians overwhelmingly agreed they possess a unique identity, separate and distinct from all other countries, despite the economic integration with the United States, and moreover, they agreed that Canadians could thrive in the new millennium by keeping their own values and would not become more like Americans even as the two countries drew closer together economically.[37] A 2003 Ipsos-Reid poll showed that almost three out of four Canadians supported NAFTA and were in favour of even greater integration with the North American economy.[38] With the stroke of his pen, Chrétien – like Mulroney – had relegated to the dustbin of history all the fears of past politicians regarding the fate of Canadian sovereignty should there be economic integration with the United States. Freer Canada-US trade was no longer seen by Canadians as a threat to national identity, but as a necessary element in Canada's well-being. This view most assuredly persisted until November 2024, when Donald J. Trump won the presidential election and vowed within days to impose 25 per cent tariffs on all products entering the US from Canada and Mexico until both countries took actions to stop the flow of illegal drugs and migrants. Throughout the campaign he had said repeatedly that tariffs were a 'beautiful' word, and he was determined to use them to bring manufacturing back to the United States. To many, Trump was an existential threat to Canada.

On 29 November Prime Minister Justin Trudeau visited Trump at his resort at Mar-a-Lago, hoping to convince the president-elect that the NAFTA that had been re-negotiated with Trump and became the United States-Mexico-Canada Agreement (USMCA) on 1 July 2020 was in the economic interests of all three nations. But Trump was dismissive and tormented Trudeau about Canada becoming the fifty-first state and the prime minister or Canadian hockey great, Wayne Gretzky becoming the Governor of Canada while sticking to his threat of punitive tariffs on Canada. Canadians were horrified and angry that Trump would threaten their economy with his tariffs and undo the economic relationship that had benefitted Canada so admirably since the Canada-US trade deal was signed on 2 January 1988, and came into effect on 1 January 1989. His talk of annexation further fuelled Canadian anger, igniting throughout the country a level of Canadian patriotism and determined resistance against the US unlike anything seen in a century. At the height of his unpopularity and with an imminent election on the horizon, Trudeau chose to resign and was replaced by Mark Carney,

---

[37] Chris Wood, 'The Vanishing Border', *Maclean's*, 20 December 1999, 29, 33; Statistics Canada, 'Trade', 2004, https://www150.statcan.gc.ca/n1/pub/11-402-x/2006/1130/ceb1130_000-eng.htm.
[38] Ipsos-Reid, 'Seven in Ten (70%) Support Canada's Involvement in North American Free Trade Agreement (NAFTA)', 8 June 2003, https://www.ipsos.com/en-ca/seven-ten-70-support-canadas-involvement-north-american-free-trade-agreement-nafta.

a former governor of both the Bank of Canada and Bank of England, who immediately dismissed Parliament and called a general election for 28 March 2025. The election became a referendum on President Trump and who was best to protect Canada in a moment of great chaos and uncertainty. Prime Minister Carney, who had helped manage crises in England with Brexit and in Canada during the 2008 financial crisis, convinced enough Canadians that he had the experience and steady hand to navigate Canada through the crisis created by President Trump. Vowing to make the United States pay for its scuttling of the Canada-US trade relationship and President's Trump's treatment of Canada, he was rewarded with a minority government. The days of economic goodwill between Canada and its closest neighbour appear to have come to an end, although it is not at all certain what will emerge in its place and how Canada can find new markets for its exports and new partners for its imports if, indeed, the special relation with the US is over as Carney has so often said.

IMAGE 12 Rally for a united Canada in Montreal, five days before Quebec voters cast ballots on the sovereignty referendum. https://www.gettyimages.ca/detail/photo/canadians-rallying-for-unity-royalty-free-image/535321470?searchscope=image%2Cfilm&adppopup=true.

12

The Quebec referendum, 1995: To leave or to stay in Canada?

On the 30th of October 1995, Canada's future as a country teetered on collapse. Across the land that evening, most people were glued to their home television sets or gathered in crowds to watch large screens as results began pouring in on the referendum to determine whether the province of Quebec should pursue separation or stay in Canada. The federal government, under Liberal Prime Minister Jean Chrétien, prepared for the worse, even removing military aircraft from the province lest they be claimed by a separatist government formally backed in its quest by a democratic vote. A public opinion poll taken the week before Quebeckers voted on the referendum, showed support for separation, with the 'yes' side having a commanding seven-point lead.

Getting to this potentially cataclysmic point was a long time coming, being built upon Quebec nationalism and dissatisfaction with the Canadian federation that had been growing for nearly a half century – or maybe longer, going all the way back to French Canadians' opposition to conscription in the First World War, or maybe even to the 1759 British victory over the French on the Plains of Abraham. In 1918, Joseph Francoeur had proposed a motion in the province's Legislative Assembly arguing for Quebec's secession; it never came to a vote, but the motion does indicate the extent to which Quebec felt alienated from the rest of Canada. This sense of dissatisfaction with the status quo gained momentum with Quebec's 'Quiet Revolution', a period of major social, political and economic changes in Quebec that began with the election of Liberal Jean Lesage as premier in 1960. Quebeckers became far more secular, redefined their identity and sought greater recognition for themselves from English-speaking Canada. The slogan of the Quiet Revolution was 'Maîtres chez nous' (Masters in our own house). The province turned to state capital as a means of economic development, limiting control by foreign interests and ensuring that new jobs created by the state would be filled by French-speaking Quebeckers.[1]

The Quiet Revolution signalled the desire for substantial change in Quebec's place in Confederation. Lesage established a ministry of federal–provincial relations, and the premiers of Quebec that followed him assumed themselves to be equal to the prime minister of Canada. Increasing numbers of Quebeckers believed that their provincial government should control many of the social programmes managed and paid for in Ottawa. The province opted out of several federal–provincial programmes throughout the 1960s, most notably the Canadian Pension Plan (CPP) and Youth Allowances (which had been implemented to support families with children under 18 years of age who remained in some type of educational institution).[2]

With the June 1966 provincial election, conservative Union Nationale leader Daniel Johnson became the premier of Quebec. He had campaigned on the slogan 'Égalité ou Indépendance' and pushed hard for constitutional change that would recognize Canada as the union of two nations rather than of ten provinces. But Johnson's more ardent nationalism failed to satisfy many Quebeckers. There were those who sought immediate independence from Canada and they looked to Pierre Bourgault's Rassemblement pour l'indépendance nationale and the Ralliement national, which, together, captured 9 per cent of the popular vote in 1966. The following year, the independence movement became a more potent force: René Lévesque, one of the early figures in the Quiet Revolution, left the provincial Liberals to create the Mouvement Souveraineté-Association that in 1968 became the Parti Québécois (PQ), of which he was the leader until 1985, when he resigned, largely for reasons of ill-health.[3]

Liberal Lester B. Pearson defeated Progressive Conservative John Diefenbaker and was the prime minister of Canada from 1963 to 1968, when he was succeeded by Pierre Elliott Trudeau. Pearson tried to understand and accommodate Quebec. He appointed a Royal Commission on Bilingualism and Biculturalism that recommended that French and English be provided for all federal government services. He reached out to the intellectuals and union leaders in Quebec who feared the rise of separatism. Most notably, he convinced three leading French Quebeckers – the academic Pierre Trudeau, journalist Gérard Pelletier and labour leader Jean Marchand – to join the federal government. They refused to accept the premise of Quebec being the homeland of French-speaking Canadians; rather, their position was that the development and protection of French was a federal government

---

[1] Michael Gauvreau, *The Catholic Origins of Quebec's Quiet Revolution, 1931–1970* (Montreal and Kingston: McGill-Queen's University Press, 2005).
[2] Dale Thomson, *Jean Lesage & the Quiet Revolution* (Toronto: Macmillan of Canada, 1984).
[3] Marguerite Paulin, *René Lévesque: Charismatic Leader*, trans. by Jonathan Kaplansky (Montreal, Quebec: XYZ Publishing, 2004).

responsibility and that French- and English-speaking Canadians should have equal support across Canada.⁴

Quebec seemed to be drifting towards greater radicalization. On 31 May 1963, *Time* magazine published an article with the headline 'Bombs in the Quiet Land' as over an eleven-week period, a series of explosions targeting federal government buildings in Quebec had killed a security guard and injured several others. The violence was attributed to the Front de libération du Québec (FLQ), which *Time* described as 'a lunatic fringe of violent nationalists whose aim is the secession of French-speaking Quebec from the rest of English-speaking Canada'.⁵

Pearson made attempts to repatriate Canada's constitution, the British North America Act, 1867 (BNA Act), but was blocked by Quebec. Since Confederation, whenever Canada's Parliament sought to amend the BNA Act, it had to make a request to the British House of Commons. Pearson saw this as a slight to Canadian nationhood. He tried to change the procedure by building on the work of E. Davie Fulton, who had been the minister of Justice in Diefenbaker's Cabinet. A dominion–provincial conference in 1960 had agreed that Ottawa should have the consent of all ten provinces before changes were made by the federal Parliament to a variety of constitutional items, including the official status of the French and English languages, education rights, the assets and legislative powers of a province, and the amending formula. Pearson sought to finalize the Fulton proposal in 1964 when Guy Favreau, his minister of Justice, presented a new proposal that retained the main features of the Fulton formula, but added provisions granting Parliament exclusive power to make amendments to Canada's Constitution concerning the executive government of Canada, the Senate and the House of Commons. At a 1964 conference, all the premiers agreed with the proposed procedure, but later, amid stiff opposition in Quebec, Premier Lesage changed his mind.

Pearson's 'three wise men' ran successfully in the 1965 general election, and in 1967, Pierre Trudeau joined Pearson's Cabinet as minister of Justice and attorney-general. Many looked to the charismatic Trudeau to finish the job of repatriating the constitution – which, in fact, he did, but it took until 1982. Pearson resigned from politics in 1968 and Trudeau, the new leader of the Liberal Party of Canada, was sworn in as prime minister on 20 April. Outside of Quebec, Trudeau was viewed positively as someone prepared to stand up to the province. Inside Quebec, he was far less favoured. This was made abundantly clear to the world on 24 June 1968, one day before the federal election that Trudeau had called. Rioting separatists in Montreal showered Trudeau, in the grandstand viewing the Saint-Jean-Baptiste Day

---

⁴Raymond B. Blake, *Canada's Prime Ministers and the Shaping of a National Identity* (Vancouver: University of British Columbia Press, 2024), 119–29.
⁵'Bombs in the Quiet Land', *Time*, 31 May 1963.

parade, with rocks and bottles. But he refused to flee. The following day, he was re-elected to the House of Commons, and the Liberals captured 45 per cent of the popular vote and the first federal majority government since 1958.[6]

Pierre Trudeau believed in a strong central government to ensure rights for all citizens. On 17 October 1968, his government introduced a bill that became the Official Languages Act of 1969. Building on the programme of language training that began in the federal public service in 1964, this Act established English and French as official languages in the federal civil service, all Crown corporations and all federal courts where either minority linguistic group constituted at least 10 per cent of the population.[7]

Robert Bourassa led the Quebec Liberal Party to a decisive victory in April 1970, and it seemed that the radical nationalist element remained on the margins of Quebec society. That soon proved an illusion. On 5 October, the FLQ kidnapped British diplomat James Cross in Montreal. It demanded that the FLQ manifesto be read over the radio and television and that all convicted or detained FLQ members be released. The Quebec government agreed to the former, refused the latter and offered the kidnappers safe passage out of Canada in exchange for Cross's release; that same day, a second FLQ cell kidnapped Pierre Laporte, the Quebec minister of Labour.

Quebec asked Ottawa for help. The federal government responded by proclaiming the existence of a state of 'apprehended insurrection' in Quebec and on 16 October invoked the War Measures Act, passed by the Borden government in 1914. The army was despatched to Quebec, civil rights were suspended and the FLQ was banned. More than 465 people were arrested, most of whom were never charged with any crime. Two days later, the FLQ strangled Laporte and stuffed his body into the trunk of a car; Cross was released in exchange for safe passage of the kidnappers to Cuba.

The vast majority of Quebeckers did not support revolutionary liberation movements. In 1973, they gave Bourassa a second overwhelming victory, though the Parti Québécois captured 30 per cent of the popular vote. Following that election, René Lévesque convinced his PQ members to accept sovereignty-association with Canada rather than outright independence. This meant that Quebec, though politically independent from Canada, would continue in an economic partnership with it. In 1976, when it was elected to government, the PQ promised that it would not unilaterally declare independence from Canada but would hold a referendum on sovereignty-association during its first term in office. That referendum was held in 1980. Voters were asked: 'Do you agree to give the Government of

---

[6]John T. Saywell, *Canadian Annual Review of Politics and Public Affairs, 1968* (Toronto: University of Toronto Press, 1969), 3–4, 46–52.
[7]Matthew Hayday, *They Want Us to Learn French: Promoting and Opposing Bilingualism in English-Speaking Canada* (Vancouver: University of British Columbia Press, 2015).

Québec the mandate to negotiate the proposed agreement between Québec and Canada?'[8]

Two developments in the final days of that campaign decisively turned the tide against the sovereigntists, the *oui* side of the question. First, Lise Payette, a highly respected Québécoise feminist and PQ minister of Consumer Affairs, Co-operatives, and Financial Institutions, offhandedly referred to women supporting the *non* side as 'Yvettes', after a symbolic compliant young girl familiar to most women from their elementary school days. Then, she called Madeleine Guay, the wife of provincial Liberal leader Claude Ryan, an 'Yvette'. This immediately mobilized a virtual army of opposition from women and sympathetic media that bolstered the federalist cause. More than 14,000 women staged a massive 'Yvette' rally in the Montreal Forum to support the *non* side.[9]

Second, Pierre Trudeau intervened. At the time that the PQ announced the referendum, Trudeau had retired from politics after losing the June 1979 federal election to the Progressive Conservatives led by Joe Clark. The PQ were delighted that Trudeau – their long-time nemesis – was gone; they saw Clark, an English-speaking Albertan, who, at thirty-nine, had become the youngest prime minister in Canada's history, as no match for Lévesque. The PQ had not, however, counted on Clark's government surviving only nine months and Trudeau returning as prime minister in early 1980. In perhaps his most eloquent and momentous speech, delivered at Paul Sauvé Arena in Montreal on 14 May 1979, Trudeau proclaimed: 'We won't let this country die, this Canada, our home and native land ... We are going to say to those who want us to stop being Canadians, we are going to say a resounding, an overwhelming No!'[10] Just under 60 per cent of Quebeckers who voted in the 1980 referendum agreed with this sentiment.

Nevertheless, Trudeau made it clear that a *non* vote should not be interpreted as an indication that everything was fine with the way Canada operated. He promised constitutional reform, but never spelled out just what that meant, and it is unlikely that he contemplated greater powers for Quebec; nor did he mention his hope to create a Charter of Rights and Freedoms that would be the basis of a new Canadian citizenship transcending ethnicity and particularism. Shortly after the 1980 referendum, Trudeau met the premiers at the prime minister's residence in Ottawa. His earlier attempts to reach a new constitutional accord had ended in failure when

---

[8]'Referendum on the 1980 Sovereignty-Association Proposal for Québec', www.electionsquebec.qc.ca/en/results-and-statistics/referendum-on-the-1980-sovereignty-association-proposal-for-quebec/.

[9]Monique Bégin, *Ladies, Upstairs!: My Life in Politics and After* (Montreal and Kingston: McGill-Queen's University Press, 2018), 342–54, The First Quebec Referendum.

[10]Pierre Elliott Trudeau, *Transcript of a Speech Given by the Right Honourable Pierre Elliott Trudeau at the Paul Sauvé Arena in Montreal on 14 May 1980* (Ottawa: Office of the Prime Minister, 1980), 15.

Quebec refused to ratify proposals agreed upon in Victoria in 1971. When in 1975 the premiers had gathered for their annual meeting, Trudeau invited them to consider a constitutional conference. Frank Moores, premier of Newfoundland and Labrador and chair of that year's conference, replied that, among other matters, the premiers wanted to consider the distribution of powers and control over resources. But no progress was made that year. Indeed, this was a period of poisoned relations between the prime minister and the premiers. The Supreme Court of Canada heard eighty constitutional cases between 1975 and 1980 dealing with the division of federal-provincial powers; this was two more than it had heard over the previous quarter century.[11]

When in September 1980, Trudeau and the first ministers met to discuss the Constitution over dinner, he was dismissive. He characterized the premiers' list of priorities as a provincial 'shopping list',[12] and before dessert arrived left the formal dinner he was hosting. Essentially, Trudeau wished to see Canada embrace a civic nationalism – one that would replace all forms of ethnic nationalism – based primarily on a shared language, culture and heritage. Less than a month after that September dinner meeting, Trudeau took to the national airwaves to tell Canadians that he would be proceeding unilaterally with constitutional reform. He promised an amending formula, a commitment to the principle of equalization and the reduction of regional disparity, and a Charter of Rights and Freedoms. Eight opposing premiers – known as the 'Gang of Eight' – insisted that by bypassing the provinces and proceeding alone, Trudeau was violating the basic principle of Canadian federalism. When they challenged his right to proceed, the Supreme Court ruled that Trudeau stood on firm legal grounds, but had violated convention, or the accepted but unwritten rules of constitutional practice that substantial provincial consent was required before the federal government amended the BNA Act.

Trudeau relented and invited the premiers to another round of negotiations in November 1981. There, the English-speaking premiers broke with Lévesque and agreed to a deal with the federal government. Quebec saw the constitutional compromise as a betrayal – 'the night of the long knives' as it became known – isolating it from the constitutional process as the federal government and English-speaking provincial politicians hammered out a deal in an Ottawa hotel suite. The provinces were able to force a few amendments, such as a new clause granting them legislative authority over natural resources, including their export, provided the producing province did not discriminate in prices or supplies available to other provinces. Despite Trudeau's insistence on a people's Constitution, in

---

[11] Blake, *Canada's Prime Ministers and the Shaping of a National Identity*, 181–90.
[12] Peter Russell, *Constitutional Odyssey: Can Canadians Become a Sovereign People?* (Toronto: University of Toronto Press, 2004), 110.

the end this was another example of elite accommodation and compromise. The Quebec legislature voted seventy to thirty-eight to reject the proposals, but ratification did not depend on provincial consent. On 17 April 1982, Queen Elizabeth II gave royal assent in Ottawa to Trudeau's constitutional package. The Constitution Act, 1982, contains the Canadian Charter of Rights and Freedoms and other provisions, including the rights of Indigenous peoples and the procedures for amending Canada's Constitution. It renames the British North America Act, 1867, the Constitution Act, 1867. With this legislation, Canada achieved its full independence, as it could now legally make changes to its Constitution without approval from Britain.[13]

In 1984, newly elected Progressive Conservative Prime Minister Brian Mulroney promised to achieve national reconciliation by bringing Quebec into the Constitution. Robert Bourassa's Liberals defeated the Parti Québécois in 1985, and it, too, made constitutional reform a top priority. Bourassa laid out five minimum conditions to be met if Quebec were to sign the new Constitution: (1) explicit recognition of Quebec as a distinct society; (2) increased powers for Quebec over immigration; (3) limitations on federal spending power; (4) recognition of Quebec's veto rights; and (5) participation by Quebec in the appointment of judges to the Supreme Court. Other premiers, also seeking more power, supported Quebec. Canada's political leaders at this time failed to consider that Canada's political culture had changed since 1982. The Charter of Rights and Freedom had created among Canadians the sense that all citizens had rights, and fundamental to this was the notion of no special status for anyone, or any area, including the belief that no single province should have a veto over proposed constitutional changes.

When, in April 1987, Mulroney and the premiers began the process to secure Quebec's signature on the 1982 Constitution, they reverted to the traditional method of negotiating behind closed doors. Initially, this produced success, as on 3 June 1987, the Meech Lake Accord was introduced. This document proposed amendments to the Canadian Constitution: it recognized Quebec as a distinct society; strengthened the relative powers of the provinces against those of the federal government; called for an annual constitutional conference to discuss such issues as Senate reform; and gave the provinces more control over immigration. Many Canadians welcomed Meech, and, in Parliament, the Liberals and the New Democrats (NDP) were generally supportive. Most of the early criticism, largely from academics, was dismissed. Then Pierre Trudeau voiced his concerns and opposition mushroomed. The 'distinct society' clause was seen to be an assault on the

---

[13]Roy Romanow, John Whyte and Howard Leeson, *Canada ... Notwithstanding: The Making of the Constitution, 1976–1982* (Toronto: Thomson Carswell, 2007).

equality principle that Canadians had come to regard as fundamental to their liberal democracy.[14]

All provincial legislatures had to ratify the Meech Lake Accord within three years of its introduction. Within a few months, however, several of the premiers who had forged the deal were replaced by determined critics. The most vociferous among them was Clyde Wells, the new premier of Newfoundland and Labrador. On 6 April 1990, his province's House of Assembly rescinded its earlier approval of the Meech Accord. Further aggravating matters, Indigenous leaders and the territorial governments complained about their exclusion from the process that produced Meech. Canada's western provinces were dissatisfied over the absence of Senate reform in the Accord and wanted change from an appointed upper house to a democratically elected one. The Senate issue gave the fledgling Reform Party the ammunition it needed to launch a major offensive against both Meech and the Mulroney government. On 12 June 1990, Elijah Harper, an Oji-Cree from Red Sucker Lake in Manitoba and the first treaty Indian elected to a provincial legislature, refused to give his consent to a motion that would provide for the initiation of hearings on the Meech Lake Accord. Harper protested the exclusion of First Nations from the constitutional process. Manitoba did not vote on the Meech Lake Accord, and that scuttled the ratification process. Reaction to the defeat of the Meech Lake Accord was severe. Lucien Bouchard, regarded as Mulroney's most prominent MP from Quebec – who had served as secretary of state and then minister of the Environment – resigned from the federal government and from the Conservative Party, arguing that Meech Lake had been a bare minimum for Quebec. Charismatic and described as being like a 'storm cloud',[15] Bouchard expressed the vision of a more sovereign Quebec with profound passion and conviction.

With six other disgruntled MPs, Bouchard created the Bloc Québécois (BQ) as a new separatist party in the House of Commons with a mandate to protect Quebec's interests in Ottawa. With support for independence growing in Quebec, Bourassa declared that for the federation to survive, radical reform was essential. He provided a deadline of 26 October 1992 for the federal government to propose something to Quebec. After that, he would hold a referendum on either renewed federalism or sovereignty. In the words of many, Quebec's Premier Robert Bourassa had 'put a knife to the throat of English Canada'.[16] The federal government appointed

---

[14]Pierre Trudeau, 'Say Goodbye to the Dream of One Canada', in Roger Gibbins, ed., *Meech Lake and Canada: Perspectives from the West* (Edmonton: Academic Printing and Publishing, 1988), 66.

[15]Mario Cardinal, *Breaking Point Canada Quebec: The 1995 Referendum* (Toronto: CBC/Bayard Canada Books, 2003), 134.

[16]Robert Fulford, 'The Knife to Canada's Throat', *National Post*, 5 April 2014, nationalpost.com/opinion/robert-fulford-the-knife-to-canadas-throat.

former Commissioner of Official Languages Keith Spicer to engage with Canadians in a Citizens' Forum on Canada's Future. Some 400,000 people participated. Spicer's report concluded that Canadians 'strongly disapprove of government policies which seem to promote the rights of groups over individuals',[17] and as such, would not accept special privileges for any one province.

When the federal and provincial governments restarted efforts on the Constitution, Ontario's NDP Premier Bob Rae, who later ran unsuccessfully for the leadership of the Liberal party of Canada, insisted that representatives of Canada's First Nations join the discussions with federal, provincial and territorial leaders. In August 1992, a deal was reached that slightly altered the Meech Lake Accord to give Bourassa what he thought he needed to win a referendum on keeping Quebec in Canada. Most significantly, the new proposal, called the Charlottetown Accord, recognized Quebec as 'distinct' based on its large French-speaking majority, unique culture and civil law tradition. By trying to define the basis and parameters of 'distinct society', the result displeased both sides: French Quebeckers thought it too narrow, while many in English-speaking Canada saw it as favouring one province. The Charlottetown Accord was presented to Canadians in a fall 1992 national referendum and was defeated, 54 per cent against to 46 per cent in favour.[18]

The federal Liberals, led by Jean Chrétien, regained power with a majority government in the general election held on 25 October 1993. Even in view of the failure to reach a constitutional deal with Quebec and the growing discord in that province, Chrétien did not seem to take the threat of separatism seriously. A weak economy and government cutbacks, meaning less money was being distributed to demonstrate the federal government's importance to people's welfare, were also contributing to discontent. Parti Québécois leader Jacques Parizeau was now leading the provincial campaign for independence. Outwardly, he may have seemed an unlikely person for the role, as he exuded characteristics of an anglophile. He held a doctorate from the London School of Economics and, when speaking English, was quite antiquarian British in his use of words and mannerisms. But Parizeau was experienced and respected, having served as finance minister in René Lévesque's provincial government. He became the PQ leader in 1987, but lost the 1989 provincial election. With the failure of both the Meech Lake and Charlottetown Accords stoking anger in Quebec, Parizeau was victorious in the provincial election of 12 September 1994, securing a majority government in a campaign in which he promised a referendum on

---

[17]'Citizens' Forum on Canada's Future: Report to the People and Government of Canada', publications.gc.ca/site/eng/9.699760/publication.html.
[18]Karlo Basta, *The Symbolic State: Minority Recognition, Majority Backlash, and Secession in Multinational Countries* (Montreal and Kingston: McGill-Queen's University Press, 2021), 63–85.

independence the following year. Parizeau's main opponent in that election was Daniel Johnson, Jr. Although well-known and respected – in business and politics, and the son of a former premier – the Liberal Party he led seemed stale, and Johnson himself appeared tepid on why Quebec should be satisfied with the Canadian federation. Mario Dumont, leader of the newly established Action démocratique du Québec (ADQ), which expressed a softer version of Quebec nationalism than the PQ, received 6.5 per cent of the vote in 1994 and one seat, for Dumont himself in Rivière-du-Loupe. Nevertheless, the ADQ captivated the emotions of many young people, with Dumont being only twenty-four years old and offering a fresh vision. In the 2007 Quebec provincial election, Liberal Premier Jean Charest was returned with a minority government, while the ADQ made a major breakthrough that made Dumont the leader of the official Opposition in the National Assembly of Quebec.

Two months after the PQ's 1994 victory at the polls, Lucien Bouchard was admitted to hospital with what was believed thrombophlebitis in his left leg. Two days later, it was revealed he was in mortal danger with what was called 'flesh-eating disease', where about half of reported cases were fatal. Much of his diseased leg and hip had to be amputated. Bouchard received heartfelt expressions of support from across Canada. In his hospital bed, Bouchard had scribbled a note, "Que l'on continue – merci" ("Let us carry on – thank you"), apparently for his medical team but in the context of the sovereignty debate the message quickly took on considerable political significance. After a week, he was removed from the critical list. Through this struggle, in Quebec, and particularly among sovereigntists, he became almost a mythical figure, symbolic of courage and determination and was treated like a hero at events where he would limp in using his cane. Bouchard handed the job of attacking the Liberals in Ottawa to his BQ lieutenants, Gilles Duceppe and Michel Gauthier, and focused his efforts on Quebec – to build support for sovereignty.

On 6 December 1994, in the National Assembly of Quebec, Premier Parizeau introduced An Act Respecting the Sovereignty of Quebec. It laid out a strategy to independence as well as post-independence relations with Canada. Quebec would continue to use the Canadian dollar and negotiate its own foreign agreements. The PQ started public consultations on the shape sovereignty was to take. The provincial Liberals rejected participation in these, stating that the PQ was being deceitful because, according to provisions in the Act, once given the mandate to negotiate independence, the people of Quebec would not be guaranteed a subsequent vote on the result. Indeed, many federalists worried that the 'yes' side, even if just squeaking by in a referendum – no matter how opaque the question on sovereignty – would declare independence from Canada.

Bouchard and Parizeau disagreed on the timing of the referendum. Parizeau wanted to establish a date for the vote – as promised within a year of being elected premier – but Bouchard favoured waiting until conditions appeared clear for winning. Bouchard maintained that a question to Quebec voters should leave open the idea of an economic association with Canada. While Parizeau was on vacation and out of contact, this was endorsed by Parizeau's second in command, Deputy Premier Bernard Landry. Upon his return, Parizeau, though annoyed, demonstrated pragmatism, stating that he, too, would consider a formal association with Canada if it was a good deal for Quebec. The question to which Quebeckers were asked to respond was unveiled on 7 September, and it read, in part: 'Do you agree that Quebec should become sovereign, after having made a formal offer to Canada for a new economic and political partnership?'[19] Many described the question as unclear; Louis Rukeyser, host of the Wall Street Business Week Show, said that 'if Quebecers understand ... it ... they all deserve a PhD'.[20]

The date for the referendum was set for 30 October. Prime Minister Chrétien firmly believed the sovereigntists would be soundly defeated, and polls taken in September also pointed to this result. On the sovereigntist side, pressure mounted to give Bouchard a leading role. On 7 October, Parizeau announced Bouchard would be the chief negotiator to achieve a new deal with Canada. Bouchard brought charisma and a new excitement to the campaign. He confidently declared that Canada would have no choice but to negotiate with Quebec, while at the same time he also assured people that talks would be practical, calm and constructive. By 12 October, polls showed the 'Oui' side gaining ground. Federalists warned of the horrid consequences of separation for Quebec, predicting tens of thousands of jobs lost, the end to social programmes, a bankrupt provincial government and the end of equalization payments to Quebec from Ottawa. Still, the tide continued turning against the federalists, with Bouchard making this into an ever more emotional crusade. In the federal government, panic set in when an internal Liberal poll taken on 19 October showed the 'Yes' side ahead by 54 per cent to 46 per cent, though other surveys pointed to a near tie. Their momentum also increased by being able to bring Mario Dumont into the Yes camp, by stressing that any path to independence would have to include a partnership with Canada. By contrast, the provincial Liberals under Daniel Johnson did not seem to have a compelling vision or message that connected at an emotional level, and for far too long, the Chrétien Liberals did not seem to take the separatist threat seriously. Even with polls turning towards sovereignty, there remained among many federalists – based on results in the 1980 referendum – the certainty that, when people actually marked their ballot, caution or fear of turmoil, would bring at least 2–3 per cent back to the NO side. Also, if losing, federalists insisted they would challenge the

---

[19]'1995 Referendum on Québec's Accession to Sovereignty', https://www.electionsquebec.qc.ca/en/results-and-statistics/1995-referendum-on-quebecs-accession-to-sovereignty/.
[20]Cardinal, *Breaking Point Canada*, 155.

legitimacy of the question asked as a basis for Quebec to pursue, let alone declare, independence.

Federalists insisted that Chrétien, despite his low popularity in Quebec, should take a much more active and public role. On 22 October, in a joint statement with Daniel Johnson, Jr, Chrétien announced that Quebec was a 'distinct society'. Many people, however, dismissed this statement as symbolic and cynical, pointing out that it was not enshrined in Canada's Constitution and, as such, had no legal implications. In the homestretch, the size of 'Yes' side rallies – and their energy and excitement – grew. Sovereigntists anticipated victory. On 25 October, five days before the vote, in a sombre televised address to the nation, Prime Minister Chrétien promised that Quebec would receive a veto on any constitutional change.[21]

The country seemed on the precipice of disaster. In the days leading up to the referendum, federal assets, including military equipment, were quietly moved out of the province, lest they be claimed by a sovereigntist government. Newspapers in Quebec printed the names of some 200 prominent federalists said to be open to negotiating the terms of Quebec's departure from Canada. Complicating things for the 'Yes' side, however, was opposition from Quebec's Indigenous peoples. A week before the vote, the Inuit of Northern Quebec and Cree of James Bay held their own referendums, achieving results that showed overwhelming support for remaining in Canada. The Mohawk of Kahnawake, who in 1990 had taken up arms to resist encroachment onto their reserve land, indicated they might violently resist being forced out of Canada.[22]

From federalist supporters came the idea of expanding on a planned 'No' rally in Montreal scheduled for 27 October. Both Air Canada and VIA rail helped with deeply discounted fares. From Ottawa, some 13,000 people left for Montreal on 200 buses. In all, the rally reached some 150,000 people. Those who travelled to Montreal to participate in the rally were committed to keeping Quebec in Canada and wanted to demonstrate to Quebecers that their Canada very much included the province of Quebec. Sovereigntists, however, cast the rally as a cynical effort to manipulate the results of the coming referendum, as well as possibly being an illegal action, because the money spent to mount the rally meant that the 'No' campaign exceed the $5 million allowable cap on expenses for each side.

On 30 October 1995, some 450 journalists from around the world arrived in Quebec to cover the referendum results as they came in. The major US television networks shifted their flagship evening news broadcast location to Montreal. There was great concern in the United States, especially from

---

[21] Jean Chrétien, 'Address to the Nation', Ottawa, Office of the Prime Minister, 1995, https://www.collectionscanada.gc.ca/primeministers/h4-4011-e.html.
[22] Chantal Hébert, *The Morning After: The 1995 Quebec Referendum and the Day That Almost Was* (Toronto: Knopf Canada, 2014).

Washington and leaders in several border states, over what a fractured Canada would mean for commerce. Secretary of State William Christopher angered sovereigntists by suggesting that the US government hoped for Canada to remain as one.

The number of eligible voters totalled just under 5.1 million. Across the province, the weather was decent on 30 October, and it was predicted that turnout would exceed the 88 per cent who voted in the 1980 referendum. Results started coming in just after 8.00 pm. Within a half hour, the 'Yes' side took the lead with 56 per cent support. This had, however, been anticipated as eastern Quebec, the first to report, was regarded as the sovereigntists' strongest electoral area. To achieve victory, 'Yes' supporters knew they had to build a healthy lead ahead of the Montreal ballots being counted. They soon encountered disappointments. The Jean Talon district in Quebec City, which the sovereigntists had hoped to win, voted 'No', and though Saguenay went 'Yes', the margin was lower than the goal of three-quarters support. With 40 per cent of polls reporting, the 'Yes' side clung to a 50.7 per cent to 49.3 per cent lead. Indeed, by 8.30 pm, many on the 'Yes' side realized they would fall short. Within an hour, with 3 million votes counted, the 'No' forces jumped ahead by 6,000 votes, and by 10.20 pm, with 97 per cent of ballots counted, that margin had grown to 43,000 votes. Results showed an astonishing 94 per cent turnout, with the federalist campaign attaining 50.58 per cent of the votes compared with 49.42 per cent for the sovereigntists.

Federalists celebrated, or more accurately breathed a sigh of relief, given the razor-thin margin of victory. Lucien Bouchard expressed disappointment, insisted the cause of independence was far from dead, but stressed that the democratic will of the people had to be respected. Concern was expressed that Jacques Parizeau would not be as gracious in defeat. Throughout the night, he grew angrier, as he had not emotionally prepared himself for a possible defeat. He took little solace from those who stressed that the sovereigntist side had come much closer than in 1980 and was now on the cusp of a future victory. Indeed, some opined it was better to have lost, rather than winning, by such a narrow margin, as a strong mandate was essential to forge ahead with such a monumental change as independence. Bouchard's speech at the Palais des congès ended with the declaration 'Don't give up hope, because the next time will be the right time'.[23] Parizeau took to the stage at 11.15 pm, the last speaker. He set aside his prepared remarks, and at one point angrily declared: 'It's true that we were beaten but we were beaten by what? By money and ethnic votes'.[24] Some cheered. But

---

[23]Cardinal, *Breaking Point Canada*, 397.
[24]'Money and Ethnic Votes: The Words That Shape Jacques Parizeau's Legacy', *Toronto Star*, 2 June 2015, www.thestar.com/news/canada/money-and-ethnic-votes-the-words-that-shape-jacques-parizeau-s-legacy/article_3eec173e-f913-5b2d-9e20-b991eef2c48f.html.

most listeners immediately understood that these comments discredited the sovereigntist claim that they embraced the idea of a pluralistic Quebec. Parizeau's outburst stoked fears that, as a separate country, Quebec would be favouring those who were of clear French-Canadian background. The next day, Parizeau announced he was retiring from politics. Pressure mounted on Chrétien to move quickly to show real progress for Quebec. This was also essential because the next month Lucien Bouchard received support to assume the PQ leadership and the premiership, a position into which he was officially sworn on 29 January 1996.

Before that point, in late November, Chrétien tabled a motion in the House of Commons declaring Quebec 'distinct' and assuring that future constitutional change would require provincial unanimity, measures he rammed through Parliament with his majority government. The federal government also transferred to Quebec (and the other provinces) greater jurisdiction over labour, training and immigration, and promised to limit federal spending on social policy without provincial consent. Ottawa also moved to set rules for any future referenda in Quebec.[25] In September 1996, it asked the Supreme Court to decide on the legality of a unilateral provincial declaration of independence. The Court ruled that Canada was based on a set of shared values, including federalism, democracy, constitutionalism, the rule of law and respect for minorities, and that no province had the constitutional right to secede unilaterally. The Court also said that Canada had an obligation to negotiate separation if a clear majority in any province voted in favour on a clear referendum question. Following the Supreme Court's ruling, Ottawa passed Bill C-20, known as the Clarity Act in 1998 requiring any referendum to be clear on the question of independence and the result to have a clear majority although it did not state what constituted a clear majority. According to Bill C-20, only the House of Commons has the power to vote on the clarity of the question and whether or not the referendum result demonstrated a clear majority.[26]

After this near-death experience for the country, it seemed that Canadians, including Quebeckers, lost the appetite to pursue arguments over the Constitution or separation. Within a decade, all those who played key roles in the 1995 referendum on both sides were no longer on the political stage. Still, from time-to-time, polls indicate heightened support for sovereignty, though not like the fever pitch that came in October 1995. In April 2025, such support barely topped 30 per cent, this also being influenced by fears from American President Donald Trump's comments

---

[25]Robert A. Young, 'Jean Chrétien's Quebec Legacy: Coasting, Then Stickhandling Hard', in Lois Harder and Steve Patten, eds., *The Chrétien Legacy: Politics and Public Policy in Canada* (Montreal and Kingston: McGill-Queen's University Press, 2006), 37–61.
[26]*Reference re Secession of Quebec*, [1998] 2 S.C.R. 217, 161 DLR (4th) 385, http://www.canlii.org/ca/cas/scc/1998/1998scc63.html.

about Canada being better off as America's fifty-first state. After the national trauma of October 1995, there has been no movement to go through the process of drawing up another question about Quebec's place in Canada and having people vote on the matter. Almost by osmosis, or quiet acquiescence, it appears that this second referendum by creating such drama – and angst – has resulted in acceptance. Canadians have accepted Quebec, de facto, as being distinct, and Quebec, for now, despite its ongoing disputes over power sharing in the federation, has to this point accepted that staying in Canada is its best option.

IMAGE 13 Michael Stark (left) and Michael Leshner celebrate their marriage following a successful Ontario court ruling, 10 June 2003. The Canadian Press/Tim Clark, CP174945751.

13

Same-sex marriage, 2005: A changing nation

Tuesday, 10 June 2003, was a sunny day in Toronto. It turned out to be especially bright for Michael Leshner and Michael Stark. Accompanied by their lawyer, they rushed to Osgoode Hall, as the Ontario Court of Appeal was to deliver its ruling on the legality of same-sex marriages. Leshner, a Crown attorney, had for some time campaigned for gay rights. On this day, he fervently believed they were finally 'going to pass the finish line'. Indeed, he and Stark had 'bought rings ... suits ... [and] had our hair done'.[1] At 10.00 am paper copies of the verdict were distributed, and a long-fought fight had finally been won. As the court began to orally deliver the result, Leshner and Stark picked up their marriage licence at Toronto City Hall and then, fearing a government appeal, rushed to the courthouse for a civil ceremony. With about forty people, mostly from the media gathered in an adjacent room, it was not long before photos of their first kiss as a married couple appeared in newspapers around the world, including in the *New York Times*, *Le Monde*, and even in the Communist state-owned *China Daily*.

The government did not appeal the 10 June 2003 unanimous ruling in *Halpern* v. *Attorney General of Canada* that the exclusion of same-sex couples from marriage violated section 15 of the Canadian Charter of Rights and Freedoms. That decision by the province's Court of Appeal legalized same-sex marriage in Ontario; moreover, it made Canada the first country to legalize same-sex marriage through a court ruling. A month later, same-sex marriage was made legal in British Columbia; in 2004, Saskatchewan, Manitoba, Quebec, Nova Scotia, Newfoundland and Labrador, as well as Yukon Territory followed; as, in 2005, did the country's remaining provinces and territories. On 20 July 2005, Canada's Parliament passed 'an Act respecting certain aspects of legal capacity for marriage for civil purposes' – the federal Civil Marriage Act – and it immediately came into force.

---

[1] www.cbc.ca/newsinteractives/features/same-sex-marriage-canada-lgbtq.

Changing mores with respect to traditionally proscribed gender roles have generated intense discomfort, when not outright hostility from Canadians. Acceptance of same-sex couples, whether married or not, or homosexuals as parents or simply as part of Canada's social fabric has been a long and hard-fought battle. Homosexuals have been portrayed as deviants, dangerous and mentally ill. Anything perceived as giving rise to or condoning homosexuality threatened these prejudices, deeply ingrained in society and in the law. In accordance with sodomy laws, sex between men was a crime in this country from the earliest colonial days to 1969, when omnibus changes were made to the Criminal Code of Canada.

Prior to Confederation, there was the story of George Markland. He was a member of Upper Canada's Family Compact, that small tight network of men who from the 1810s to the 1840s dominated the legislative, bureaucratic, economic, judicial and religious centres of power in the colony. Markland's political career ended abruptly because of rumours he was having illicit relationships with men who came to his office sometimes in the evenings. In May 1838, Markland was accused of improper conduct. An inquiry was ordered by Lieutenant Governor Sir George Arthur. Witnesses came forth claiming Markland had had liaisons with several young men. He was presumed to be guilty. On 28 August, his career in shambles, Markland agreed to resign as inspector general, and in return, the inquiry was dropped. George Markland lived the rest of his life in virtual isolation and never again held any public office.

Some decades later, in Old Montreal, in a sting operation in 1869, police raided the premises of Moise Tellier, owner of a supposed notorious hangout for homosexuals. The *Montreal Star* reported the incident, stating, 'Tellier's business is nominally to keep a small shop for apples, cakes, and similar trifles. But the business is only a cloak for the commission of crimes that rival Sodom and Gomorrah ... It has been watched'. The police and media generally agreed that something of a homosexual nature was going on; Tellier was involved and implied to be for some time; and had sexually propositioned a constable. Moise Tellier was apprehended, tried and fined $20, although it is not clear what the actual charge was.[2]

Such prejudices, police raids and enforcement of laws that criminalized homosexuality remained strong and unabated. In 1927, under the editorship of Strathearn Boyd Thomson, one of Toronto's social elites, the tabloid newspaper, *Hush* (later renamed *Hush Free Press*), was founded. An instant success, it soon had a wide readership right across the country, publishing very personal stories, reports of government corruption and sensationalized

---

[2]Hamish Copley, 'Tales from the Champ-de-Mars, part 1: The Moise Tellier Trial', in *The Drummer's Revenge*, LGBT history and politics in Canada, 4 May 2016, https://thedrummersrevenge.wordpress.com/2016/05/04/tales-from-the-champ-de-mars-part-1-the-moise-tellier-trial/; and Craig Jennex, *Out North: An Archive of Queer Activism and Kinship in Canada* (Toronto: The ArQuives: Canada's LGTBQ2+ Archives, 2020), 15.

accounts of gay and lesbian life, with headlines such as 'Love-Sick Pansy Boys', in the 5 June 1930 edition,[3] or 'Winnipeg's "Pansy" Traffic: More Police Vigilance Required on the Streets', at the top of the front page of the 19 May 1932 edition. Earlier, in 1928 and into 1929, *Hush* published a number of articles about the banned lesbian novel, *The Well of Loneliness*, by British author Radclyffe Hall, and the infamous obscenity trial that followed its publication. These formed part of a 'special series of articles' dealing with lesbianism, 'one of the vilest of the hidden vices of modem society'. One of the writers pointed out what he characterized as a 'peculiar legal anomaly', stating that 'while male persons guilty of unnatural acts are diligently prosecuted and heavily punished ... like conduct between females, strange as it may seem, appears to come outside the cognizance of the Law'. Accordingly, the writer concluded, lesbians were 'shameless females beyond the law'.[4] In addition to sodomy being a crime, in 1892, section 178 of the first Criminal Code of Canada made 'gross indecency' between men illegal. This included anything indicative of same-sex attraction, such as dancing, kissing or simply touching. In 1953, section 178 was extended to women.

During the Second World War, to free up more men for frontline action overseas, some 50,000 Canadian women were recruited for various auxiliary roles in support of the military. The Women's Royal Canadian Naval Service (WRCNS) was formed in 1917, disbanded in 1919, and reformed in 1939; initially WRCNS members served as cooks, despatch riders and sail-makers. In 1941, the Canadian Women's Auxiliary Air Force was established and renamed the Women's Division of the Royal Canadian Air Force (WDs) the following year; these women had administrative, clerical and other comparable roles. Also in 1941, the Canadian Women's Army Corps (CWAC) was created; most of these women served in Canada although some went overseas, and most worked as secretaries, cooks, mechanics and in other needed trades. By and large, Canadians accepted these as emergency measures. Nevertheless, there also arose a 'whispering campaign',[5] in which it was said that such women would lose their femininity and be exposed to lesbians.

Efforts were made to keep gays and lesbians from coming to Canada, most blatantly in Canada's 1952 Immigration Act, which placed restrictions on admitting 'prostitutes, homosexuals, and degenerates'.[6] Attention focused on exposing gays and lesbians in the military, as they were assumed to compromise cohesion, and in government roles that involved security, as they were considered susceptible to blackmail from Soviet and other

---

[3] Jennex, *Out North: An Archive of Queer Activism and Kinship in Canada*.
[4] See Steve Maynard, '"Hell Witches in Toronto": Notes on Lesbian Visibility in Early-Twentieth-Century Canada', *Left History* 9, no. 2 (Spring/Summer, 1994): 191–205.
[5] Ruth Roach Pierson, *They're Still Women after All: The Second World War and Canadian Womanhood* (Toronto: McClelland & Stewart, 1986), chapter 4.
[6] Jennex, *Out North*, 14.

Communist agents. It was common practice for police or RCMP officers to be placed undercover at bars or at other places considered to be gay gathering spots (as happened in the Tellier incident). Surveillance also involved mail opening and phone tapping and interrogating suspected sexual partners. The RCMP built a network of informants and files on thousands of suspected homosexuals. Those in the military who were identified as homosexuals were forced to resign. Interrogations would last for hours where the accused would be threatened with a dishonourable discharge unless giving up the names of others. 'One day, chillingly, I realized I was undergoing somewhat heavy-handed investigation', recalled Harold, a long-serving naval officer stationed in Ottawa as an assistant director. 'He [the military investigator] turned in my direction and said, "I have received allegations that you are a homosexual. What do you have to say?" To have admitted homosexuality would have caused my immediate dismissal and the destruction of the basis on which I had built my life'.[7]

Nine thousand such individuals had been identified by 1968 and their names put on lists. Those who were in the Civil Service and the military were forced to resign or assigned to mundane roles. The campaign against homosexuals was kept secret. There were no committee hearings where people were called to give testimony or to publicly divulge names, as in the famously televised ones that Wisconsin Senator Joseph McCarthy chaired in the early 1950s to root out suspected Communists in the United States. In Canada, knowledge of these campaigns to identify homosexuals remained hush-hush, especially in queer communities where people knew it was essential to practise discretion and secrecy.

In the early 1960s, seeking to improve their identification of homosexuals, the RCMP connected with Frank Wake, at Ottawa's Carleton University. With funding from the federal Department of Health and Welfare, Professor Wake, whose specialization was Criminal Sexual Psychopathy, began work on what the RCMP derisively called the 'fruit machine'. Never proven effective and abandoned by authorities in 1967, the programme sought to identify homosexuals through the response of their pupils to visual stimuli, word association, attention span and blood volume flow, as well as from a series of 'masculinity-femininity tests'.[8]

With growing restlessness, especially among youth, over what many considered excessive conservatism, traditionalism and the emphasis on conformity since the end of the Second World War, social attitudes began to shift in the 1960s. Young Canadians, particularly university students, demanded change. They wanted a different life from that of their parents

---

[7]Gary Kinsman and Patrizia Gentile, *The Canadian War on Queers: National Security as Sexual Regulation* (Vancouver: University of British Columbia Press, 2010), 116.
[8]www.cbc.ca/arts/the-fruit-machine-why-every-canadian-should-learn-about-this-country-s-gay-purge-1.4678718.

and grandparents, and they spearheaded change in music, fashion and many of the values of an earlier generation. The US civil rights movement and youth protest against the military draft (conscription) and the war in Vietnam helped fuel the movement in Canada. Moreover, these years saw a growing women's rights and liberation movement, which for many women meant workplace and legal equality and beyond that the right to control their own bodies. This led to demands, and successes, on access to birth control, including to the contraceptive pill, and for access to legal abortions.

Tolerance and progressivism with regard to same-sex couples appeared to gain steam, if slowly. One such indication was the stunning rise to prominence of Pierre Elliott Trudeau. First elected to the House of Commons in 1965, he served as justice minister and attorney general in Lester Pearson's Liberal government and then as prime minister of Canada. Across the country, people were captivated by this unconventional figure in Canada's corridors of power – by 1968 their excitement was even described as 'Trudeaumania'. A bachelor in his late forties, with his flamboyant style, charisma and sex appeal, Pierre Trudeau seemed to symbolize the mood of the Swinging Sixties. He spoke often of a Canada that was becoming less staid, more diverse, modern and accepting. As justice minister, he raised formerly taboo topics like abortion, divorce and homosexuality, and on 21 December 1967, he introduced Bill C-195, the 'Omnibus Bill', in the House of Commons. The bill called for massive changes to the Criminal Code of Canada with proposed revisions to abortion laws, the legalization of lotteries, restrictions on gun ownership and legalization of police breathalyzer checks. The section that attracted the most attention, however, was its proposal to decriminalize 'homosexual acts' performed in private. Explaining the bill, Trudeau said, 'It's bringing the laws of the land up to contemporary society ... Take this thing on homosexuality. The view we take is, there's no place for the state in the bedrooms of the nation. What's done in private between adults doesn't concern the Criminal Code'. The week before the bill was introduced, however, Pearson announced that he would be retiring from politics the following spring. In April 1968, Trudeau won the Liberal leadership convention called to replace Pearson, making him prime minister. Bill C-195 died on the Order Paper during the 1967–8 Session, but after the general election held on 25 June 1968, which the Liberals won by landslide, it was reintroduced as Bill C-150 that December by John Turner, the new justice minister.

On 14 May 1969, after heated debates, the Criminal Law Amendment Act, 1968–9 passed third reading in the House of Commons by a vote of 149 to 55. This was a massive 126-page, 120-clause amendment to the criminal law and criminal procedure of Canada. It decriminalized homosexual acts and homosexuals nationwide and allowed abortion under certain conditions; lotteries were thereby regulated; rules for gun possession were tightened; and new offences were written into law, e.g., for drinking and driving, making harassing phone calls, misleading advertising and cruelty to animals.

Winning a clear majority government, Trudeau's promise was to create a just society. Yet, for all the progressive noises, Trudeau's government did not make it easier for Canadian women to have an abortion, nor did it condone homosexuality. Nevertheless, Trudeau is remembered for declaring, 'We're not going to send policemen into the nation's bedrooms'.[9] In part, this was his response to the widespread outrage over a 1967 decision by the Supreme Court of Canada affirming a twenty-year jail sentence handed to Everett Klippert of Saskatchewan for being classified as a dangerous sex offender, though, in actual fact, his real 'crime' was being gay. Yet, during the leaders' debate leading to the 1968 federal election, Trudeau said that he was 'separating the idea of sin and the idea of crime', adding that those who engaged in certain activities would have to answer to their God for their sins, not the police.[10] In 1971, Klippert's sentence was reversed, and he was freed. In 2017, the Justin Trudeau government formally apologized to Klippert and issued a compensation package to those charged, convicted and punished simply because they were gay.

Demands for rights for homosexuals had started to gain momentum. The famous 'Stonewall Riots' in New York City in 1969, for example, where gay men engaged in violent resistance in response to vicious police raids on the Stonewall Inn in Greenwich Village, gave impetus to a gay rights movement that also came to Canada. Calls for gay rights were also encouraged by the greater sexual liberation that occurred in the 1970s. Gays and lesbians became more visible, including as characters on popular television shows, even if often still portrayed in a comedic, flamboyant, effeminate, stereotyped manner. Quebec, in a bold move in 1977, became the first province in Canada to include protection of sexual orientation in its Human Rights Code, making it illegal to discriminate against homosexuals in employment, housing and public accommodation.

Gays and lesbians organized groups and campaigns for more rights and to raise awareness of the discrimination they faced. The Gay Alliance towards Equality (GATE) was founded in Vancouver in 1971 and later added a chapter in Toronto. The University of Western Ontario's Homophile Association was formed in 1970; after a time, it moved off-campus, and in 1975 became the Homophile Association of London (HALO). The Zodiac Friendship Society of Saskatoon was created in 1972. The Gay Montreal Association/Association Homophile de Montreal was active in the early 1970s. The decade also saw the opening of gay and lesbian bookstores and theatre companies. Gay groups organized fundraising events, such as those to support Douglas Wilson, a University of Saskatchewan graduate student who, in 1975, was suspended from supervising student teachers because of

---

[9] www.cbc.ca/archives/no-place-for-the-state-in-the-bedrooms-of-the-nation-1.4681298.
[10] 'Federal Elections: 1968 Leaders' Debate', at 1:48:18, CBC Archives, https://www.cbc.ca/player/play/1842543948.

his involvement in gay liberation activities. Such activism mushroomed, and by the end of the decade, there were at least thirty such organizations in some fifteen communities across Canada.

Nevertheless, the 1970s continued to see police raids, such as on bathhouses, with gay men arrested for engaging in sexual activity, which remained illegal outside the parameters of two consenting adults, twenty-one years of age and older, and in a private setting. In 1977, Toronto police and the Ontario Provincial Police (OPP) raided the offices of Canadian Gay Archives and The Body Politic, then arguably the most prominent publisher specializing in material for the queer community. Several of those involved were charged with distributing 'obscene, indecent, immoral or scurrilous'[11] material. Eventually brought to trial, they were acquitted, though their complaints to Ontario Attorney-General Roy McMurtry were never answered. Facing down such opposition, the Gay Archives grew, held conferences and workshops, and published works on gay leaders. It earned charitable status in 1981, which significantly helped its financial position and enabled its continued growth.

Gay groups fought back against prejudice through the courts, one example being the activism of the Gay Alliance Toward Equality. In 1973, GATE launched a human rights complaint against the *Vancouver Sun* for refusing to publish a paid advertisement for a queer publication named *Gay Tide*. Although GATE lost, the case made it all the way to the Supreme Court of Canada, which in its decision cited freedom of the press and argued that 'homosexuality was offensive to most people'.[12]

Some queer groups took to public protest. As early as 1971, several came together on Parliament Hill in Ottawa to condemn the discrimination they faced that, they charged, federal politicians were doing nothing to mitigate. 'There's no homosexual problem in Canada', declared one of their leaders.

> There's a heterosexual problem. It is they who have made the laws to protect themselves from us. They're the ones who employ the RCMP to identify us, isolate us from our jobs ... [and] control the schools that teach hatred of homosexuals. They're the ones who control the churches that label us sinners. They're the ones who control the courts that label us criminals. No longer![13]

In 1977, Barbara Thornborrow went public against the Canadian Forces Special Investigations Unit (SIU) after it had precipitated her departure from the military when love letters from her girlfriend and her possession of gay and lesbian publications were uncovered. That same year, anti-gay prejudice

---

[11] Jennex, *Out North*, 15.
[12] Ibid., 108.
[13] Ibid., 121.

spiked in the wake of the murder of twelve-year-old Emmanuel Jacques in Toronto. Lured into an apartment with the promise of money to help move furniture, Jacques was sexually assaulted and killed by a homosexual assailant. The ensuing outrage across Canada, including intense anti-gay sentiment, saw the shutting down of numerous adult stores and body rub parlours rumoured to be frequented by homosexuals.

Through the late 1970s, protests and activism by gay and lesbian groups grew across Canada. These actions were stoked by a visit to Canada by the American 1950s and 1960s celebrity pop singer, Anita Bryant, who later became known for campaigning against queer rights, leading a coalition called Save Our Children. In 1978, Bryant toured Canada as part of Renaissance International's Christian Liberation Crusade; more than 1,000 people came out in Toronto to protest her presence. Towards the end of the decade, gay and lesbian groups and their supporters raised some $90,000 to help pay the legal defence costs of more than twenty men arrested at a police raid of a downtown Toronto bathhouse known as The Barracks. In May 1981, the Toronto Gay Street Patrol was formed. Its members, though dedicated to non-violence, completed self-defence training to prevent and cope with attacks on homosexuals. But police raids did not abate. On 5 February 1981, some 300 suspected homosexuals were arrested by Toronto police at four known gay bathhouses; this was the largest mass arrest in Canada since the 1970 October Crisis when the federal government imposed the War Measures Act to suppress the violent Front du libération du Québec (FLQ). More than 90 per cent of the charges made during the bathhouse raids were eventually dropped, and thirty-five years later, in 2016, Toronto police issued an official apology. These raids galvanized Toronto's LGBTQ community to fight for their rights and their political voice.

The 1980s brought the catastrophic impact of the Acquired Immunodeficiency Syndrome (AIDS) epidemic. In Canada, AIDS killed thousands of young men, and brought more intense, and open, prejudice with people referring to AIDS as the 'gay disease' and as God's judgement against homosexuality. Gays responded with groups like the AIDS Committee of Toronto, established in 1983, and three years later, the Canadian AIDS Society formed as an umbrella organization to counter growing anti-gay sentiment. The RCMP scaled back its surveillance to find homosexuals, and rule changes allowed gays to appeal the denial of a security clearance. Still, the RCMP, as well as the Canadian Security Intelligence Service (CSIS), created in 1984, maintained anti-gay hiring practices. From February 1986, in response to a Military Charter Task Force, service personnel were no longer required to report suspected homosexuals to their commanding officer. Canada's military continued to purge gays and lesbians, and it was known that many military commanders unofficially tolerated violence against suspected homosexuals in their ranks. By the end of the decade, however, further signs of Canadians' increasing acceptance of homosexuals and progress with respect to their rights did come. On 29 February 1988,

British Columbia's Svend Robinson of the New Democratic Party (NDP) became the first openly gay member of Canada's Parliament, though not until 1994 did Bloc Québécois MP Réal Ménard become the second.

The 1990s brought other wins for what is now called the 2SLGBTQ+ community. The acronym represents two-spirit, lesbian, gay, bisexual, transgender, queer and additional people who identify as part of sexual- and gender-diverse community, terminology that continues to evolve. Gays and lesbians carried their fight forward through the courts. With increased visibility and growing public support came legislative and policy wins. In 1992, the ban against homosexuals serving in the military was lifted. Also in August 1992, in a landmark decision that came to be called 'the Leshner Ruling', the Ontario Human Rights Commission, in the matter of the Ontario Public Service Pension Plan, ruled in favour of extending survivor benefits to persons in same-sex conjugal relationships. It was Michael Leshner who filed the complaint, and as a Crown attorney for the province (and thus a member of the Public Service Pension Plan), he was taking his own employer to court. Leshner argued that the denial of survivor benefits to his same-sex partner – Michael Stark, who he met in 1981 and married in 2003 – constituted a contravention of the Ontario Human Rights Code. The Commission agreed and ordered the province to set up a 'parallel arrangement' to disburse these benefits. Over the years, the couple took part in various protests, Pride parades and media interviews. But beyond trying to shift public opinion and gain traction politically, Leshner opted for a legal strategy to advance the fight for equal rights for gays and lesbians.

The broad trend pointed to increased acceptance and success in attaining equality. This progress was bolstered by references to Canada's 1982 Charter of Rights and Freedoms, particularly section 15(1), which states, 'Every individual is equal before and under the law and has the right to the equal protection and equal benefit of the law without discrimination and, in particular, without discrimination based on race, national or ethnic origin, colour, religion, sex, age or mental or physical disability'.[14] Although there is no mention of sexual orientation – an omission interpreted by many as deliberate – the intent or philosophy evident in section 15(1) of the Charter has been used to great effect in advancing rights for gays, lesbians and all others who identify as part of the queer community.

Several provincial Human Rights codes, during the 1990s, identified discrimination based on sexual orientation as unacceptable, as did the federal Human Rights Code in 1996. The previous year, Ontario – soon followed by British Columbia, Alberta and Nova Scotia – permitted same-sex couples to adopt children. In 1997, Canada's military began considering same-sex benefits. The Supreme Court of Canada, in 1999, ruled that same-sex couples should have access to the same government benefits as extended

---

[14] www.justice.gc.ca/eng/csj-sjc/rfc-dlc/ccrf-ccdl/resources-ressources.html#copy.

to all common law and married couples. As the millennium closed, a legally recognized marriage still applied solely to the union between one man and one woman. But the political, and legal, winds were shifting.

In December 2000, at the Metropolitan Community Church of Toronto, Pastor Brent Hawkes began issuing banns of marriage in advance of performing wedding ceremonies for two same-sex couples – Kevin Bourassa and Joe Varnell, and Anne and Elaine Vautour – whom he married on 14 January 2001. This was the first legal same-sex marriage in North America. The banns form did not require the spouses' gender to be specified. Local and national media covered the event and were joined by international organizations such as Agence France Press, Reuters, Associated Press, *Time*, *Newsweek*, *Ms.*, *Salon*, *Mother Jones*, a Japanese television crew and also the Christian Broadcast Network. Even Canada's governor general was there, if only in spirit: at one point during the service, the minister told the congregation that Governor-General Adrienne Clarkson had sent her regrets and well wishes to the happy couples. Similar marriages followed, and all were later validated with the Ontario Court of Appeal's landmark ruling in 2003 but backdated to 2001.

Issuing banns of marriage is a fully legal way to have a marriage performed without the need for a city-issued marriage licence. Marriages performed under either process – after issuing banns or after presenting a marriage licence – require certification by the provincial registrar. Thus, banns-based marriages created a legal vacuum that forced a court case. Over the course of the year, several other same-sex couples, among them Hedy Halpern and Colleen Rogers, as well as Michael Leshner and Michael Stark, joined a court challenge that began hearings at the Ontario Superior Court in November 2001. The argument was that, like withholding benefits, denying same-sex couples the option to marry violated their equality rights under the Charter of Rights and Freedoms.

The Ontario Superior Court, in *Halpern et al. v. Attorney General of Canada et al.* ruled in 2003 that not recognizing same-sex unions as legal was a violation of Canada's Charter of Rights and Freedoms. 'Same-sex couples are capable of forming long, lasting, loving and intimate relationships', the Court declared. 'Denying same-sex couples the right to marry perpetuates the contrary view, namely, that same-sex couples are not capable of forming loving and lasting relationships, and thus same-sex relationships are not worthy of the same respect and recognition as opposite-sex relationships. The Court does not accept that'.[15]

In spring 2003, a House of Commons Standing Committee on Justice and Human Rights began hearings across Canada on how best to recognize same-sex unions. In Canada, both the federal and provincial governments

---

[15] www.cbc.ca/newsinteractives/features/same-sex-marriage-canada-lgbtq.

share jurisdiction over marriage laws. The federal government, through Parliament, has the power to legislate on the definition of marriage and divorce. Provinces, on the other hand, have the authority to regulate the solemnization of marriage (the ceremony) and issue marriage licenses. The Committee travelled to a dozen cities and heard from 475 witnesses. Although often quite profound and intense disagreements were heard, the broad consensus pointed to growing support for equality: while in 1993, 37 per cent of Canadians surveyed supported same-sex marriages, by 2002, that proportion stood at 53 per cent. Liberal Prime Minister Jean Chrétien indicated that the federal government was disposed to move in that direction, but he also said that the courts would have the final word. The Halpern case had been taken to the provincial Court of Appeal, and its verdict on 10 June 2003 reaffirmed the initial decision. On 28 June 2005, Canada's Parliament passed the Civil Marriage Act. The free vote in the House of Commons was a momentous victory for gays, lesbians and their many allies, but the fact that the count was 158 to 133 clearly demonstrated division, discomfort and continuing reluctance among many Canadians to fully accept queer communities. Governments in Canada were pleased that these cases were taken to the courts, because the decisions gave them cover to move in a direction still politically charged and divisive.

Canada was the third country worldwide to legalize same-sex marriages, after the Netherlands and Belgium. Others followed, often rapidly. By 2023, marriage equality had come to most US states, Europe and Oceania, as well as to several countries in South and Central America. In Africa, only South Africa had moved in this direction, and in Asia, only Taiwan.

Momentum continued for acceptance and equality for queer communities in Canada. The federal Conservative government under Stephen Harper came to power in January 2006. During that election campaign, Harper promised to hold a free vote to settle the same-sex marriage issue, once and for all. Though many Conservative MPs were known to be opposed to same-sex marriage, they did not seek to reverse the Civil Marriage Act, realizing that it would cost them politically and likely produce reversals in the courts. In early December 2006, a motion asking the government to introduce legislation to restore the traditional definition of marriage without affecting civil unions and while respecting existing same-sex marriages – which would have required Conservative support to proceed – was defeated, 175 to 123. Also in 2006, responding to a parliamentary committee report entitled *Equality for All*, it was decided that excluding sexual orientation from any of Canada's Human Rights codes, provincial or federal, constituted a violation of the Charter of Rights and Freedoms. In another free vote in the House of Commons, this was supported by a count of 153 to 76.

With greater recognition, public support and legal victories, the number of same-sex marriages in Canada tripled between 2006 and 2011, to the point where they were largely normalized. Canada's international image became one of being a gay-friendly country. In 2006, Montreal hosted the first-ever World Outgames that brought tens of thousands of queer athletes from more than 100 countries to the city. The 2010 Winter Olympics that was held in Vancouver provided a separate building – named Pride House – for gay athletes. Annual Pride parades in Canadian cities have become massive events, with politicians from all major political parties joining in support. In 2014, WorldPride in Toronto became the largest ever queer gathering and included a mass wedding for 115 same-sex couples. Pride flags now fly at countless public events, and in high schools gay-straight alliances have flourished, building understanding and mutual respect among the young. Also of great significance was that in November 2017, Prime Minister Justin Trudeau issued an official apology on behalf of the federal government – and the nation – for the purging of gays and lesbians from the public service and the military, especially during the 1950s, 1960s and 1970s. Their criminal records were expunged, and financial compensation was paid to those who had lost their employment and equally important, Trudeau said 'for the oppression of the lesbian, gay, bisexual, transgender, queer, and two-spirit communities, we apologize. We were wrong. We are sorry. And we will never let this happen again'.[16] In 2024, some 65 per cent of Canadians believed that same-sex couples should have the right to legally marry.[17] Still, many religious groups, particularly Catholics and evangelical Protestants, successfully argued in court for exemptions to perform and recognize such unions, arguing not only Charter Rights protecting Freedom of Religion, but also that 'God creates and orders marriage between a man and a woman', for the purpose of procreation, and that 'scripture prohibits homosexual relationships'. However, Canada's United Church, among many other denominations, declared marriage as 'a union in which the covenant between God and humanity is mutually expressed and experienced'[18] and that same-sex relationships equally reflected that covenant.

By no means has homophobia or transphobia disappeared in Canada, a fact that is sometimes shockingly expressed. In 2018, in Toronto, Bruce McArthur pleaded guilty to eight counts of the first-degree murder of gay men. Gays are still compelled by law to disclose to any sexual partner that they have HIV/AIDS, a requirement that criminalizes them discriminately as the disease can be spread by anyone, or through the transmission of blood. Most recently, in 2024, in an action widely condemned as transphobic, New Brunswick, Alberta and Saskatchewan issued an order requiring teachers to inform the parents of anyone under the age of sixteen if their child was

---

[16]'Remarks by Prime Minister Justin Trudeau to Apologize to LGBTQ2 Canadian', 28 November 2017, https://www.pm.gc.ca/en/news/speeches/2017/11/28/remarks-prime-minister-justin-trudeau-apologize-lgbtq2-canadians.
[17]https://www.statista.com/statistics/1317351/public-opinion-same-sex-marriage-canada/.
[18]Pamela Dickey Young, *Religion, Sex and Politics: Christian Churches and Same-Sex Marriage in Canada* (Halifax and Winnipeg: Fernwood Publishing, 2008), 59, 69.

identifying themselves using a different pronoun from the gender on their birth certificate. In Saskatchewan, to retain the requirement, the provincial government used the notwithstanding clause in the Charter of Rights and Freedoms to override that document's protections of individual liberties. 'Some unsupportive families have kicked their kids out of the house or resorted to physical violence. Shredding the rights of students is repulsive', said Harini Sivalingam, director of the Equality Program at the Canadian Civil Liberties Association. Eric Bell, who founded Queen City for All, an advocacy organization to promote inclusion in Regina schools, bluntly concluded, 'There is no other way to describe it other than bigotry and transphobia and homophobia'.[19] Recent polls indicate that Canadians may be becoming less tolerant, reflecting growing social conservatism across North America and large parts of Europe over the 2020s. While some 74 per cent of Canadians polled in 2023 agreed that transgender people should be legally protected from discrimination in housing, employment and access to public places, this had dropped from 78 per cent two years earlier, and when it came to accepting them displaying affection in public, support over the same period declined from 48 to 40 per cent. With respect to trans males competing in women's sports, only 21 per cent were supportive in 2023.[20]

For 2SLGBTQ+ communities, the Canada of the 2020s is far cry from what the country was like in previous decades. With increasing speed and scope, the current generation has witnessed a transformational expansion of rights. Gay marriages are no longer an anomaly. Recent and monumental victories, and the general acceptance – and even normalization – of gay life remain a very new phenomenon and belie a past and sometimes still a present where discrimination and ostracism are widespread. Certainly, courageous protests in pursuit of greater rights within the gay community set a strong foundation upon which their full legal equality has been established. Yet, in the minds of many people, this is not only controversial, but viewed as immoral, making newfound victories seem tenuous. Homophobia remains deeply entrenched, and, in a more conservative milieux, surfaces with strength, as the trans community is currently experiencing. Canada's legalization of same-sex marriages was a landmark affirmation of Charter rights and established the country as a worldwide leader in supporting queer communities. Still, there remain several battles for 2SLGBTQ+ communities to win so that Canada unequivocally reflects its reputation as one of the world's best countries in being gay-friendly.

---

[19] nationalpost.com/news/saskatchewan-students-pronoun.
[20] Ipsos, 'Canadians Support Protection of The LGBT+ Community, but Declining Support May Indicate a Step Back in Progress', 1 June 2024. https://www.ipsos.com/en-ca/canadians-support-protection-lgbt-community-but-support-declining.

IMAGE 14 In Act of Reconciliation, Canada Apologizes for Aboriginal Abuses. Canadian Prime Minister Stephen Harper (R) and National Chief of the Assembly of First Nations Phil Fontaine (2R) pause before walking into the House of Commons on Parliament Hill, 11 June 2008.

14

Statement of apology, 2008: Activism, dialogue, truth – towards reconciliation

On behalf of the Government of Canada, on Wednesday, 11 June 2008, in a special joint session of the House of Commons and the Senate, Prime Minister Stephen Harper delivered a 'Statement of Apology to Former Students of Indian Residential Schools'. This was a seminal moment, for as the prime minister declared, 'The treatment of children in Indian Residential Schools is a sad chapter in our history'. It was the first time that Canada officially took responsibility for attempting to assimilate its Indigenous, peoples – First Nations, Inuit and Métis – most especially by placing their children in government-sponsored residential schools, where many became victims of physical, sexual and psychological abuse, the effects of which lasted for generations, even to this day. For more than four decades, former students of residential schools had campaigned to have the government and the various religious orders recognize the abuses that had occurred at those schools and provide compensation for their abuses and mistreatment. The Government of Canada had responded incrementally. In 1998, it issued a Statement of Reconciliation acknowledging the abuses suffered by former students and established the multi-million-dollar Aboriginal Healing Foundation. In 2003, the Alternative Dispute Resolution process was launched which provided an out-of-court mechanism to determine compensation and offer psychological support. In 2006, the Canadian government, the churches and Indigenous organizations reached a class-action agreement with legal counsel for former students to address the legacy of residential schools. The comprehensive Indian Residential Schools Settlement Agreement (IRSSA) provided a $1.9 billion compensation package for all former residential school students through a Common Experience Payment (CEP) and an Independent Assessment Process (IAP) for claims of abuse. The apology was not wholly a gesture of magnanimity on the part of the Prime Minister even if he did choose to do so in Parliament and in a televised broadcast. It was part of the IRSSA settlement.

In the thirteen-minute statement, televised on Canadian Broadcasting Corporation (CBC) and the Aboriginal Peoples Television Network (APTN) channels,[1] Harper described the federal government's 'role in the development and administration of these [residential] schools'. This policy began in the 1870s, with the last such school closing only in 1997. 'Two primary objectives of the Residential Schools system', explained Harper, 'were to remove and isolate children from the influence of their homes, families, traditions and cultures, and to assimilate them into the dominant culture'. Moreover, 'these objectives were based on the assumption Aboriginal cultures and spiritual beliefs were inferior and unequal'. 'Indeed', as the prime minister was surely embarrassed to acknowledge, 'some sought, as it was infamously said, "to kill the Indian in the child"'. Owning up, Harper proclaimed, 'today, we recognize that this policy of assimilation was wrong, has caused great harm, and has no place in our country'.[2]

Despite the federal government's decades-long determination to assimilate them, in spite of official statutes curtailing their rights – including the right to vote and the right to legal representation in making complaints to the government – Indigenous people survived these neo-colonial, even genocidal policies, and they have prevailed. Their numbers have consistently been increasing, from 113,000 in 1921 to a quarter million in 1951, and a half million by 1971, until another fifty years later, more than 1.8 million people in Canada (5.0% of the population of Canada) self-identified as an Indigenous person on Canada's 2021 Census of Population.[3]

The prime minister described and addressed the harms done by the Residential Schools system. Across the country, there had been 132 such 'federally-supported schools', most of them 'operated as "joint ventures" with Anglican, Catholic, Presbyterian or United Churches'. Harper stated that 'the Government of Canada built an educational system in which very young children were often forcibly removed from their homes, often taken far from their communities. Many were inadequately fed, clothed and housed. All were deprived of the care and nurturing of their parents, grandparents and communities'. He acknowledged that 'First Nations, Inuit, and Métis languages and cultural practices were prohibited in these schools', and further, 'tragically, some of these children died while attending

---

[1] See, e.g., 2008 Federal Apology to Residential School Survivors, https://www.youtube.com/watch?v=aQjnbK6d3oQ.

[2] 'Prime Minister Harper Offers Full Apology on Behalf of Canadians for the Indian Residential Schools System' (Hereafter, Harper's Apology), https://www.rcaanc-cirnac.gc.ca/eng/1100100015644/1571589171655.

[3] 'An Update on the Socio-economic Gaps between Indigenous Peoples and the Non-Indigenous Population in Canada: Highlights from the 2021 Census', https://www.sac-isc.gc.ca/eng/1690909773300/1690909797208.

residential schools and others never returned home'. Then the prime minister announced: 'The government now recognizes that the consequences of the Indian Residential Schools policy were profoundly negative and that this policy has had a lasting and damaging impact on Aboriginal culture, heritage and language'. He asserted that 'while some former students have spoken positively about their experiences at residential schools, these stories are far overshadowed by tragic accounts of the emotional, physical and sexual abuse and neglect of helpless children, and their separation from powerless families and communities'.[4]

How did this momentous change in the government's attitude come about? One way to historicize the changes is to consider how political leaders (both Indigenous and non-Indigenous) since the nineteenth century confronted Indigenous peoples even though we acknowledge that such an approach does not always capture the whole Indigenous perspective that often motivated new directions at the state level.[5] Almost from the earliest days of Confederation, and certainly with the Indian Act, a Canadian federal law that came into force in 1876, together with the Department of Indian Affairs (DIA) and its agents, the lives of Indigenous people were kept severely constrained. The Act has been a central piece of legislation impacting First Nations peoples in Canada, often viewed as a tool of colonial control and assimilation. It controls such matters as Indian status, defining who is legally considered 'Indian' and therefore eligible for certain benefits and rights; and the structure of First Nations bands (governing bodies) and the management of Indian reserves (land set aside for First Nations). Although it has been amended numerous times, including in 1985 to address sex-based discrimination in the Act, allowing women who lost status through marriage to regain it, the Indian Act continues to be a significant factor in the relationship between the federal government and First Nations in Canada and the cultures, economies and communities of First Nations communities. It is now accepted that historically the Act facilitated policies like residential schools that caused severe intergenerational trauma for many First Nations communities. Well into the twentieth century, the DIA came down hard on any attempts at Indigenous political organization and activism, and it took until 1960 for Indigenous persons to be granted the right to vote in Canada's federal and provincial elections.

Starting soon after the First World War, however, organized demands for changes in the relationship between Indigenous peoples and the Canadian government became increasingly apparent and increasingly harder for

---

[4]Harper's 'Apology'.
[5]Anne Trépanier, for instance, notes how the historical record tends to ignore the political engagement of Indigenous peoples in the nineteenth-century. See her, *De l'hydre au castor: Imaginaire et représentations de la Confédération dans la presse de l'Amérique du Nord britannique, 1844-1867* (Quebec: Éditions du Septentrion, 2024).

the Canadian state to ignore. More than 3,500 Indigenous men enlisted in Canada's military during the Great War. Among them was Lieutenant Frederick Ogilvie Loft (1861–1934), (known in Mohawk as Onondeyoh, meaning 'beautiful mountain') of the Six Nations of the Grand River, who went overseas with the 256th Infantry Battalion of the Canadian Expeditionary Force (CEF). After the Armistice, Indigenous veterans were not treated the same as the non-Indigenous men with whom they had served. They were denied access to such programmes as loans to purchase land because state officials deemed them, but not non-Indigenous veterans, unable to cope with debt. As a response to the rising frustrations of Indigenous veterans, Fred Loft established the League of Indians of Canada (LIC) in December 1918. The LIC was the first organization in Canada that aimed to see 'all Indians being united in one great association'.[6]

Lumberman, journalist, civil servant, author, activist, army officer and Mohawk pine tree chief, Loft knew deeply and intimately just how difficult, indeed, impossible in many respects was life for an Indigenous person of Canada.[7] Raised Anglican, he grew up speaking both English and Mohawk. Although not among the children who were 'forcibly removed from their homes',[8] at age twelve, Loft spent a year at a Residential School, and later had this to say about the experience: He remembered that he 'was hungry all the time, did not get enough to eat ... In winter the rooms and beds were so cold that it took half the night before I got warm enough to fall asleep'. He was later enrolled in community schools, graduated in bookkeeping from the Ontario Business College in Belleville, and in the next years held various jobs, including as a reporter covering the general election of February 1887. Prime Minister John A. Macdonald had in 1885 extended the federal franchise to all central and eastern Canadian male status Indians who met the property qualification; however, this right was withdrawn in 1898, at which time Wilfrid Laurier was prime minister. Loft was known to be 'a staunch Liberal', and somewhere around 1890, Ontario Liberal Premier Oliver Mowat appointed him to the bursar's office of the Asylum for the Insane in Toronto, a position Loft held until 1926. Illustrative of attitudes at the time are the words of Goldwin Smith in 1891. He had been a professor of history at Cornell University (1868–72) before moving to Toronto. Considered one of Toronto's 'leading intellectuals', he 'dismissed the native North American in two sentences: "The race, everyone says, is doomed ... Little will be lost by humanity"'.[9]

As well as his 'day job', Fred Loft did a lot of writing in which he drew attention to various Indigenous causes. In a letter to the Toronto *Globe*,

---

[6]Donald B. Smith, Loft, Frederick Ogilvie. (Hereafter, Smith, 'Loft'.) https://www.biographi.ca/en/bio/loft_frederick_ogilvie_16E.html.
[7]Smith, 'Loft'.
[8]Harper's 'Apology'.
[9]Smith, 'Loft'.

dated 7 November 1896, he explained his desire for 'greater autonomy for the First Nations'. The DIA 'should more readily adhere to our decisions and wishes, as expressed through the wisdom of our respective councils, rather than submit, as has too often unfortunately been the case, to dictation'.[10] The issue of submitting to 'dictation', rather than engaging with First Nations would come up time and again for more than a century.

The Lofts had an extensive social circle that included 'ministers, doctors, lawyers, and heads of organizations', who all 'counted Fred Loft as a friend'. This did not mean that Torontonians were unaware that the Loft was an Indigenous person. For a while, the Lofts lived on the same street as Toronto's senior police magistrate, who described his neighbour as 'a respectable gentleman of fairly good education, and much better qualified for the franchise than 95 per cent of those who have it'. In 1908, Loft published articles in the *Globe* 'on the future of the "Indian"' and also, in 1909, a series on 'the Indian and education' in *Saturday Night*. He described Residential Schools as 'veritable death-traps', and called instead for day schools on reserves.[11]

In 1907, Loft wrote an important letter to Prime Minister Laurier. In it, he explained his decision to apply for the post of superintendent of the Six Nations, the top federal job in the Grand River community. 'There is perhaps nothing I have desired in my life more than becoming if possible the Superintendent of the Six Nations of Brant; should it be considered by your Government that one of themselves would be capable of performing the duties of the office'. The Six Nations Council approved his application. The government, however, turned him down. Ten years later, the Council still wanted Loft as their superintendent, and again recommended his appointment, and again his application was denied. In August 1917, the Six Nations Council conferred on Fred Loft 'an honour given only to the most outstanding members of the Grand River Iroquois Confederacy': a pine tree chieftainship. Months later, as the Council's representative, Loft met with King George V at Buckingham Palace.[12]

On returning to Canada from his deployment overseas, Loft set to work seeking better conditions for Indigenous people. The federal government had in 1911 amended the Indian Act 'to permit the expropriation of reserves adjacent to or within large towns', a change denounced by the League of Indians of Canada. Loft wanted the government to improve the education it offered Indigenous children with additional day and high schools on reserves, and this was made one of the main objectives of the LIC.[13] In a statement of principles, the LIC asserted: 'Not in vain did our young men die in a strange land; not in vain are our Indian bones mingled with the soil

---

[10]Ibid.
[11]Ibid.
[12]Ibid.
[13]Ibid.

of a foreign land for the first time since the world began; not in vain did the Indian fathers and mothers see their sons march away to face what to them were unknown dangers'.[14] The organization listed a variety of issues that had long angered Indigenous people across Canada, and for which they were seeking redress from the federal government, including not only the destructive impact of educational policies and administrative practices, but also the poor economic and health conditions on reserves, the loss of reserve lands, the failure of the state to recognize Indigenous land rights and the restrictions imposed on hunting and trapping rights.

In encouraging membership and attendance at the LIC's annual meetings, Loft sent circulars to band chiefs and individuals alike, largely at his own expense. In one such circular letter, dated 26 November 1919, he argued that Indigenous people needed to 'free themselves from the domination of officialdom'. As the LIC's first president and secretary-treasurer, Loft expended enormous energies in trying to respond to every and any complaint that reached him. The Toronto *Daily Mail and Empire* asserted in his obituary that, before and after organizing the LIC, Loft 'travelled for years almost continuously fixing up a trapper's dispute, appealing to officials at Ottawa for justice to his clients, after the war helping the Indian veterans who were entitled to pensions'.[15]

Fred Loft met his nemesis in the person of Duncan Campbell Scott, who had joined the DIA in 1880 and from 1913 until 1932 served as its deputy superintendent general of Indian Affairs. Throughout his long career with the DIA, Scott aggressively promoted and enforced policies that marginalized Indigenous people, especially with regard to Indigenous spirituality. Under his direction, in 1920 the Indian Act was amended to require school attendance by Indigenous children between the ages of seven and fifteen, and because there were no Day Schools available for many students, residential schools were the only option.[16]

Scott was unhappy with the LIC's stated principles and demands. He regarded Loft as a subversive and the LIC as a roadblock to efficient administration. To destroy the LIC's effectiveness, he focused on its leader. Under a 1920 amendment to the Indian Act, Scott tried to have Loft's Indian status removed, to enfranchise him, in effect. Before a special committee of the House of Commons, Loft presented the LIC's position on compulsory enfranchisement, stating it was not opposed, 'so long as it is based upon educative ideals and a proper training for the eventual assumption of the individual for the higher status of citizenship involving

---

[14]Quoted in Timothy Winegard, *For King and Kanata: Canadian Indians and the First World War* (Winnipeg: University of Manitoba Press, 2012), 182, 184.
[15]Smith, 'Loft'.
[16]https://gladue.usask.ca/node/2408; and https://nctr.ca/education/teaching-resources/residential-school-history/.

all its responsibilities'. But how, Loft continued, could the government consider such a policy when 'scarcely five per cent of the adult population of the reserves are capable of corresponding intelligently'. This 'reveals him as a moderate', and shows Loft to be 'anxious for his people to enter into the larger society around them'.[17]

In 1922, Mackenzie King's government abolished compulsory enfranchisement. Scott's attempt to have Loft's Indian status removed failed, but he still considered Loft a radical, and certainly not 'a moderate'. Scott saw assimilation as the best solution to what he called the 'Indian' problem: 'Our objective is to continue until there is not a single Indian in Canada that has not been absorbed into the body politic'.[18] In hopes of embarrassing the federal government into changing its policies, the Ontario-based Six Nations took their case for self-government to the League of Nations in Geneva, which deemed the matter an internal one.

The LIC's growth was hampered by relentless opposition to it from the DIA, as well as by Loft's limited resources. A 1927 amendment to the Indian Act barred Indigenous people from hiring lawyers to pursue grievances against the government. Loft remained active. The *Toronto Daily Star*, on 17 November 1932, reported Loft's contention that jailing some 'Indians' for poaching under provincial game laws was contrary to their rights under the British North America (BNA) Act. This outspokenness inevitably caught Duncan Scott's attention, and in the early 1930s he considered criminal charges against Loft for attempting to raise money for land-claim issues. Loft's health was deteriorating, however; he died in Toronto in July 1934. As the historian Donald B. Smith has put it, 'The First Nations of Canada owe a great deal to Onondeyoh/Fred Loft, an early 20th-century political visionary'.[19]

During the Second World War, Canada's Indigenous people again answered the call. More than 4,200 First Nations individuals, including seventy-two women, enlisted, together with thousands more Métis, Inuit and non-Status Indians. They served without official recognition of their Indigenous identity. They participated in the domestic effort on the 'home front', donating and helping in humanitarian and patriotic causes, as well as working in war industries in unprecedented numbers. Yet, as happened after the First World War, Indigenous veterans of the Second were not afforded the same benefits as non-Indigenous veterans. Many found the return to societal racism and marginalization difficult after the acceptance they had experienced in uniform. The result was an increase in Indigenous political

---

[17] Smith, 'Loft'.
[18] Jonathan Peyton and Robert L. A. Hancock, 'Anthropology, State Formation, and Hegemonic Representations of Indigenous Peoples in Canada, 1910–1939', *Native Studies Review* 17, no. 1 (2008): 55, 63.
[19] Smith, 'Loft'.

activism. Although by the time Fred Loft died, the LIC had become largely defunct, except for branches in Alberta and Saskatchewan; other leaders and other organizations took up furthering Indigenous peoples' interests nationwide.

In 1939 the Indian Association of Alberta (IAA) was formed, the North American Indian Brotherhood was established in 1945, the Federation of Saskatchewan Indians (FSIN) in 1946, the National Indian Brotherhood (NIB) in 1968, and its successor, the Assembly of First Nations (AFB), was chartered in 1985. With the harrowing years of the Great Depression and then the Second World War finally over, Canada's federal government faced tremendous pressure for major changes to social and citizenship rights. As the country looked to its government to create a new social order, Indigenous people could no longer be ignored. In 1946 Mackenzie King initiated a Parliamentary review of the Indian Act. Through the DIA and its powerful agents, the Indian Act had given Ottawa almost complete control over Indigenous identity, political structures, governance, cultural practices and education, while seriously restricting the freedoms of Indigenous individuals. The state began a process of reforming the Indian Act, but as usual, without consulting Indigenous peoples. In face of their objections, however, the government – for the first time – finally reached out to First Nations communities for input from them. This resulted in some significant revisions to the legislation. When, on 20 June 1951, a new and revised Indian Act received royal assent, some of the most offensive political, cultural and religious restrictions had been removed, including the ban on ceremonies such as the potlatch and the sun dance. For the first time, First Nations communities were able to launch land claims against the government, and First Nations women were able to vote in band council elections. Nevertheless, many discriminatory features remained, including state control of Indigenous child welfare, prohibitions on First Nations people possessing intoxicants or being intoxicated and status women losing their rights if they married a non-status person.

John George Diefenbaker was prime minister from 1958 to 1963. More than any other Canadian prime minister to that point, he sought to improve conditions for Indigenous people. From his years as a defence attorney in Saskatchewan, he knew first-hand of the exclusion and discrimination they faced, and he promised to do better. Indigenous people must have the vote, he insisted – and without abrogating or diminishing their status and existing treaty rights – and in March 1960 those recognized as 'Indians' under the Indian Act were granted the federal vote. The enfranchisement clause in the Act, a process that resulted in a person no longer being considered an 'Indian' under federal legislation and being removed from their band, was dropped in 1961 (although compulsory enfranchisement when Indigenous peoples met certain government-prescribed conditions had been eliminated earlier). Canada's first Indigenous senator, Akay-na-muka (James Gladstone) of the Blood reserve of the Blackfoot Nation in Alberta, was appointed by Diefenbaker.[20] Moreover, unlike his predecessors and many of his contemporaries, Diefenbaker acknowledged the contributions to Canada made by Indigenous people. The 'broad outlines [of] the confederation of peoples we know as Canadians today', he said, were 'in many ways foretold by the Indian and Eskimo peoples who in years gone by maintained related cultural, social and economic organizations within the boundaries of what is Canada today'. The earliest arrivals to Canada worked with Indigenous peoples, forging the outline of the nation together, building the great transcontinental railways which followed Indigenous routes.[21]

In April 1963, Lester B. Pearson succeeded Diefenbaker as prime minister. Pearson, too, recognized that the nation had to do better in improving conditions for Indigenous peoples, as articulated in the increasing demands coming from their leadership. In 1964 he commissioned Howard B. Hawthorn, a British Columbia anthropologist, to investigate the lives of Indigenous peoples in Canada. *A Survey of the Contemporary Indians of Canada: Economic, Political, Educational Needs and Policies*, known as the Hawthorn Report, came out in 1966. It asserted that Indigenous peoples are the most disadvantaged population in the country. The Report famously designated them as 'Citizens Plus', recommended increased services for Indigenous peoples and 'recognized the need for a specialized Indigenous government system, but it also argued that the significance of treaties should be reduced'.[22] Pearson promised to reorganize certain government departments to provide for the special needs of Indigenous peoples and the development of the North. To encourage community development for the benefit of Indigenous peoples, amendments to the Indian Act were planned, but there was little progress on that file by the time Pearson retired from politics in 1968.

Pierre Elliott Trudeau succeeded Pearson. He also acknowledged that Indigenous peoples had been marginalized since Confederation, adding they must be fully included as equals. Accordingly, in the House of Commons, on 25 June 1969, Jean Chrétien, his minister of Indian Affairs and Northern Development (as the DIA had been renamed), unveiled what became an extremely controversial document entitled *Statement of the Government of Canada on Indian Policy*, better known as the White Paper. As far back as in 1896, Fred Loft had asked that Indigenous communities be part of the conversation, 'rather than submit[ting], as has too often unfortunately been the case, to dictation',[23] and, indeed, Mackenzie King had begun such a

---

[20]Notes for an address by the Prime Minister, the Rt. Hon. John G. Diefenbaker, on *The Nation's Business*, 19 May 1960, John George Diefenbaker Fonds (JGDF), MG01/VII/A/507, University of Saskatchewan Archives.
[21]Notes for Response to Toast to Canada, UBC Dinner, Vancouver, 25 September 1958, JGDF, MG01/VII/A/706, vol. 22, SA.
[22]'The Hawthorn Report (1967)', https://www.mulroneyinstitute.ca/node/3961.
[23]Smith, 'Loft'.

process. Nevertheless, the White Paper hardly paid attention to any concerns Indigenous leaders raised during the consultation process.

The criticism of the rigorous efforts by the Canadian government since 1867 to remove the culture, language and life skills of Indigenous communities has overwhelmingly been directed at Canada's first prime minister, John A. Macdonald; however, all of the country's prime ministers share responsibility for perpetrating this national shame. When in 1968 Pierre Trudeau became prime minister, most Canadians failed to grasp the enormity of this history, or the extent to which these were still the prevailing conditions. Trudeau was a champion of individual rights, and the White Paper embodied that rhetoric: he proposed the full-scale integration of Indigenous peoples into mainstream society. It was not a path favoured by Indigenous organizations. A firestorm of protest ensued led by Harold Cardinal, president of the Indian Association of Alberta, and the White Paper was immediately countered with the 'Red Paper'. Indigenous leaders became further incensed when Trudeau stoked the fire by stating that the disadvantaged position of Indigenous peoples was attributable not to federal policy or to racial prejudice but to their special status. Taken together, this sparked forceful opposition from right across the country and with it a new era of Indigenous political organizing. The 1969 White Paper was a lost opportunity for reconciliation, especially considering the magnitude of unresolved Indigenous issues. Asking Canadians to correct their distorted views and misunderstanding about Indigenous peoples and asserting that 'those who are furthest behind should be helped most', Trudeau simply withdrew the proposal, while reiterating his opposition to special status for any group.[24]

Even if Trudeau opposed special status for Indigenous people, Aboriginal rights are included in the Constitution Act, 1982 recognized in section 35 of the Charter of Rights and Freedoms (1) 'The existing aboriginal and treaty rights of the aboriginal peoples of Canada are hereby recognized and affirmed, [and (2) that] "aboriginal peoples of Canada" includes the Indian, Inuit and Metis peoples of Canada'.[25] That did not come easily, however. There was no recognition of existing treaty rights and the importance of Indigenous-state relationships in Trudeau's initial proposal for patriation in 1980. This section was included only after a Parliamentary Special Joint Committee on the Constitution recommended its inclusion following strong representation from Indigenous organizations who were not consulted initially about the new constitution but successfully fought to have their title and rights enshrined and protected as constitutional powers were transferred from Britain to Canada. Even then, this section was dropped from the draft on

---

[24]Raymond B. Blake and John D. Whyte, 'Pierre Trudeau's Failures on Indigenous Rights Tarnish His Legacy', *The Conversation*, 10 June 2021, https://theconversation.com/pierre-trudeaus-failures-on-indigenous-rights-tarnish-his-legacy-162167.

[25]Constitution Act, 1982 Section 35, https://indigenousfoundations.arts.ubc.ca/constitution_act_1982_section_35/.

the dramatic evening of 4 November 1981, when the premiers (with the exception of Quebec's) agreed to a constitutional deal with Trudeau and only re-inserted it following sharp criticism and intensive lobbying and public demonstrations from both Indigenous and non-Indigenous Canadians. Also noteworthy was the addition of the word 'existing' at that time to the phrase 'aboriginal and treaty rights' when first ministers finally included the section in the constitution. Section 37 required that a constitutional conference be called within one year to deal with matters concerning the Indigenous peoples of Canada, including the identification and definition of their rights, and stipulated that representatives of Indigenous Canadians be invited to participate. As a result, two additional sections were added in March 1983: (1) for greater certainty, in subsection (1) 'treaty rights' include rights that now exist by way of land claims agreements or may be so acquired, and (2) notwithstanding any other provision of this Act, the aboriginal and treaty rights referred to in subsection (1) are guaranteed equally to male and female persons.[26] When those rights were entrenched in the constitution, they became part of the country's highest law. Indigenous rights are not, however, defined in the constitution. This step has been largely up to the Supreme Court of Canada, and substantial progress has been made there. Through such cases as Calder, Delgamuukw, Marshall, Tsilhqot'in and Daniels, Indigenous rights have been interpreted to embody a range of cultural, social, political and economic rights, including the right to land, as well as to fish, to hunt, practise one's own culture and to establish treaties.

Calder (1973) recognized, for the first time, that Aboriginal title has a place in Canadian law. In Delgamuukw (1997), the Supreme Court found that claims to traditional lands had to show exclusive occupation of the territory by a defined Aboriginal society at the time the Crown asserted sovereignty over that territory. In that same case, the Court ruled that the oral histories of Aboriginal peoples were to be accepted as evidence proving historic use and occupation. Tsilhqot'in (2014) further clarified the requirements for establishing Aboriginal title, ruling that Aboriginal title rested on three criteria: proof of Aboriginal occupation, and then continuity and exclusivity of use. The landmark Daniels case (2016) addressed the lingering question of whether the Crown owes the same fiduciary duty to Métis and non-status Indians as it does to 'Treaty Indians'. The Court held that Métis are a distinct people, and that Métis and non-status Indians are 'Indians' for the purpose of Parliament's law-making. The Court also ruled that, in order to advance reconciliation, two relevant sections of the constitution should be read together: Section 91(24), which states that the federal government has exclusive authority over 'Indians and Lands reserved for Indians', and section 35, which states that '(1) the existing aboriginal and treaty rights of the aboriginal peoples of Canada are hereby recognized and affirmed. (2) In

---

[26]Roy Romanow, John Whyte and Howard Leeson, *Canada . . . Notwithstanding: The Making of the Constitution, 1976–1982* (Toronto: Carswell/Methuen, 1984).

this Act, "aboriginal peoples of Canada" include the Indian, Inuit and Métis peoples of Canada'.

The Marshall decision (1999) is particularly noteworthy. Donald Marshall Jr. was not only a Mi'kmaq leader and activist, but also one among several Indigenous young men across Canada wrongly convicted of serious crime. In 1971 he was sentenced to life in prison, but released only in 1982, having served nearly eleven years for a murder he did not commit; he was officially acquitted by the Supreme Court of Nova Scotia in 1983. A decade later, Marshall was convicted on charges of fishing out of season and without a licence. In a landmark ruling in 1999, the Supreme Court of Canada held that the Peace and Friendship Treaties signed by the Crown before the Royal Proclamation in 1763 affirm the right of Mi'kmaw, Wolastoqiyik and Passamaquoddy peoples of Atlantic Canada to earn a 'moderate' commercial livelihood from fishing and hunting, subject only to conservation requirements.

On becoming prime minister in 1984, Brian Mulroney spoke of Canada's founding peoples as French, British and Indigenous: he was the first to do so. He also insisted Indigenous people must participate fully in the nation's economic and political well-being. In his opening remarks at the mandated First Ministers' Conference on the Rights of Aboriginal Peoples in April 1985, he praised Indigenous people for maintaining their cultural identity despite decades of adversity, expressly stating that they were 'part of our national heritage, part of how we define ourselves as a society, something to be celebrated, not ignored'. The social indicators of disparity, however, as experienced by Indigenous peoples in terms of unemployment, high incidences of alcoholism and suicide, inadequate educational facilities and substandard housing are the other side of the heritage of Indigenous tenacity and perseverance. Those issues must be addressed as Indigenous peoples were not, insisted Mulroney, 'seeking the best welfare system in the world'. The key to improving their lives, he said, was through 'constitutional protection for the principle of self-government'. Unlike other groups in Canada, Mulroney singularly pointed out, Indigenous people did not have the institutions to determine their own cultural and political development, despite the progress being made through the courts. The path to their success lay in self-government, and he asked Canadians not to fear that but see it as a way to remedy injustices and create a better Canada.[27]

In 1991 Mulroney appointed the Royal Commission on Aboriginal Peoples (RCAP), giving it a mandate 'to examine the economic, social, and cultural situation of the Aboriginal peoples' of Canada. Nevertheless, when Mulroney began his constitutional odyssey with the Meech Lake Accord in 1987 with the aim of getting the Province of Quebec signed on to the

---

[27]First Ministers' Conference on the Rights of Aboriginal Peoples, *Press Conference of Prime Minister Brian Mulroney* (Ottawa: 2–3 April 1985), https://primarydocuments.ca/first-ministers-conference-on-aboriginal-constitutional-matters-verbatim-transcript-press-conference-of-prime-minister-brian-mulroney/.

constitution, Indigenous peoples were, again, excluded. When Meech failed to be ratified by all of the provinces, Mulroney again embarked on discussions with first ministers, but this time, also with representatives of four national Indigenous associations. In late August 1992, the Charlottetown Accord was concluded with, among other things, provisions for Indigenous self-government; however, in a national referendum held on 26 October 1992, it, too, was defeated. To this day, Indigenous self-government remains a work in progress for most First Nations in Canada but there has been some success. Since 1975, Canada has negotiated and signed twenty-six modern treaties with Indigenous groups in Canada, eighteen of which contain self-government provisions or associated self-government agreements. One testament to the strength of Indigenous and Inuit political leaders and to the flexibility of Canadian political institutions is Nunavut, a province-like jurisdiction in Canada's north with Inuktitut as an official language of the new territory. As part of the 1993 Nunavut Land Settlement Agreement, it was stipulated that the Northwest Territories be divided and territory set aside as a homeland for the Inuit. After several years of negotiations, Nunavut, meaning 'Our Land' in Inuktitut, was officially created on 1 April 1999, and it is administered by a body called the Nunavut Tungavik Incorporated, which, as a large capital and landholder, is a major player representing the Inuit interests in Nunavut.

In 1993, Jean Chrétien followed Mulroney as prime minister. He, too, admitted that Canada had failed Indigenous peoples: he promised to reverse injustices against Indigenous peoples and protect their languages, values and cultures. The Royal Commission on Aboriginal Peoples was another important step in bringing Indigenous peoples into the story of Canada. When it reported in 1996, the RCAP made 440 recommendations for improving the relationship between Indigenous peoples and the Canadian government and Canadian society as a whole. The Commission's recommendations were largely ignored. Although he talked constantly of working with Indigenous communities to strengthen their capacity for economic and social development and to expand community-based justice approaches, Chrétien's response to the RCAP's work was incrementalist and piecemeal at best, focusing at different times on Indigenous children and youth, urban Indigenous people, and Indigenous people's health, education and good governance.[28] The Chrétien government did take one important initiative. On 7 January 1998, Indian Affairs Minister Jane Stewart delivered an address in Ottawa 'on the occasion of the unveiling of Gathering Strength – Canada's Aboriginal Action Plan'. The prime minister was conspicuous

---

[28]Michael Murphy, 'Looking Forward without Looking Back: Jean Chrétien's Legacy for Aboriginal-State Relations', in Lois Harder and Steve Patten, eds., *The Chrétien Legacy: Politics and Public Policy in Canada* (Montreal and Kingston: McGill-Queen's University Press, 2006), 161–80; Canada, Department of Indian Affairs and Northern Development, *Gathering Strength: Canada's Aboriginal Action Plan* (Ottawa: Minister of Public Works and Government Services, 1998).

by his absence, although various Indigenous leaders were in the audience. Stewart opened her statement with, 'Elders, Chiefs, Commissioners, my colleagues, leaders, honoured guests, ladies and gentlemen. I have been looking forward to this opportunity to speak to you about the work of the Royal Commission on Aboriginal Peoples and to speak in the broadest terms about the relationships between Aboriginal and non-Aboriginal people in this country'. She agreed with the RCAP's commissioners where they said, 'The main policy direction, pursued for more than 150 years, first by colonial then by Canadian governments, has been wrong'. Therefore, continued Stewart, 'the time has come to state formally that the days of paternalism and disrespect are behind us and that we are committed to changing the nature of the relationship between Aboriginal and non-Aboriginal people in Canada'. Then, in the 'Statement of Reconciliation' portion of this address, Stewart declared, 'the Government of Canada today formally expresses to all Aboriginal people in Canada our profound regret for past actions of the federal government which have contributed to these difficult pages in the history of our relationship together'. As well as other steps for renewal, Stewart announced, 'Our commitment began today with the Statement of Reconciliation and the $350 million for healing to address the legacy of physical and sexual abuse at residential schools'.[29]

The new millennium has seen the political leaders of various countries around the world make apologies to their Indigenous peoples for past injustices.[30] The prime minister of Canada admitting that its government had been oppressive and had promoted the perniciousness of colonization is an important step in reconciliation with Canada's historically marginalized communities. Harper's 2008 Statement of Apology furthers 'the process of expunging guilt' for historical injustices.[31] As with other apologies, Harper's was not only about remembering a dreadful chapter in the nation's past, but also about beginning a healing process: 'The government recognizes that the absence of an apology has been an impediment to healing and reconciliation'.[32]

'To the approximately 80,000 living former students, and all family members and communities', Harper announced on 11 June 2008, 'the Government of Canada now recognizes that it was wrong to forcibly remove children from their homes and we apologize for having done this'. Moreover, he made it known that 'years of work by survivors, communities,

---

[29]'Address by the Hon. Jane Stewart on the Occasion of the Unveiling of *Gathering Strength – Canada's Aboriginal Action Plan*', Ottawa, 7 January 1998, https://www.documentcloud.org/documents/2724282-1998-Address-by-the-Honourable-Jane-Stewart.html.

[30]For a list of some 20+ countries that have done so, see, e.g., Apologies to Indigenous peoples, https://en.wikipedia.org/wiki/Apologies_to_Indigenous_peoples.

[31]Jason A. Edwards and Lindsay R. Calhoun, 'Redress for Old Wounds: Canadian Prime Minister Stephen Harper's Apology for the Chinese Head Tax', *Chinese Journal of Communication* 4, no. 1 (2011): 73–89.

[32]Harper's 'Apology'.

and Aboriginal organizations culminated in an agreement that gives us a new beginning and an opportunity to move forward together in partnership'. He mentioned that, in September 2007, implementation of the Indian Residential Schools Settlement Agreement (IRSSA) had begun.

And just the week before, on 1 June 2008, what Harper characterized as 'a cornerstone of the Settlement Agreement', the Indian Residential Schools Truth and Reconciliation Commission (TRC), was established, with a mandate to document the history and lasting impacts of the Residential Schools system on students and their families.[33] The TRC presented its final report in 2015, which included '94 Calls to Action', and in a concluding statement identified the treatment of Indigenous children in Residential Schools as 'cultural genocide'.[34] In 2018 the Department of Indigenous and Northern Affairs was replaced with two new departments, Crown-Indigenous Relations and Northern Affairs. In 2021 the Government of Canada made 30 September a federal statutory holiday, naming it the National Day for Truth and Reconciliation; by 2023 it was also a holiday for all provincial employees in New Brunswick and Nova Scotia, and for all workers in British Columbia, Manitoba, Northwest Territories, Nunavut, Prince Edward Island and the Yukon. Today, it is hard to find a public institution or major enterprise in Canada that has not taken steps to build a new relationship with Indigenous peoples.

Harper's 2008 apology marked a significant moment towards better relations between the government, Canada's Indigenous peoples and all Canadians. The path to that moment was long and difficult. Indigenous peoples' activism, nation-to-nation dialogue (finally), changes to Canada's constitution, judicial rulings and public attitudes all combined in launching what are still but the beginnings of a new relationship between Indigenous people and everyone else in Canada. At last, however, though progress remains slow, the path forward is based on the recognition of rights, respect, cooperation and partnership. That the prime minister of Canada could make this apology in June 2008 to the survivors of Canada's Residential Schools, and having made it, win re-election in October that year and again in 2011 shows that not only the Government of Canada, but all Canadians more generally now recognize and accept that reconciliation with Indigenous peoples is essential to national well-being. Indeed, opinion polls showed in 2024 that a clear majority of Canadians feel optimistic that meaningful progress towards reconciliation will happen in their lifetime.[35]

---

[33] Prime Minister's Office, Prime Minister Stephen Harper, 'Prime Minister Harper Outlines the Government's Achievements for Aboriginal Canadians', Halifax, 2 November 2007, http://www.pm.gc.ca/eng/media.asp?category=2&id=1887.

[34] Government of Canada, 'Truth and Reconciliation Commission of Canada', https://www.rcaanc-cirnac.gc.ca/eng/1450124405592/1529106060525.

[35] 'Reconciliation and Relations with Indigenous Peoples', Environics Research, 2024, https://www.environicsinstitute.org/docs/default-source/default-document-library/reconciliation-and-relations-with-indigenous-peoples6864b722-6a8e-4d24-bcc1-5467039e9b83.pdf?sfvrsn=9903a9e_1.

IMAGE 15 Part of the truckers convoy that shut down downtown Ottawa, 22 January 2022. https://www.alamy.com/ottawa-ontario-canada-28th-january-2022-sign-saying-truckers-for-freedom-on-front-of-large-truck-during-the-blockades-of-freedom-convoy-protest-image470267643.html?imageid=CCCFD88C-4F66-4446-803B-65402DA55C5B&pn=1&searchId=9b66dec-487da299abca2140cde9d1044&searchtype=0.

15

The freedom convoy, 2022: Canada in the Covid-19 pandemic

Shortly before Christmas 2019, reports surfaced from the city of Wuhan, China, of several cases of a deadly new infectious disease caused by the severe acute respiratory syndrome coronavirus 2 (SARS-CoV-2). The disease was soon labelled Covid-19. Although claims were made that it originated from a local laboratory, a recently published study 'concludes that there's almost no chance the virus originated from a lab leak'. According to 'strong but circumstantial evidence' the new virus jumped from infected animals to humans at wet markets, specifically involving 'the wildlife trade in the Huanan Seafood Wholesale Market' in Wuhan.[1] The disease spread rapidly. By the end of January 2020, there were nearly 10,000 confirmed cases in China alone. Canada's first-known case of Covid-19 was reported on 23 January 2020 of a man who had recently visited Wuhan. The wife of Canada's Prime Minister, Sophie Trudeau, tested positive for the disease on 13 March, after a visit to London, England. Covid-19 was spreading throughout Canada, and by the end of March, it accounted for sixty-nine reported deaths. Before a vaccine for it was developed, no effective medical treatment existed for Covid-19. Fears were mounting that there would be a recurrence of something similar to the Great Influenza Epidemic of 1918–20, caused by the H1N1 subtype of influenza A, that had infected about a third of the world's population, and killed 25 million or more people.

On 30 January 2020, Dr Tedros Adhanom Ghebreyesus (Tedros), director general of the UN's World Health Organization (WHO), convened a second meeting of the International Health Regulations (2005) Emergency Committee 'regarding the outbreak of novel coronavirus 2019 in the People's Republic of China, with exportations to other countries'. The Committee

---

[1] www.cbc.ca/news/canada/saskatoon/where-did-covid-19-originate-saskatoon-lab-helps-with-genetic-analysis-that-points-to-animal-market-1.7386847.

learned that 1,370 'of the confirmed cases' in China were severe and 170 people died, while 124 people recovered and were discharged from hospital. But there were now '83 cases in 18 countries. Of these, only 7 had no history of travel in China'. The statement about the meeting noted that 'the Committee believes that it is still possible to interrupt virus spread, provided that countries put in place strong measures to detect disease early, isolate and treat cases, trace contacts, and promote social distancing measures commensurate with the risk'.[2] That same day, acting on this information and advice, the WHO director general declared the outbreak of Covid-19 a 'Public Health Emergency of International Concern'.[3]

Less than two months later, on 11 March 2020, Dr Tedros announced, 'There are now more than 118,000 cases in 114 countries, and 4,291 people have lost their lives'. He then expressly proclaimed Covid-19 a worldwide pandemic and called on countries 'to take urgent and aggressive action' to try to contain the disease as much as possible. He advised that 'if countries detect, test, treat, isolate, trace, and mobilize their people in the response, those with a handful of cases can prevent those cases becoming clusters, and those clusters becoming community transmission'. Moreover, apparently aware of how any such measures would be received, the WHO chief pointed out that 'all countries must strike a fine balance between protecting health, minimizing economic and social disruption, and respecting human rights'.[4]

Starting with China, communities around the world shut down. People were ordered to remain indoors except for controlled access to obtain essential needs. By the end of 2020, daily Covid-related deaths stood at some 10,000 globally, eventually exceeding 50,000 in Canada and 7 million worldwide over the life of the pandemic.

On 18 March 2020, the Trudeau government began banning most international air traffic into Canada. The following weekend, the international border with the United States was closed, except to maintain essential services. With active encouragement from governments, numerous employers, including all those in the public sector, shifted to remote, at-home, work. In-person gatherings of more than a few people were outlawed. There was no or limited in-person access to retail establishments, people were to keep at least a metre apart, and customers had to follow directional arrows to minimize the spread of the virus.

---

[2] www.who.int/news/item/30-01-2020-statement-on-the-second-meeting-of-the-international-health-regulations-(2005)-emergency-committee-regarding-the-outbreak-of-novel-coronavirus-(2019-ncov).
[3] www.who.int/publications/m/item/covid-19-public-health-emergency-of-international-concern-(pheic)-global-research-and-innovation-forum.
[4] www.who.int/director-general/speeches/detail/who-director-general-s-opening-remarks-at-the-media-briefing-on-covid-19–11-march-2020.

Governments, pharmaceutical companies, researchers and the expertise of many others were harnessed to produce a vaccine against Covid-19 as quickly as possible, and by the end of 2020, vaccines started to become available worldwide. Soon after the first vaccines were rolled out, governments in many countries, including Canada, started to demand proof of vaccination from people before they could enter public places and, eventually, before they could cross the international border between Canada and the United States. This sparked protests, especially from truckers, many of whom saw their livelihoods threatened.

On 9 December 2020, Health Canada authorized the first Covid-19 vaccine in Canada, manufactured by Pfizer-BioNTech. It was rolled out in phases: phase one began on 15 December, 'with a pilot project in Toronto and Ottawa' and included 'the vaccination of over 2,500 health care workers'.[5] For some time, demand for vaccines outstripped supplies. Priority lists detailing who was to get inoculated first were developed, starting with essential workers and the elderly, especially those in long-term care homes, for whom Covid carried a far greater risk of being deadly. As the availability of vaccines increased, countless employers and public places of all types in Canada instituted vaccine and mask-wearing mandates. Provincial governments developed apps, and provided certificates, so people could prove they had been vaccinated. Despite opposition from those who feared adverse effects from a vaccine which they thought had been inadequately tested and/or from those who insisted that compliance with such measures was a personal choice in a free and democratic society, Canada's governments – both provincial and federal – maintained that restrictions were justified to protect the health of the general population. If someone refused vaccination, or other restrictions, they would have to accept their exclusion from many places, including unvaccinated children being kept from attending schools or, if ordered back to work in person, the potential loss of employment.

Initially, there was optimism that the shutdowns and restrictions would not last long. Even the most pessimistic predictions assumed the crisis would last just a few months. But it only worsened in 2021. As the months passed, with more and more government-imposed restrictions in efforts to contain Covid-19, increasing numbers of Canadians grew doubtful about their necessity. People were suffering psychologically, with enforced isolation, and in many cases, economically and socially as their movements were increasingly constrained. Canadians were becoming fatigued with the profound and, to many, seemingly all-too-encompassing restrictions on their daily lives. Protests grew.

The federal government set up support programmes to keep businesses and families financially above water. This included provisions for very generous economic relief. For those in businesses that had lost at least 30

---

[5] https://news.ontario.ca/en/release/59607/ontario-begins-rollout-of-covid-19-vaccine.

per cent of their revenue during the pandemic, Ottawa introduced a subsidy covering up to 75 per cent of employees' salaries, and in April 2020, it passed the Canada Emergency Response Benefit (CERB) that provided a taxable benefit of $2,000 monthly, for a maximum of four months, for those who had lost their jobs due to Covid. Yet, in many places, with premises shut, and people laid off, the costs to individuals and to the economic well-being of the country became a dire concern. Provinces loosened restrictions, some faster than others, and especially as vaccines became generally available, pressure mounted for a return to normalcy. Frustrating in this context were also the seemingly false starts, which made people more anxious, despondent and distrustful of government expertise, including that of the national and provincial chief medical officers who were key in establishing the levels of restrictions. Between March and Christmas 2020, in Saskatchewan, for example, the limits on indoor crowd size went down from 25 to 10, back up to 15 and then 30, then back down to 15, to 10 and even as low as 5. In Quebec, people had to observe a curfew set at 8 pm. In Ontario, in 2020 alone, the provincial government introduced some 200 orders-in-council to deal with Covid. The prime minister was advised by many to follow suit: now that most Canadians were vaccinated, only a minority would have their freedoms impacted, and it was said, for good reason.

The prime minister was also gearing up for an election, and he was counselled that taking a strong position on Covid measures would be a popular position, underlining his strong leadership throughout the pandemic. On 20 September 2021, Justin Trudeau was re-elected, though his mandate remained virtually unchanged, as the Liberals gained only two additional seats, remaining in a minority position with 157 of 338 seats, and just 32.6 per cent of the popular vote. But Trudeau was true to his word, and by the end of the next month, Canadians were required to show proof of Covid vaccination to board a plane or train.

Over the course of 2021, questions emerged about whether Covid-related restrictions violated Canada's Constitution, more particularly the 1982 Charter of Rights and Freedoms. As far as Canada's governments were concerned, emergency health and safety safeguards were paramount. Nevertheless, the speed at which restrictions mounted during the pandemic opened debate over whether constitutional rights were getting due consideration, and if their abrogation was proportional to the risks. It was pointed out that section 6(2) of the Charter guaranteed the right to move and to take up residence and 'pursue a livelihood' anywhere in Canada. Yet, quite early in the pandemic, apart from any action from the federal government, several provinces, starting with New Brunswick and Quebec, barred entry from other parts of the country except for essential services, and to enforce this, police checkpoints were established. In many provinces, those who returned from other parts of Canada and elsewhere were compelled to go into a fourteen-day isolation period to ensure they had not contracted Covid, a measure that proved difficult to enforce.

Critics also pointed to sections 7 and 9 of the Charter, which addressed the requirement not to deny rights 'except in accordance with the principles of fundamental justice'.[6]

Canadians generally complied with the issued restrictions and supported the prime minister's approach. Fear was rampant over rapidly rising mortality rates broadcast daily in the media, often including horrifying images of temporary morgues established because of the large numbers who were dying of the disease. Canada's mortality rate from Covid-19 remained significantly lower than across most of Europe and much lower than in the United States, where resistance to and the imposition of restrictions across states were markedly different. But protests mounted worldwide. In 2021, France faced protests against vaccine mandates imposed that summer. In the United Sates, protests were fuelled in part by President Donald Trump's opposition to wearing masks. Growing opposition in Canada mirrored what was going on internationally. Canadians objecting to their governments' restrictions called the measures heavy-handed and disproportionate. Starting on 31 March 2021, Ontario, for example, introduced expanded powers for police which, some feared, gave authorities the means to undertake unrestricted spot checks on people to ensure they were vaccinated.

On 16 November 2021, Brigitte Belton, a truck driver from Wallaceburg, Ontario, was stopped by the Canadian Border Services Agency (CBSA) at the Windsor-Detroit crossing because she was not wearing a mask. Belton made a video that she posted on TikTok, in which she proclaimed: 'This isn't my country. In Canada, we're no longer free'.[7] Conditions would, in fact, soon become more restrictive, because at this point, Belton and others were not actually required to prove they had been vaccinated. A month before the Belton incident, however, US President Joe Biden's administration announced that, starting in 2022, full vaccination would be required of any foreign national crossing into the United States, including those driving commercial trucks. Three days after Belton posted her video, the Trudeau government announced it would be mirroring the requirement set in the United States, and that similar restrictions on those entering Canada would start on 15 January 2022.

Initially, there was confusion about the extent to which the new rules would apply. On 12 January, a CBSA employee told a Canadian Broadcasting Corporation (CBC) reporter that truckers would be exempt. Responding the next day, a joint communique from Canada's federal ministers of health, transport and public safety made clear this was not the case. On 14 January, Tamara Lich, who had established herself as a vocal opponent of government Covid restrictions, started a crowdfunding

---

[6]www.justice.gc.ca/eng/csj-sjc/rfc-dlc/ccrf-ccdl/.
[7]Paul Wells, *An Emergency in Ottawa: The Story of the Convoy Commission* (Toronto: Southerland House, 2023), 20.

account on GoFundMe under the name 'Freedom Convoy 2022', and through social media, namely, Facebook, began organizing a nationwide protest. Canadian truckers had had experience with convoy-based protests before this; for example, in 2019 many of them organized against what they considered to be excessive energy costs.

Although the Freedom Convoy was initially sparked by restrictions seen as threatening the livelihood of truckers, it morphed into a larger, broader movement that portrayed Covid measures as a cudgel used by what was called the 'deep state' to exert unprecedented and unwarranted controls, including restrictions on speech, creating what was termed a woke society steeped in liberalism, political correctness and identity politics that Prime Minister Trudeau was seen as exemplifying. Canadian protest demonstrations received increasing coverage on American newscasts, particularly on right-wing outlets, that portrayed Canada, and especially Justin Trudeau, as authoritarian. In February 2022, for example, Fox News, the most prominent conservative-minded US television network, falsely claimed that police in Canada mounted on horseback boasted about trampling protestors.

The restrictions on truckers that were fully put into place by 22 January 2022 ignited the Freedom Convoy, which, as it gained steam, transformed into a broader, angrier, conspiratorial movement, and was defined by those who were opposed to it as racist, misogynist and a homophobic right-wing amalgam. That day, truckers from across the country set out in convoy for Ottawa. They were led by Tamara Lich, a well-known activist, who organized for the right-wing Western-Canadian based Maverick Party and the anti-government Yellow Vest protests in France, and Chris Barber, a Canadian trucking company operator from Swift Current, Saskatchewan. The truckers were soon joined by numerous others who believed that their governments were undermining their freedoms, specifically by compelling inoculation to enable participation in society. Many of them believed that the vaccine had not been adequately tested to prove its efficacy and to ensure against potentially adverse side effects. Truckers focused their objections directly on the federal government. Convoy participants demanded the end of all mask and vaccine mandates. They rejected the idea that the federal government in its fight to control Covid was acting for the public good and asserted, instead, that it was destroying fundamental liberties. Hundreds of their vehicles descended upon the nation's capital, grinding it to a halt, blocking access routes into the city's core, including to Parliament, and occupying the streets of downtown Ottawa neighbourhoods. The origins of this melee, the court cases that ensued, and disagreements and disputes over whether Canada's government had demonstrated contempt for democracy before and after the Freedom Convoy's presence in Ottawa surfaced, rapidly intensified, and to some extent, remain unresolved to this day.

The opposing sides on mandates became ever more entrenched and increasingly looked upon the other as an enemy. While a determined minority spoke of freedoms being trampled, the other side, reflecting the views of most Canadians, cast anti-vaxxers and those opposed to masking, as uninformed, as rejecting science, as 'free riders' putting many others at risk, and as motivated by right-wing conspiracy theories. Such characterizations, on both sides, were also conveyed and magnified through traditional media, spread wildly by social media and echoed by politicians and other public leaders.

The Freedom Convoy that reached Ottawa was not the only anti-government protest in this period. In January 2022 alone, there were nearly 200 anti-vaccine demonstrations across Canada, more than double the number that occurred during all of 2021. In this charged atmosphere, as the Freedom Convoy rolled out across Canada, beginning mainly in British Columbia and Ontario, along the journey to Canada's capital, things ground to a halt in numerous communities, as truckers slowly moved through main thoroughfares. By 29 January, hundreds of trucks had arrived in Ottawa, converging on Parliament Hill and the surrounding blocks in the downtown. Secondary protests occurred in provincial capitals and at international border crossings. Overall, across Canada, it has been estimated that some 200 commercial trucks, 650 personal vehicles and 10,000 people participated in these demonstrations.

The uprising initially presented itself as a working-class protest. Leaders and participants said that Covid-19 restrictions were undermining the ability of ordinary folks to make a living. Indeed, the fact that truckers converged on 'white-collar' Ottawa was symbolic of an anti-elite message they sought to convey. With the broadening number of people who became involved, the protest changed, however, or, as some have contended, was hijacked by various extremists and became an unruly anti-government mob. Among others, such views were expressed by the *Toronto Star*, which described those who descended on Ottawa as 'threaten[ing] journalists ... spit[ing] on them or threaten[ing] violence in general'.[8]

Canadians, though increasingly fatigued, if not frazzled, by Covid-19 and the array of restrictions that governments imposed, were not sympathetic to the protesters, especially since, by early 2022, nearly 90 per cent of Canadians had had at least one Covid vaccination. One poll taken in late January revealed that 61 per cent of Canadians felt that the unvaccinated should pay the full cost of their medical care if contracting Covid. In Quebec, Premier François Legault flirted with the idea of charging the unvaccinated an additional tax.

In Ottawa, the situation grew increasingly tense. Downtown neighbours Victoria De La Ronde and Zexi Li became ever more frustrated with and fearful of the truckers occupying their neighbourhood, and they publicly

---

[8] www.thestar.com/news/gta/physical-assaults-spitting-on-older-people-and-children-among-soaring-number-of-anti-asian-hate/article_e64fe1ce-0178-5016-b22e-481de05a736d.html.

pleaded with police to intervene. Both lived alone, and La Ronde is blind. Li filed an injunction, citing constant, excessive noise and harassment. 'The impact on my physical well-being was – is – quite extensive', De La Ronde later testified. She said she could not sleep and that her lungs hurt because of the fumes billowing from trucks. Li said she was harassed when wearing a mask. 'They would blast their horns at me with a smile on their faces. And then they would cheer in unison and almost take joy in my flinching'. Some residents fought back; for instance, there were reports of eggs being thrown at the truckers from apartment balconies.

Ottawa's municipal government came under intense criticism. Citizens charged it with minimizing the threat in its early stages, and, as such, being unprepared, enabling pretty much unfettered access for trucks into the city's core, and for others to set up supply routes from Ottawa's inner perimeter, by the main Via Rail train station. Ottawa's chief of police, Peter Sloly, could not provide an adequate answer as to why things so quickly spiralled out of control, except to say that, initially, the police could not legally block roads and that the trucks had a right to use all streets. Within a day, as the truckers parked their vehicles and essentially shut down much of the city, 85 per cent of stores in the downtown Sparks Street pedestrian shopping district ceased operations. One home with a Pride flag flying out front had its back step soiled with faeces. Ottawa's Mayor, Jim Watson, cast the truckers as engaged in 'despicable behaviour', and criticized the provincial government of Doug Ford and the federal government for not rapidly making additional law enforcement personnel available. Police Chief Sloly was harangued into resigning, especially as the RCMP and Ontario Provincial Police (OPP) claimed that he had never provided them with details on what was needed to maintain order.

Reports surfaced claiming that the Freedom Convoy was receiving donations from foreign sources, presumably right-wing ones, but this was never validated. News coverage also emphasized the protestors' coarse behaviour, including flying flags representing the slave-owning American Confederacy – though those displaying them said this represented rebel opposition to government autocracy – as well as Nazi swastikas, and also, in the course of their encampments, 'defacing the Terry Fox Statue, urinating on the Tomb of the Unknown Soldier, dancing on the tomb of the Unknown Soldier, [and] harassing and taking food from homeless people'.[9] The Parliament Buildings were untouched and the Centennial flame which has burned since 1967 was never extinguished. It was no repeat of 6 January 2021 in the United States but the situation in Ottawa was described as a 'siege' or 'occupation', with residents essentially being held hostage in their homes, unable to come and go, subjected to a constant barrage of air horns that left many traumatized. There were reports of several protesters being

---

[9]Wells, *Emergency in Ottawa*, 22.

armed. By contrast, the protesters presented themselves as defending liberties, as diverse, and as a kind and supportive family-friendly community, where dances were held and food was shared. They asked to meet with Trudeau, but this overture was rejected, especially because the prime minister cast them as extremists.

Increasing numbers of Ottawa residents demanded that the police clear out the protestors who were also portrayed as being inspired by President Donald Trump's Make America Great Again (MAGA) movement, and by some of its members' storming the Capitol Building in Washington, DC, on 6 January 2021. Shocking to many Canadians was that the police – in trying to prevent violence and things spiralling out of control – were seen shaking hands with and even hugging some protestors. At this same time there was a blockade on the Canadian side of the Alberta-Montana border crossing that started on 29 January and went on for two weeks. Four of those protestors at Coutts, Alberta, were arrested. Linked to a far-right American group called Diagalon, they were charged with conspiring to murder RCMP officers as uncovered in trucks joining that blockade were a 'cache of guns, ammunition, a machete, and body armour'.[10] Blockades were established at several other border crossings with the United States, including at Sarnia and Windsor, Ontario, and at Emerson, Manitoba. Events in Canada were widely publicized around the world and helped spark similar protest activities elsewhere, including in the United States, France, Belgium, the Netherlands, the United Kingdom, Cyprus, Austria, Australia, New Zealand, and Saint Pierre and Miquelon.

On Sunday, 6 February 2022, Ottawa Mayor Jim Watson declared an emergency. Five days later Ontario Premier Doug Ford did the same. This provided law enforcement authorities a wider scope of powers with which to respond, and in the process, placed increased pressure on the federal government to intervene. On 14 February, Prime Minister Trudeau met virtually with the country's premiers and made clear his intent to invoke the Emergencies Act to deal not only with the situation in Ottawa, but also with ongoing blockades at the international border, and smaller, shorter, but still very disruptive convoys that, to varying extents, were shutting down other Canadian communities. This was the first time this legislation, which had replaced the War Measures Act, was used since its introduction in 1988. Prime Minister Trudeau had had enough. After three weeks, and with no prospect of the Ottawa occupation dissipating, on Valentine's Day, 14 February 2022, he invoked the Emergencies Act.

Law enforcement officers, some of them on horseback, armed with tactical gear, moved slowly, truck by truck, to remove the demonstrators from Ottawa. In some cases, that required the use of stun grenades and pepper spray. Authorities claimed that several officers were assaulted and that some

---

[10]Ibid., 24–32.

of the protestors tried to grab their weapons. The demonstrators were accused of placing children at the front to stymie authorities. Police in Ottawa made 273 arrests and laid 422 charges. In all, by 31 March 2022, the Ottawa Police Service laid 533 criminal charges against 140 individuals connected with the Freedom Convoy and towed away or impounded 110 vehicles. As well, and as permitted under the Emergencies Act, some 280 bank accounts worth about $8 million were frozen for being used to fund the protestors. In the months that followed, several participants in the Freedom Convoy were brought to trial, including its leaders and founders, Tamara Lich and Chris Barber, on 17 February 2022. Both were criminally charged with mischief, intimidation, obstructing a highway, obstructing a police officer and counselling others to commit the same offences. They asserted they were peacefully exercising their Charter rights of expression, association and peaceful assembly. Artur Pawlowski, a pastor who participated in the Coutts, Alberta, international border blockade, was sentenced to ninety days in prison. Denied probation instead of imprisonment because he refused to recognize his actions as wrong, a crowd of 200 supporters gathered at the Lethbridge courthouse, shouting 'hold the line',[11] which was a popular rallying cry among the Freedom Convoy participants. Pat King, another leader of the protests, was found guilty on five counts, including one count each of mischief, counselling others to commit mischief and counselling others to obstruct police.

It was also the case that any time the Emergencies Act was declared in force, the legislation required that within sixty days a public inquiry be arranged to assess whether such an extreme response was justified. The government-appointed Commissioner Justice Paul Rouleau of the Ontario Court of Appeal hired a team of lawyers who questioned seventy-six witnesses. The process started on 13 October 2022, went on for six weeks, and those who testified included merchants, residents, truck drivers and law enforcement personnel, and concluded with Prime Minister Justin Trudeau himself. Those representing or supporting the protestors expressed scepticism about the Commission, predicting it would result in a whitewash. Rouleau was known as a Liberal, having worked on former Liberal Prime Minister John Turner's 1983 party leadership campaign, and then as a senior staffer in Turner's office.

To reach its conclusions, the Rouleau Commission was tasked to consider the 'evolution and goals of the convoy and blockades; their leadership, organization and participants; the impact, role, and sources of misinformation and disinformation, including the use of social media; the impact of the blockades, including their economic impact; and the efforts of the police and other responders prior to and after the [Emergencies Act's] declaration'. The Commission was guided by the legal definition of

---

[11] *Toronto Star*, 19 September 2023.

a national emergency as an 'urgent and critical situation that exceeds the capacity or authority of the province to deal with it, and that cannot be effectively dealt with under any other law of Canada'.[12]

Rouleau was convinced that the government had made its case, in large part because provincial governments had shown that they were either unwilling or unable to respond effectively, and there was the distinct possibility of isolated protests becoming an uncontrollable nationwide phenomenon that would threaten public order, national health and Canada's economy. Rouleau made clear that he was not making a legal argument, as this was a Commission report, not a trial, and as such his conclusions should not be taken as setting precedent.

Court cases did, indeed, follow after the Freedom Convoy was dismantled. In mid-2023, Manitoba's Court of Appeal upheld a decision from the Court of King's Bench that public health restrictions on free assembly did not violate section 1 of the Charter of Rights and Freedoms that speaks of balancing between individual rights and the 'interests of society'.[13] In a statement made in January 2024, based on an appeal brought forward from the Canadian Civil Liberties Association, the Canadian Constitution Foundation, the Canadian Frontline Nurses and several individuals, Justice Richard Mosley, a federal court justice who specializes in national security and anti-terrorism matters, disagreed with the Rouleau Commission, asserting that the Freedom Convoy did not present a level of threat beyond the ability of normal law enforcement and legislation to effectively manage. He pointed out that though the weapons found in trucks and the actions of some protestors revealed violent intent, this was far from being a 'threat to national security'.[14] Mosley stressed that the standard for imposing the Emergencies Act had to be kept very high and invoked only as a 'last resort'.[15]

It was well within the ability of the Ontario government to have better resourced and responded to events in Ottawa and that improved de-escalation training for law enforcement personnel would have prevented matters from coming to such a contentious point, something borne out by far more successful police interventions to Covid-related protests in other cities worldwide, and even in other communities across Canada. Also, federal government Privy Council documents revealed that while Ontario's premier, Doug Ford, supported Trudeau's imposition of the Emergencies Act, others were opposed, stating that, in their jurisdiction, things remained calm. Quebec's premier François Legault warned against implementing the legislation, claiming it would invoke bitter memories of Pierre Trudeau's

---

[12]*Report of the Public Inquiry into the 2022 Public Order Emergency*, vol. 1, *Overview*, February 2023, www.publicorderemergencycommission.ca/files/documents/Final-Report/Vol-1-Report-of-the-Public-Inquiry-into-the-2022-Public-Order-Emergency.pdf.
[13]Winnipeg *Free Press*, 20 June 2023.
[14]Edmonton *Journal*, 27 January 2024.
[15]Halifax *Chronicle Herald*, 27 January 2024.

introduction of the War Measures Act in October 1970, which many Quebeckers, especially francophones, have considered an overreaction to the Front du Libération du Québec, and really designed to crush a burgeoning, non-violent, separatist movement.

Justin Trudeau's government made clear that it would appeal Mosley's ruling based on the conviction that the Freedom Convoy presented a clear and present danger to Canada's economic health, social cohesion and constituted authority. This, in turn, generated criticism. Leah West, a former national security lawyer and a professor at Carleton University, noted that the only evidence of serious violence was in Coutts, Alberta, which was handled there, not in Ottawa.[16] Many suggested the federal government could have diffused matters by simply listening to grievances from those who led the Freedom Convoy, and that carrying on this process would 'only further inflame Pandemic-era division'.[17] Anger was also fed by Trudeau's ongoing characterization of the Freedom Convoy, and other protestors, as 'foreign-funded white supremacists'[18] to continue justifying his government's implementation of the Emergencies Act.

Despite the recent, contentious and sometimes violent disputes, an October 2024 edition of *US News and World Report* named Canada – based upon international surveys – as the world's friendliest country.[19] Canadians are portrayed internationally as polite, especially when compared with their southern neighbours. Yet, numerous events in the country's history, and within its current population, belie such characterizations. On several occasions, Canada's government imposed draconian legislation to crush dissent, such as in the World Wars, to quell the perceived threat of radical socialism following the First World war, and to vanquish the FLQ.

In more recent times, however, Canada has been presented as a nation where its 1982 Charter of Rights and Freedoms is revered and as symbolizing the country's commitment to protect individual rights, to tolerance, to civility and to respect for dissent. The limits of this, and indeed Canada's reputation, as a safe, calm, land were blatantly challenged with the rise of and the means government used to defeat the Freedom Convoy. In those tense weeks, and months, in the midst of the Covid-19 pandemic, many Canadians showed a profound distrust of, and even violent opposition to, government, were outrightly hostile to their fellow citizens, and, in many cases, embraced racist tropes and conspiracy theories.

---

[16]Dale Smith, CBA/ACB National, Hindsight 2022, 24 January 2024, https://nationalmagazine.ca/en-ca/articles/law/in-depth/2024/hindsight-2022.
[17]Saint-John *Telegraph Journal*, 25 January 2024.
[18]Edmonton *Journal*, 24 January 2024.
[19]www.usnews.com/news/best-countries/rankings/friendly.

On 5 May 2023, the director general of WHO posted this statement: 'With great hope I declare COVID-19 over as a global health emergency'.[20] For more than twelve months, the pandemic 'has been on a downward trend', he said, with immunity increasing due to the highly effective vaccines developed in record time to fight the disease, and infections. Death rates have decreased and the pressure on once-overwhelmed health systems has eased. The WHO chief noted that the impact of the pandemic had 'exposed political fault lines, within and between nations. It has eroded trust between people, governments and institutions, fuelled by a torrent of mis- and disinformation'. The end of the emergency was a moment to celebrate, and he paid tribute to the 'incredible skill and selfless dedication of health and care workers' worldwide. In that WHO statement, it also says, 'Many mistakes were made, including a lack of coordination, equity and solidarity, which meant that existing tools and technologies were not best used to combat the virus'.[21]

The truckers' Freedom Convoy exposed a baser, harsher side of Canadian society and, in the minds of a lot of people, a federal government all too ready to deny freedoms. The Trudeau government made extraordinary efforts during the Covid-19 pandemic to protect the nation's health and, in its view, public safety and economic stability, while retaining overall majority support for its restrictions and reactions. Nevertheless, the measures that the Trudeau government took facilitated or worsened bitter divisions in the country and attracted unprecedented worldwide attention, not only for standing firm in face of violent opposition, but also for prompting questioning about Canada's foundational attachment to the rule of law and the protection of freedoms.

---

[20] https://x.com/DrTedros/status/1654484522358939650?ref_src=twsrc%5Etfw%7Ctwcamp%5Etweetembed%7Ctwterm%5E1654484522358939650%7Ctwgr%5E3b2fda07e5a52d6d735ddf5667e1a4ae938a394f%7Ctwcon%5Es1_&ref_url=https%3A%2F%2Fnews.un.org%2Fen%2Fstory%2F2023%2F05%2F1136367.

[21] https://news.un.org/en/story/2023/05/1136367.

Index

100th anniversary. *See* centennial project (1967)

Aboriginal Healing Foundation (1998) 203
Acquired Immunodeficiency Syndrome (AIDS) epidemic 196, 200
Action démocratique du Québec (ADQ) 182
Alternative Dispute Resolution process (2003) 203
Anderson, Benedict 17
Anderson, J. T. M. 49
anti-conscription riots, Quebec City (1918) 55–6, 65
    French-Canadian wartime discord 56, 59–60
    martial law 56
Ash, Stuart 131
Asia Pacific Economic Co-operation (APEC) 168
Assembly of First Nations (AFB) 210

Barber, Chris 224, 228
Beatty, Bruce W. 130
Bennett, Richard B. 89–90
Bennett, W. A. C. 140
Berger, Carl 158
Berton, Pierre 134
Beveridge Report (1942) 115
Biden, Joe 223
Bill C-20, Clarity Act 186
Bill C-60, Recognition and Protection of Human Rights and Fundamental Freedoms 144–5
Bill C-195, 'Omnibus Bill' 193
Bissoondath, Neil, *Selling Illusions: The Cult of Multiculturalism in Canada* 153
Bloc Québécois (BQ) 23, 180, 197

Bonne Entente movement 59
Borden, Robert 55–6, 58–66, 72, 74, 87–8, 143, 158, 176
Bouchard, Lucien 180, 182–3, 185–6
Bourassa, Henri 59, 63
Bourassa, Robert 176, 179–80
Bourgault, Pierre 174
Bowell, Mackenzie 36
British North America Act, 1867 (BNA Act) 13, 15, 18, 20–1, 28, 143–4, 175
    federal government jurisdiction 36
    minority education rights 20, 60
    Ottawa's responsibilities 20
    principal goal 28
    qualified 'person' for Senate 75–6
Broadbent, Ed 166
Brodie, Janine 93
Brown, George 14, 17, 30
Bruchési, Paul (Quebec Archbishop) 65
Bryant, Anita 196
Bush, George H. W. 167

Calder case (1973) 213
Campbell, Kim 168
Canada Day 2, 130, 137, 164
Canada Development Corporation (CDC) 160
Canada Emergency Response Benefit (CERB) 222
Canada First movement (1868) 31, 34
Canada Health Act, 1984 (CHA) 8, 126
Canada Pension Plan, 1966 (CPP) 125–6, 138, 174
Canada-US Automotive Products Trade Agreement, 1965 (APTA/Auto Pact) 159, 165–6
Canada-US Free Trade Agreement (CUSFTA) 9, 164–6, 168

Canada-US Reciprocal trade agreement (1935) 159
Canadian Broadcasting Corporation (CBC) 131, 133, 146, 163, 169, 204, 223
Canadian Charter of Rights and Freedoms (1982) 9, 39, 52, 143–4, 149, 178–9, 189, 197–9, 201, 212, 222, 229–30
   aboriginal and treaty rights 212–13
   criticisms 154
   equality of status and 152
   multiculturalism and diversity, policy of 152–3, 155
   'Night of the Long Knives'/*Nuit des longs couteaux* 150
   notwithstanding clause 151, 201
   reasonable accommodation, immigrant communities 154
'Canadian clause' 103
Canadian Historical Association 2–3
Canadian Labour Congress (CLC) 90, 120
Canadian Manufacturers Association 161
Canadian Medical Association (CMA) 120, 124
Canadian Multiculturalism Act (1988) 52, 153
Canadian National Railway (CNR) 133
Canadian Red Cross 70
Canadian Women's Army Corps (CWAC) 79–80, 191
Canadian Women's Suffrage Association 69
Cardinal, Harold 212
Carney, Mark 10, 25, 169
Carney, Pat 164
Cartier, George-Étienne 17–19, 21, 28
Centennial of Confederation Act (1963) 129
centennial project (1967) 8
   celebrations 133–4
   centennial buildings, construction of 129
   Centennial Commission 129–32
   Centennial Flame, Parliament Hill 131–3, 226
   Centennial Train 133
   commemorative coins 130
   de Gaulle speech 134–5
   designation for 1 July 130
   Expo 67 133–4, 140
   logo 131
   national symbols and anthem 130–1
   new Canadian flag 130
   Pearson's initiatives 138–9
   song 131, 133
Charles III, King 3
Charlottetown Accord 181, 215
Chinese Immigration Act (1923) 49
Chrétien, Jean 153, 168–9, 173, 181, 183–4, 186, 199, 211, 215
Churchill, Winston 107
Civil Marriage Act (2005) 10, 189, 199
Clarity Act (1998) 186
Clark, Champ 158
Clark, Joe 147, 150, 177
Clinton, Bill 168
Colville, Alex 130
Common Experience Payment (CEP) 203
compulsory enfranchisement 208–10
Confederation process 136–7
   federal and provincial government 20, 24–5
   federalism 18–19, 21
   100th anniversary (*see* centennial project (1967))
   motives 17–18
   New Brunswick 21–2, 24
   Newfoundland 15, 21, 24
   Nova Scotia 13–25
   politicians in Maritime colonies 17, 21
   Prince Edward Island 15, 21, 24
   Quebec Conference 17–18, 21
   Rupert's Land, acquisition of 28–33
conscription
   anti-conscription riots, Quebec City 55–6, 65
   Australia, rejection of 58
   exemption 55, 62, 64, 66
   French-Canadian battalions 62
   impact on national unity 67
   Military Service Act (1918) 63, 65–6, 72
   NSB and 61

parade against, Victoria Square (1917) 54
Constitution 178–9
  BNA Act (*see* British North America Act)
  Charter of Rights and Freedoms (1982) 150–5
  cultural and linguistic equality 145, 147
  Parliament of Canada, power to amend 144
  Patriation Reference (1981) 150
  Trudeau constitutional goals 147–9
Constitution Act (1982) 9, 39, 143, 151, 155, 212
Co-operative Commonwealth Federation (CCF) 8, 76–7, 90–1, 93, 114–15, 117–20, 122, 124
  health care, publicly funded 118
  Medicare 8, 91, 113–14, 119–24, 126, 166
  public medical insurance 120
  universal comprehensive health coverage 119, 124
Covid-19 pandemic 219–20
  anti-vaccine demonstrations 225
  ban on international air traffic 220
  Canada's first case 219
  CERB 222
  mortality rate 223
  protests on restrictions 223–4 (*see also* Freedom Convoy (2022))
  shutdowns and restrictions 221–2
  vaccines 221
Crerar, Thomas 73
Criminal Code of Canada 88–9, 190–1, 193
Criminal Law Amendment Act (1968–9) 193
Cross, James 176
cultural genocide 10, 38, 217

Daniels case (2016) 213
de Gaulle, Charles 133–5
  speech, 1967 134–5
Delgamuukw case (1997) 213
Dempsey, Lotta 79
Dennison, Flora 72

Department of External Affairs (DEA) 101–2, 160
Department of Indian Affairs (DIA) 11, 205, 207–11
Dewdney, Edgar 27
Dickens, Charles, *A Tale of Two Cities* 14
Diefenbaker, John George 108, 110–11, 119, 124–5, 129, 133, 144–5, 159, 174–5, 210–11
  improving conditions for Indigenous people 210–11
Discover Canada: The Rights and Responsibilities of Citizenship 154
Dominion Day/Canada Day 115, 121, 125, 130–3, 137
Dosanjh, Ujjal 153–4
Douglas, Tommy 8, 90–1, 112
  Birch Hills speech 119
  early life 116
  Medicare 8, 91, 113–14, 119–24, 126, 166
  political prominence 117
  public health portfolio 117
Doukhobors 44–5, 49
  Sons of Freedom 45
Dumont, Mario 182–3

Economic Council of Canada 159–60
Eden, Anthony 107
Eisenhower, Dwight D. 109
Emergencies Act (1988) 11, 227–8
Empire Settlement Act (1922) 49
Expo 67, International and Universal Exposition 133–4, 140

Fairclough, Ellen 80
Family Allowances Act (1945) 115
federalism 18–19, 21, 25, 147
  cooperative federalism 138
  renewed federalism 147–8, 180
Federalism for the Future (1968) 145
Federation of Saskatchewan Indians, 1946 (FSIN) 210
Female Employees Fair Remuneration Act (1951) 80
Fenians 22

First Ministers' Conference on the Rights of Aboriginal Peoples (1985) 214
First Nations 36–9, 139, 150, 180–1, 203–5, 207, 210, 215
First World War 7, 44, 46–7, 49, 66–7, 70, 72–4, 78–9, 86–7, 92, 100, 130, 173, 205, 209, 230
Fisher, John 129
Fitzpatrick, Charles 65
flag of Canada 8, 111, 130
Flavelle, Joseph Wesley 86
Ford, Doug 226–7, 229
Foreign Investment Review Agency (FIRA) 160
Francoeur, Joseph-Napoléon 65, 173
Freedom Convoy (2022) 11
  blockades, border crossings 227
  Emergencies Act 227–8, 230
  objections on federal government 224
  in Ottawa 218, 225–8
  protestors' coarse behaviour 226–7
  removing demonstrators 227–8
  Rouleau Commission 228–9
  Trudeau government 230–1
free trade election (1988) 157–70
  Canada-US Free Trade Agreement 9, 164–6
  Liberal campaign 166–7
  Mulroney's brand of nationalism 167
  NAFTA 9, 156, 167–9
Front de libération du Québec (FLQ) 11, 136, 175–6, 196, 230
Fulton, E. Davie 175

Garneau, Jean-Georges 59
Gay Alliance toward Equality, 1971 (GATE) 194–5
General Agreement on Tariffs and Trade (GATT) 159, 161, 168
Geneva Accords (1954) 106
Ghadar Party (1913) 42–3
Gimby, Bobby 131
Gladstone, William 24
Godfrey, John Milton 59
Goods and Services Tax (GST) 168
Goudge, Monson Henry 24
Gouin, Jean Lomer 59

Government of Canada 150
  Alternative Dispute Resolution process (2003) 203
  ill-treatment of Indigenous peoples 30–3
  Indian Act in 1876 37
  official languages 138
  Self-Government Treaty 39, 214–15
  Statement of Apology (2008) 203–5, 216–17
  Statement of Reconciliation (1998) 203, 216
  TRC 39
Great Depression (1930s) 7, 49, 76, 84, 89, 95, 115–16, 210
  Saskatchewan 115–16
Gretzky, Wayne 169
Gwatkin, Willoughby 56

Halpern v. Attorney General of Canada 189, 198–9
Hamon, M. Max, *The Audacity of His Enterprise* 33
Harper, Elijah 180
Harper, Stephen 10, 153–4, 199, 202
  apology for Indian Residential Schools system (*see* Statement of Apology (2008))
Hawthorn, Howard B., *A Survey of the Contemporary Indians of Canada* 138–9, 211
Homophile Association of London (HALO) 194
homosexuals/homosexuality 10, 190–7, 200
  decriminalization, 'homosexual acts' 193–4
  gay rights movement 194–5
  identification, RCMP 192
  lesbianism 191
  in military, forced to resign 192, 195
  Pride House, gay athletes 200
  protests and activism 196
  tolerance and progressivism to 193
Hospital Insurance and Diagnostic Services Act (1957) 119
Howe, Joseph 12

anti-Confederation efforts 13–15, 22–3
and 'better terms' for Nova Scotia 15, 23–5
Botheration Letters, Halifax's *Morning Chronicle* 22
on Nova Scotia into Confederation 13
as president of Privy Council 24
Hudson's Bay Company (HBC) 15, 28, 30, 32–3
Hughes, Sam 57–8, 60–1
Hyde Park Agreement (1941) 102, 159

immigration. *See also Komagata Maru* incident (1914)
African Americans 47
from Asia 43
from the British Isles 44
from China 46–7
Doukhobors 45, 49
of German Americans 47
Japanese and East Asians 47, 50–1
Jewish 50–1
labour shortage and 49
multiculturalism and 52
non-agricultural immigrants, denial of entry 50
prohibition by Canadian government 41, 49
Ukrainians 44–5, 48
unemployment, exacerbation of 50, 53
Immigration Act 49, 51, 89, 191
Imperial Conference, London (1926) 144
Imperial Munitions Board 60
Independent Assessment Process (IAP) 203
Indian Act (1876) 37, 139, 205, 207–10
enfranchisement clause in 210
Indian Association of Alberta, 1939 (IAA) 210, 212
Indian Residential Schools
abuse and mistreatment, Indigenous children 36, 203–7, 216–17
cultural genocide 10, 38, 217
Harper's apology, behalf of Government of Canada (*see* Statement of Apology (2008))
Loft's experience in 206–7
objectives of 204
TRC 217
Indian Residential Schools Settlement Agreement (IRSSA) 203–4, 217
Indigenous peoples 6
abuse and mistreatment, residential schools 36, 203–7, 216–17
activism 205, 209–10, 217
attempting to assimilate 10, 37, 39, 45, 139, 152, 203–5
Citizens Plus 139
development for 138–9
Diefenbaker improving conditions for 210–11
employment opportunities for 154
federal vote, granting of 210
First Nations 36–9, 139, 150, 180–1, 203–5, 207, 210, 215
Inuit (*see* Inuit people)
Métis (*see* Métis people)
Mulroney improving conditions for 214–15
Pearson improving conditions for 211
Quebec referendum opposition 184
rights and 212–14
right to self-government and self-determination 39
self-government 11, 38–9, 214–15
veterans 206, 209
White Paper (1969) 211–12
Industrial Relations and Disputes Investigation Act (1948) 95
International Control Commission (ICC) 106
Inuit people 10, 39, 150, 184, 203–4, 209, 212, 214–15

Jahn, Gunnar 99
Johnson, Daniel 140, 146, 174, 182–4
Johnson, Lyndon 159

Klippert, Everett 194
Komagata Maru incident (1914) 6–7, 42–3
apology for 52

immigration prohibition and 41–2
Sikhs on board 40
Ku Klux Klan 49

LaMarsh, Judy 130, 133
land ownership 44, 119
Lapointe, Ernest 60
Laporte, Pierre 176
Laurier, Wilfrid 47, 59, 63, 67, 143, 147, 157–9, 163, 206–7
Lavigueur, Henri-Edgar 56
League of Indians of Canada (LIC) 206–10
League of Nations (1919) 75, 100–1, 143, 209
Legault, François 225
Lesage, Jean 135, 173–5
Leshner, Michael 189, 197–8
'the Leshner Ruling' 197
Lévesque, René 146, 150, 174, 176–8, 181
Liberal Party of Canada 136, 157, 160, 175–6, 181–2
Lich, Tamara 223–4, 228
Ligue nationaliste canadienne (1903) 59
Lloyd, Woodrow 120–1, 124
Loft, Frederick Ogilvie 206–7
  criminal charges against 209
  early life and career 206
  honour from Six Nations Council 207
  Indigenous causes, working for 206–8
  LIC 206–10

Macdonald, John A. 15, 17–18, 21, 23–5, 27, 30–5, 38, 100, 163, 206, 212
  opposition to Liberals' free trade 157–8
  protectionist National Policy (1879) 157
Mackenzie King, William Lyon 41, 51, 67, 73, 84, 86, 90–3, 95–6, 103, 115, 143, 159, 163, 209–11
Macphail, Agnes 5, 68
  campaigns 74
  delegate to League of Nations 75
  early life 74
  in general election, 1921 7, 73, 80–1
  in Ontario CCF 77
  as peace activist 75, 77
  prison reforms 77
  social programmes, advocating for 76–7
Manitoba 29, 35–6, 38–9, 93, 125, 167, 180, 189, 217, 227, 229
  bilingual education, restriction of 60
  health care 117
  vote to women 71
Manitoba Act (1870) 29, 32, 34–5, 60
Marchand, Jean 174
Markland, George 190
Marsh, Leonard 92, 115
Marshall decision (1999) 214
Marsh Report. *See* Beveridge Report (1942)
McClung, Nellie 71
McDougall, William 28, 30–3
McKinney, Louise 71
Medicare 8, 91, 113–14, 119–24, 126, 166
Meech Lake Accord (1987) 179–81, 214–15
Meighen, Arthur 64, 67
Métis people
  Convention of Forty 32
  Daniels case (2016) 213
  grievances, mid-1880s 37–8
  National Committee of the Métis 31–2
  North-West Resistance 6, 15, 28, 38
  Red River settlement 29–30
  scrip process and 37
  self-determination of 31
military service. *See also* conscription
  enlistment numbers 58
  homosexuals 192, 195–7
  Royal 22nd Regiment/Vandoos 58
  Toronto 57
Military Service Act (1918) 63, 65–6, 72
Military Voters Act (1917) 64, 72
Mosley, Richard 229–30

Mouvement Souveraineté-Association 174. *See also* Parti Québécois (PQ)
Mowat, Oliver 25, 206
Mulroney, Brian 9, 153, 157, 160–9, 179–80, 214–15
   CUSFTA 9, 164–6, 168
   free trade initiative 157, 161, 162–6
   GST 168
   House of Commons announcement 162–3
   improving conditions for Indigenous people 214–15
   NAFTA 9, 167–9
   on nation-building 167
   Quebec into 1982 Constitution 179
multiculturalism 5, 9, 52, 137, 146, 152–5

Nasser, Gamal 107–8
National Battlefields Commission 59
National Energy Program (NEP) 160, 164
National Indian Brotherhood, 1968 (NIB) 210
National Labor Relations Act 85
National Policy (1879) 157
National Service Board (NSB) 61
National War Labour Board 84
New Democratic Party (NDP) 90, 112, 120, 122, 125, 166, 179, 181, 197
Night of the Long Knives/*Nuit des longs couteaux* 150, 178
Non-Aligned Movement (1961) 107
Norris, Tobias 71
North American Free Trade Agreement (NAFTA) 9, 167–9
   signing of 156
North American Indian Brotherhood (1945) 210
North Atlantic Treaty Organization, 1949 (NATO) 4, 103–4, 106, 108
North-West Resistance (1885) 6, 15, 28, 38
North-West Territories 27–8, 31
Nova Scotia 6, 13–25, 57, 84, 217
   'better terms' for 23–5
   same-sex marriage 189, 197
Numbered Treaties (1871) 36, 39

Nunavut Land Settlement Agreement (1993) 215

Official Languages Act (1969) 138, 146, 176
Ogdensburg Agreement (1940) 102, 159
One Big Union (OBU) 88
Ontario Provincial Police (OPP) 195, 226
Ontario's Regulation 17 (1912) 59–60
Orange Order 34–5
organized labour 66, 84, 95–6

Parizeau, Jacques 181–3, 185–6
Parlby, Irene 71
Parti Québécois (PQ) 146–7, 174, 176–7, 179, 181–2, 186
patriating the constitution 9, 149–50, 212
Patterson, William 117
Paul Martin, Joseph James Guillaume 83–4, 86, 94
Peace, Order and Good Government of Canada (POGG) 20
peacekeeping 4, 8, 100, 102, 104–6, 109–111
Pearson, Lester Bowles 98
   Article 2 of North Atlantic Treaty, drafting of 103–4
   career and studies 100–1
   as civil servant 101–2
   defusing Suez Crisis 99–100, 106–11
   functional principal 102
   improving conditions for Indigenous people 138–9, 211
   initiatives, centennial 138–9
   international peacekeeping 100, 102, 104–6, 109–111
   Korean War, UN negotiations 104–5
   new Canadian flag, resolution for 8, 130
   Nobel Peace Prize, 1957 8, 99, 111
Pelletier, Gérard 174
People's Republic of China (PRC) 104–5
Progressive Conservative Party of Canada 93, 119, 129, 144, 147, 157, 160–1, 174, 177, 179
protectionism 9, 157, 160, 162–4

Quebec 10
    anglophone dominance, replacing of 136–7
    anti-conscription riots (*see* anti-conscription riots, Quebec City)
    FLQ 11, 136, 175–6, 196, 230
    nationalism, rise of 8, 134–5
    sovereignty-association 147
Quebec Conference 17–18, 136
Quebec Liberal Party 60, 135, 176
Quebec Pension Plan (QPP) 138
Quebec referendum (1995) 10, 146–7
    'No' rally in Montreal 184
    question to Quebeckers 183
    support for sovereignty 186
    voters and results 185
    'Yes' supporters 173, 177, 182–5
    Yvette rally 177
Queen Elizabeth II 133, 142, 151–2, 179
Quiet Revolution 8, 135, 173–4

racism 145, 155, 209
    Anti-Oriental riots of September 1907 41
    against Black migrants 47
    prohibiting immigration 41 (*see also Komagata Maru* incident (1914))
Rae, Bob 181
Rand, Ivan 83, 86, 94–5
Rand Formula (1946) 83, 86, 94–6
Reagan, Ronald 161–2
Reciprocity Treaty (1854) 157, 159
Red River Expeditionary Force 35
Red River Resistance (1869–70) 31, 34–5, 37
Reference Re Resolution to amend the Constitution/Patriation Reference (1981) 150
Regina Manifesto (1933) 91, 117
Riel, Louis 5–6, 15, 26–8
    banishment from Canada 36
    early life 29
    hanging of 6, 27–8
    North-west Rebellion 6, 15, 28, 38
    Red River Resistance 31, 34–5, 37
Robarts, John 140
Roosevelt, Franklin Delano 102, 159

Rouleau, Paul 228–9
Royal Canadian Air Force Women's Division (RCAF(WD)) 79–80
Royal Commission on Aboriginal Peoples (RCAP) 214–16
Royal Commission on Bilingualism and Biculturalism, 1963 (B&B Commission) 137–8, 174
Royal Commission on Health Services (1961) 124
Royal Commission on the Economic Union and Development Prospects for Canada (1982) 160
Royal Commission on the Status of Women (1967) 139
Royal Proclamation (1763) 39, 214
Rukeyser, Louis 183
Rupert's Land 15, 31–2, 34
    Canadians in Red River 30–1, 34
    Red River Settlement 29–31
    sale to Canada 28–9
    Smith's negotiations with Riel 33–4

same-sex marriage 188–9, 197
    right to adopt children 197
    banns of marriage, issuing of 198
    Civil Marriage Act (2005) 10, 189, 199
    legalization 189, 199, 201
    Ontario Superior Court on 198
Saskatchewan doctors' strike (1962) 119–21
    agreements 123
    duration of 123
    Keep Our Doctors committees 121–2
    outcomes 126
    press coverage 114
    replacement physicians 122
    Swift Current Citizens Safety Committee 123
    voting to reject Medicare 121
Saskatchewan Klan 49
Saskatchewan Medical Care Insurance Act (1962) 114, 121
Scott, Duncan Campbell 208–9
Scott, Thomas 34–5
Second World War 7, 50, 77–80, 92–5, 102–3, 105, 107, 110, 115–16, 119, 138, 191–2, 209–10

Self-Government Treaty 39, 214–15
Shamrock Summit 162
Shaunessy, Thomas George 58
Sicko documentary 113
Sifton, Clifford 44
Simeon, Richard 21
Singh, Gurdit 42
Skelton, Oscar Douglas 101
Sloly, Peter 226
Smith, Donald Alexander 33–4
Smith, Goldwin 159, 206
Smith, Mary Ellen 71
social citizenship
  family allowances, providing of 84, 92
  labour militancy, rise of 86–7
  Regina Manifesto 91
  Riot Act 88–9
  UAW trade union 85–6
  unemployment insurance plan 90, 92
  Wartime Labour Relations Regulations 84–5
  work camps, Department of Defence 90
  WTLC 87
Social Gospel movement 116
Soldiers of the Soil 62
sovereignty 143–4, 147. *See also* Quebec referendum (1995)
  Constitution Act, 1982 151
  cultural sovereignty 163
  treaty making and 36
Stark, Michael 189, 197–8
Statement of Apology (2008) 203–5, 216–17
Statement of Reconciliation (1998) 203, 216
Statute of Westminster (1931) 100
Stewart, Jane 215–16
St Laurent, Louis 103, 108, 143–4, 148
Stowe, Emily Howard 69
Suez Crisis (1956) 8
  Canada as middle power 106, 110
  Israeli forces in Sinai Peninsula 109
  nationalization of Suez Canal 108
  Pearson's leadership in defusing 99–100, 106–11
  UNEF, establishment of 109–10
  uprisings by Egyptians 107

Taft, William Howard 158
Tait, Thomas 61
Tellier, Moise 190
Thatcher, Ross 120, 124
Thomson, Strathearn Boyd 190
Thornborrow, Barbara 195
Tilley, Leonard 16, 18, 21–2
Trades and Labour Congress of Canada, 1883 (TLC) 87
Treaty of Versailles 100
Trout, Jennie Kidd 69
Trudeau, Justin 11, 52, 80, 220, 222–4, 231
  Emergencies Act, implementation of 227–9, 230
Trudeau, Pierre Elliott 9, 11, 25, 52, 136, 140, 142–4, 146, 174
  Bill C-195, 'Omnibus Bill' 193
  constitutional goals 147–9
  on importance of constitution 148–9
  nationalist policies 160
  official bilingualism and multiculturalism 146
  patriating the constitution 9, 149–50, 212
  speech at Paul Sauvé Arena in Montreal 177
Trump, Donald J. 9, 169–70, 186, 223, 227
Truth and Reconciliation Commission, 2008 (TRC) 10, 39, 217
Tsilhqot'in case (2014) 213
Tupper, Charles 15, 21–2
Turnbull, Jessie 69
Turner, John 161, 166–7, 193, 228
2SLGBTQ+ community 197, 201

Unemployment Insurance Act (1940) 115
Union Government Publicity Bureau (1917) 65
United Automobile Workers of Canada (UAW) 83, 85–6, 91
United Farmers of Ontario, 1914 (UFO) 74
United Nations Emergency Force (UNEF) 8, 100, 109–10
United Nations Organization 4, 99, 102–6, 108–9

United States-Mexico-Canada
    Agreement (USMCA) 169
universal health care 8, 114. *See also*
    Medicare
  acceptance from doctors 123–4
  opposition from doctors (*see*
    Saskatchewan doctors' strike)
  Royal Commission on Health
    Services 124–5
  Saskatchewan Medical Care
    Insurance Act 114, 121
UN's Relief and Rehabilitation
    Administration (UNRRA) 102

Wake, Frank 192
Wall Street crash (1929) 49
War Measures Act (1914 & 1970) 11,
    56, 176, 196, 227, 230
Wartime Elections Act (1917) 64, 72
Wartime Labour Relations Regulations
    (1944) 84
Watson, Jim 226–7
Wells, Clyde 180
West, Leah 230
White Anglo-Saxon Protestant
    (WASP) 6
White Paper (1969) 211–12
Wilson, Cairine 76
Wiman, Erastus 159
Windsor auto strike (1945) 7
  barricade by pickets 82
  duration 83–4, 94
  Rand Formula 83, 86, 94–6

UAW Local 200 and demands 85
  union security to Canada 83, 94–6
Winnipeg General Strike (1919) 48–9,
    87–91
Winnipeg Trades and Labour Council
    (WTLC) 87
women in Canadian society. *See also*
    Macphail, Agnes
  employment options 70, 73, 78, 80
  equality and 73, 75, 79–81
  general election, 1921 73
  military jobs 79–80
  participation in elections 69
  Persons Case (1929) 7, 72, 75
  Royal Commission on the Status of
    Women (1967) 139
  social reforms, pursuing 70
  suffrage movement 69–72
Women's Division of the Royal
    Canadian Air Force (WDs) 191
Women's Franchise Act (1918) 72
Women's Royal Canadian Naval
    Service (WRCNS) 79–80, 191
Woodsworth, J. S. 88, 90, 116
World Health Organization (WHO)
    219–20, 231
Wynne, Kathleen 60

xenophobia 1, 7, 41

Zedong, Mao 104
Zodiac Friendship Society of
    Saskatoon, 1972 194